JOURNALISM ACROSS CULTURES: AN INTRODUCTION

Journalism Across Cultures: An Introduction

Levi Obijiofor
Senior Lecturer, University of Queensland

Folker Hanusch
Senior Lecturer, University of the Sunshine Coast

palgrave
macmillan

First published 2011 by
PALGRAVE MACMILLAN

Palgrave Macmillan in the UK is an imprint of Macmillan Publishers Limited, registered in England, company number 785998, of Houndmills, Basingstoke, Hampshire RG21 6XS.

Palgrave Macmillan in the US is a division of St Martin's Press LLC, 175 Fifth Avenue, New York, NY 10010.

Palgrave Macmillan is the global academic imprint of the above companies and has companies and representatives throughout the world.

Palgrave® and Macmillan® are registered trademarks in the United States, the United Kingdom, Europe and other countries.

ISBN: 978–0–230–23609–7 hardback
ISBN: 978–0–230–23610–3 paperback

This book is printed on paper suitable for recycling and made from fully managed and sustained forest sources. Logging, pulping and manufacturing processes are expected to conform to the environmental regulations of the country of origin.

A catalogue record for this book is available from the British Library.

A catalog record for this book is available from the Library of Congress.

10 9 8 7 6 5 4 3 2 1
20 19 18 17 16 15 14 13 12 11

Printed in China

For
Edith Nneka (Levi)
Stephi, Finn and Felix (Folker)

Contents

Acknowledgments

Right from the time this book was conceived through to its conclusion, a lot of people influenced its final outcome. They encouraged us in various ways; they shared ideas with us and provided valuable insights. We would like to acknowledge everyone who contributed to the success of our effort. They are too numerous to name. However, we would like to mention, specifically, Zala Volcic, who was an original member of our team that started working on this book. Zala had to withdraw from our team for family reasons. However, we are extremely grateful to her for her contributions during the original planning stages. Credit must be given to her for bringing fresh ideas and her multicultural background to the project. We enjoyed collaborating with her in teaching and research and regret very much that she had to pull out of the book.

Levi would like to acknowledge all the people who made remarkable and indelible impact on his life that is difficult to recount in an acknowledgment page. They include his parents (Caleb and Esther Obijiofor) and his wife (Edith Nneka). My parents have been the pillar that supported and motivated me throughout my primary, secondary and university education. In good times and bad times, they assisted me. I am eternally indebted to them. I am also indebted to my wife for her support and her extraordinary spirit of understanding, tolerance, patience and humour which kept me going even when I felt like giving up. My special appreciation must also go to Polycarp Emenike (Odenigbo Nanka) who has been a mentor and an inspiration to me in so many ways. I have benefited from his words of wisdom and encouragement, his work ethic, his strive for excellence in all his endeavours, his achievement record and, above all, his uncommon generosity.

Folker would like to thank Stephi and Finn for their unconditional love, support and incredible patience during a time when work encroached on family life far too often. I know it was not easy at times, and I am lucky to have you. I would also like to acknowledge my family, especially my parents, for teaching me to think for myself and to be critical. A number of other people have had formative influence on my life more generally, and they are too many to mention. You know who you are. In the context of this particular book I would like to thank: Claudia Mellado for her advice on journalism in

Latin America; Louise North, who provided valuable feedback on the topic of gender and journalism; and Thomas Hanitzsch, who allowed me to look at a forthcoming journal article and from whose expertise on comparative journalism studies more generally I have benefited incredibly.

We would both like to thank a number of people at Palgrave Macmillan, without whom this project would not have been possible. They include our commissioning editor, Rebecca Barden, who graciously granted us an extension in order to complete the book following our colleague's withdrawal. Our gratitude also goes to Paul Sng, as well as former commissioning editors Emily Salz and Beverley Tarquini who showed interest in our original proposal and saw its potential.

It is said that all works are co-operative enterprises. So is this book. If this book holds some merit, it must be attributed to the contributions of all the people we acknowledge here. If, however, there are errors in the book, we take full responsibility for them.

CHAPTER I

Introduction

Journalists operate in human societies, and consequently, how journalism is practised and the degree of freedom and autonomy that journalists exercise are affected by the existing technological, social, economic, political, cultural and legal frameworks and contexts in a globalized world. These complexities and interlocking relationships underpin not just the nature of journalism but also how it is practised, how journalists are trained, the definitions of news, those who are qualified to serve as journalists and the communication infrastructure that creates the environment that facilitates professional journalism culture.

The interdependent and interconnected nature of our world spawned by increasing globalization and technological changes underlines the importance of analysing journalism practices from a global perspective. However, quite a number of scholars have expressed dissatisfaction with the current performance of journalists and media organizations in capturing diverse issues of global concern (Cottle, 2009), including the failure to recognize and appreciate people from non-western cultures (Hafez, 2009). Thus, Wasserman and de Beer (2009, p. 428) call for 'a definition of journalism that is more inclusive of global political differences'. Although we live in a globalized world, research evidence suggests that news agendas are dominated by domestic news events, a focus on popular personalities, soft news and entertainment-driven content, concentration on regional news or 'Eurocentrism', as well as diminished attention to international news in general (see, e.g., Sutcliffe et al., 2009; Altmeppen, 2010; Joye, 2010).

This book examines theoretical and practical issues that underpin journalism across cultures. It demonstrates that journalism can be taught, practised and analysed through different epistemological backgrounds and frameworks. It examines, for example, the interface between practitioners and the technologies they use (e.g. how technology impacts on journalism practices), as well as the various frameworks that inform models of journalism education and training across the world. The book is interdisciplinary in theoretical

1

and practical approaches because we draw on other fields such as media and cultural studies, anthropology, sociology, linguistics, as well as politics and international relations. We show – through examples taken from diverse countries – how journalism can be examined through a wide variety of socio-cultural and educational contexts, including professional and practical experiences. In an increasingly globalized world, we believe a more in-depth focus on, and global insights into, journalistic cultures are important. In this context, this book is inclusive and international in scope because in it we look at issues that cut across cultures.

The book integrates major theoretical and practical approaches, including non-western and Western contexts, in exploring international journalism perspectives from around the world. As new technologies blur the boundary between content producers and content consumers (e.g. the growing phenomenon of citizen journalism or participatory journalism), increasing globalization facilitated by new technologies has compelled journalists, media owners and managers, journalism academics as well as media consumers to critically re-think news reporting and production conventions. Technological changes have also generated new business models for survival in an increasingly competitive industry. These developments have influenced not only global journalism practices but also the frameworks and pedagogies for the teaching of journalism across the world. These issues are explored in this book.

Research in journalism studies shows that similarities and differences abound across cultures, underlying the diversity that exists around the world. Specifically, studies conducted to explore journalistic professional routines, editorial conventions and socialization mechanisms show similarities in countries such as Brazil, Germany, Indonesia, Tanzania and the United States (in Hanitzsch, 2009, p. 413). Other studies, however, show that differences exist in the way journalists in different countries perceive their roles and the way they make news judgments in their professional practice (Deuze, 2002; Hanusch, 2008a). Exploration of the similarities and differences that mark journalistic practices across the world constitutes not only a valuable contribution to the scholarship of journalism studies but also an appreciation of the value of diversity in human societies. Hanitzsch (2009, p. 413) states that comparative studies in journalistic practices are important because they enrich our understanding of different countries. Thus, comparative studies have shown that 'news production is contingent on the cultural, political and historical contexts that shape the journalist's work' (p. 413), as no two countries share exactly the same culture. One value of comparative studies is that they help to draw our attention to diverse perspectives of journalism, not just the dominant Western version. This explains our interest in the phrase 'journalism cultures' rather than journalism, which suggests one conceptualization of journalism. Interest in global journalism studies therefore suggests a growing fascination for knowledge of journalistic cultures and conventions around the world. While we cite examples (in this book) from specific nations and regions, our analysis goes beyond national boundaries because, as Hanitzsch (2009, p. 416) points out, 'National borders do not necessarily correspond to cultural, linguistic and ethnic divisions, nor do they correspond to a common sense of identity.'

In comparative journalism studies, the work of Hallin and Mancini (2004) is widely cited not only for its comparative value but also for its scope and analytic rigour. For example, Hallin and Mancini's book is considered significant because it provides an important framework that enables us to explore the relationship between Western media models and media systems in non-western cultures, although the major focus of the book is on media systems in Western Europe and North America. For example, in terms of historical relationships, major European powers such as Britain, France, Belgium, the Netherlands, Italy and Germany played a key role in shaping the pre-independence and post-independence philosophies that underpinned media systems in their former colonies in Africa in the twentieth century.

In their book – *Comparing Media Systems* – Hallin and Mancini categorized Western Europe and North America into three media models, namely the Liberal Model (seen mostly in Britain, Ireland and North America), the Democratic Corporatist Model (observable in northern continental Europe) and the Polarized Pluralist Model (applicable to the Mediterranean countries of southern Europe). The authors state that one of the distinguishing elements among media systems across the world is that 'media in some countries have distinct political orientations, while media in other countries do not' (Hallin and Mancini, 2004, p. 27). In this context, Hallin and Mancini argue that journalism, as practised in every part of the world, is never neutral. As they put it, 'even where journalists may be sincerely committed to a professional ideology of "objectivity", news incorporates political values, which arise from a range of influences, from routines of information gathering to recruitment patterns of journalists and shared ideological assumptions of the wider society' (2004, p. 26). This argument reinforces the widely held view that media in every country are tied to various political and economic interests at any one time in history. Notwithstanding this point, Hallin and Mancini's book has been criticized for its excessive emphasis on Western media systems and for overlooking other perspectives that exist in other parts of the world. This is not surprising as journalism is often regarded as 'an Anglo-American invention' (Chalaby, 1996, p. 303). Wasserman and de Beer (2009) argue that the marginalization of some parts of the world (e.g. Africa) has undermined past and current scholarly attempts to construct media models and press systems. 'The end-result is too often that the Western democratic model of liberal democracy remains the implicit or explicit normative ideal against which journalism in non-western societies is measured, with media-state relations as a primary determinant of journalistic standards' (2009, p. 431).

In his analysis of the growth of French and American journalism from the 1830s to the 1920s, Chalaby (1996) argued that there were political, legal, economic, educational and language factors that encouraged the development, sustenance and dominance of Anglo-American genre of journalism. This historical dominance means that other journalistic conventions and practices in non-western societies are regarded as mere derivatives of the Anglo-American system. Although the Anglo-American model of journalism may have influenced the origins of other forms of journalism, Wasserman and de Beer (2009, p. 428) argue that 'the dominant Anglo-American view of journalism is being challenged by studies showing up the gap between theory and practice'. This again suggests that, rather than talk about one type of journalism, it is appropriate to speak of journalisms or different types of journalism. In this context, Hanitzsch (2009) has suggested that comparative journalism studies should go beyond excessive focus on Western models of journalism to explore other models of journalism. The significance of comparative analyses of journalistic practices conducted by Chalaby (1996) and by Hallin and Mancini (2004) is that they helped to draw out the major differences between Anglo-American journalism and the types of journalism that exist in other parts of the world. This is the key reason why, in this book, we constantly cite examples or draw on journalistic systems and practices that exist in other cultures.

We argue that an examination of journalism practices across cultures will enrich rather than dilute public knowledge and understanding of the similarities and differences in journalism. Previous comparative studies provide compelling evidence that similarities and differences exist in journalistic practices at the national, regional and international levels. We have therefore set out in this book to analyse systematically: the different media models and press systems that exist in various parts of the globe; how journalism is practised and taught around the world; how gender is reflected, recognized and overlooked in newsroom cultures; how new technologies have transformed the landscape of foreign news reporting; the growing debate about the role of journalists in peace and conflict reporting; the increasing commercialization of journalism and the factors that are aiding the practice; and the impact that new technologies are having on journalism practices around the world. Therefore, global perspectives and representation constitute the overarching schema of this book. Where similarities and differences exist, we have tried to identify them. Where contradictions blur arguments, we point them out. By analysing global differences and similarities in journalism, our objective is to explore the world from as diverse perspectives as are possible. This means we have deliberately refrained from presenting a framework that analyses journalism cultures in terms of the narrow and polarizing binary division of North versus South or the Manichean duality of 'light versus darkness', 'good versus evil' or 'right versus wrong'. Examining journalism in different societies in a globalized world enables us to understand what is happening in other cultural contexts. For example, as Wasserman and de Beer (2009, p. 429) point out, 'While the political-economic context of journalism studies in Africa might differ considerably from some non-western contexts like Asia, it might correspond with, for instance, Latin America, for both historical (such as the history of colonialism) and economic (as developing regions in the global economy) reasons.'

Blumler et al. (1992) have identified three ways through which comparative research in communication has contributed to knowledge. First, comparative research exposes us to communication trends and dilemmas that are not easily observable in our world. Second, comparative research has the capacity to surmount or prevail over 'space- and time-bound limitations on the generalizability of our theories, assumptions and propositions' (1992, p. 3). Comparative research can also enable us to examine and expose the implications of the disparities that exist in the way communication is structured in our larger world (pp. 3–4). Similarly, Livingstone (2003, p. 479) has identified the various values attached to comparative research, namely: to improve our knowledge of our own country and others; to examine scholarly postulation in different environments; to analyse how local audiences receive imported cultural products; and to enhance cross-cultural understanding. Nevertheless, Chang et al. (2001) examined 151 comparative international communication studies published in six leading communication journals between 1970 and 1997 and found: clear evidence of the lack of theoretical progress in comparative international communication research; few efforts to examine theoretical postulations cross-nationally; the requirement for better articulation of knowledge and assumptions that would offer productive ideas cross-nationally; and failure to observe systematic sampling methods that would yield data that are representative of the larger population (pp. 430–1).

Despite the advantages of comparative communication research, there are certain drawbacks. Comparative research is not without its difficulties, such as the complexities associated with examining different systems or time periods which may constrain 'meaningful comparison' (Blumler et al., 1992, p. 13).

Livingstone (2003, p. 491) argues that 'comparative research is challenging because one must balance and interpret similarities and differences while avoiding banalities and stereotypes'. Among the difficulties that impede comparative research are: the enormity of the differences being studied and their various components or elements, both of which would complicate the kind of meanings to be derived; and studying the differences in social systems could lead to the devaluation of the differences within the system. As Blumler et al. (1992, p. 13) point out, 'Nations and cultures are not typically homogeneous; they often encompass different language and ethnic groups, regions, and social classes that are in symbolic and pragmatic competition'. There are also methodological and theoretical dilemmas involved in comparative research, such as the danger of universalizing research approaches and theoretical frameworks that often ignore cultural distinctions or details (Livingstone, 2003; Hanitzsch, 2009). For example, research in the field of development communication which dominated intellectual discourse in the 1950s, 1960s and 1970s adopted Western-oriented approaches prescribed by communication scholars such as Daniel Lerner, Everett Rogers and Wilbur Schramm, and pushed the notion that 'development in the Third World should be measured in terms of the adoption and assimilation of Western technology and culture. The main emphasis of the work was on increasing efficiency within an accepted and unquestioned value framework' (Halloran, 1998, p. 44). As a reflection of the mood of that era, most of the research conducted at the time affirmed and emphasized the validity of Western approaches and ideologies. In the developing countries, these viewpoints underlined existing economic and cultural reliance on the West rather than the socio-cultural, political and economic sovereignty of those emerging nations (Halloran, 1998, p. 44).

By identifying the drawbacks of comparative communication research, we also acknowledge the limitations of our own work. In general, many intellectual efforts are never perfect because they serve as a reflection of the political, economic, social and cultural climate in which they are produced. Although we did not set out to accommodate inadequacies, there is, however, value in limitations that may emerge owing to changes in global geopolitical and economic systems, as well as developments generated by technological transformations. These changes, whenever they occur, will offer us an opportunity to engage in future revisions of the approaches we adopted and the arguments we made in this book in order to reflect the realities of a globalized world in the twenty-first century. Cultures are dynamic and so too are journalistic practices. The changing nature of journalism strengthens the need for scholars to revisit their work regularly. In this book, we have made conscious efforts to draw on Western and non-Western journalistic systems and practices. We have also drawn on different cultures that inform journalism practices across the world. At the heart of these differences and similarities is the need to recognize diversity. The following section provides a synopsis of the chapters that follow. This serves as a foretaste of the contents of the book.

Chapter outline

The history of media systems and press theories and the extent to which media systems influence journalistic practices and philosophies are explored in Chapter 2. The chapter analyses contemporary and past media models and theories of the press, as conceptualized by different scholars. The chapter delves beyond dominant media models to explore other global perspectives, including media systems in Africa, Latin America, the Arab world and the Middle East, media transformations in China, as well as North American and Western European media models, not forgetting the classical but controversial *Four Theories of the Press*, which is widely regarded as the vehicle that sparked scholarly interest in the construction of press systems across the world. The strengths and drawbacks of these media models and press systems are examined and critiqued in-depth. In this chapter we also draw attention to the political, social, cultural and economic factors that distinguish journalistic practices in different societies. For example, many of the past approaches to classifying media systems were examined through political economy frameworks that tended to overlook larger cultural issues (Mowlana, 1997). This chapter recognizes the impact that technological changes have had on the conceptualizations of press systems and media models, including the meanings traditionally attached to concepts such as the press. We therefore pose the question: Do existing media models still constitute an accurate representation of global media systems in the twenty-first century and are such classifications still valid?

With emphasis on journalistic practices and how journalists perceive their roles in different societies, Chapter 3 explores the various types of journalism that exist in different parts of the world. It examines the differences and similarities in journalists' professional views about their role in society. The analysis includes scholarly insights into the factors that influence journalistic practices across individual, organizational, media system and cultural levels. For example, a comparative study of national news cultures conducted in the Netherlands, Germany, Britain, Australia and the United States noted how journalists' approach to work distinguished Dutch and German practices of journalism from the Anglo-American conventions (Deuze, 2002). In terms of role perceptions, we see across different regions the various ways that journalists perceive their role. The first large-scale comparative study in this regard was conducted by Weaver (1998a) who reported results of journalists surveyed in 21 countries and territories around the world. One role perception that appeared to receive support from journalists generally was 'getting information to the public'. However, Weaver (1998b, p. 478) notes that, 'beyond these roles, there is much disagreement over how important it is to provide entertainment, to report accurately and objectively, to provide analysis of complex issues and problems, and to be a watchdog on government'. In the Arab world, Pintak and Ginges' (2008) survey showed that many Arab journalists subscribed to an active role in trying to bring change. Similarly, a study of Brazilian journalists identified three types of role perceptions – the interpretive, adversary and disseminator functions (Herscovitz, 2004). Chapter 3 also examines the debate over adoption of culturally appropriate values in journalism practices in various regions. In that context we analyse arguments for regional approaches that originated from a belief that journalism works best if it is practised in accordance with local cultural values. Many of the regional models emerged from a resistance to imported Western models which local journalists did not see as applicable to or useful in their cultural circumstances. For example, there is the contested view that Asian news media should reflect Asian values. Massey and Chang (2002, p. 992) clarify that the argument is based on the notion that 'the modern, economically strong Asian society is best built on a foundation of traditional Eastern beliefs, not transplanted Western values'. Similar debates have dominated discussion on the scholarship of African journalism. Thus, Chapter 3 offers a kaleidoscopic analysis of discussions about how culture is embedded in journalism practices and how it defines the way journalists approach their job in different social and cultural milieu.

The quality of journalism around the world is often attributed to the nature of the education and training that journalists receive. At the centre of this discussion is the question of whether journalism education should be tailored towards more vocational aspects or whether it should reflect a mix of theory and practice. These issues are explored in detail in Chapter 4. The literature on journalism education suggests that models of journalism education tend to be designed to suit the specific objectives of each country (Nordenstreng, 2009). Analysis of models of journalism education is important because, according to Gaunt (1992, p. 1), 'journalism training perpetuates or modifies professional practices and moulds the perceptions journalists have of the role and function of the media'. This chapter also reviews the current state of journalism education around the world, taking into consideration the diverse cultural, political and economic environments. To understand how and why journalists in different countries and regions are educated in various ways, we examine the history of journalism education around the world. We also provide an overview of the tensions that exist in journalism education globally, in particular the arguments for and against on-the-job and university-only models. By doing so, we hope to shed light on the benefit of journalism education models that are specific to individual cultures rather than importation of the dominant Western models that may not necessarily apply in other contexts.

One noticeable feature of journalism education around the world is the growing number of female students. Research suggests that, in some countries, women are in the majority not only in the classrooms but also in newsrooms. Chapter 5 therefore examines a range of issues relating to gender in journalism such as the institutional discrimination against women. On this point, Fröhlich (2007, p. 163) notes, on the basis of research evidence, that 'an overwhelming majority of women journalists worldwide agreed that women journalists face professional barriers that their male colleagues do not and that the top obstacle for women in management is continually proving their abilities to colleagues and supervisors'. One of the contentious issues in this area is the notion that there is a 'glass ceiling' that prevents women journalists from attaining senior editorial and management positions. Some studies have examined not just how many women are in journalism but also the way in which they carry out their job. Do women engage in journalism practice in significantly different ways from men, or are they compelled to adopt news values developed by men over several centuries? It has been argued that women journalists are assigned to report stories about fashion, entertainment and culture, while men usually report political, economic, financial and sport stories (Robinson, 2005). It has also been suggested that when women make the news, they are typecast as celebrities, victims of crime, or in clearly 'woman-centred' stories that are usually marginal to the main news agenda (Gallagher, 2010). As we highlight in this chapter, there is some evidence to suggest that some women, in an attempt to become 'one of the boys' in the profession and to be accepted as serious news reporters, adopt mainstream news values. Nevertheless, research evidence shows also a general softening of news values in recognition of the increasing participation of women in journalism.

Foreign news reporting is an important field of journalism and it has attracted intense scrutiny by professional journalists and journalism academics. Foreign news reporting is important because the way it is reported shapes the way we view people and events in other cultures, how we relate to them, and how we communicate with them (Wolter, 2006). In the decades of the

1970s and 1980s, there were widespread criticisms particularly from the developing countries about how Western news media portray people and cultures from the non-west in typically stereotyped fashion. Concerns were also raised about the disproportionate flow of overseas news from the West to the non-west and vice versa, including the quality (nature) of news about developing societies. These and other issues culminated in sustained agitations for a New World Information and Communication Order (NWICO) which dominated intellectual discussions at the United Nations Educational, Scientific and Cultural Organisation (UNESCO) in the late 1970s up to the early 1980s. Against this background, Chapter 6 analyses the changing landscape of foreign news reporting with special emphasis on how technological changes have transformed foreign reporting. The chapter argues that new technologies have significantly affected the way foreign news is reported, including the quantity, frequency, speed of coverage, global coverage of news events, and the growing participation of news consumers – citizen journalists – in the collection, production and distribution of foreign news. Despite technological influences, research suggests that media attention to foreign news is declining in much of North America and Western Europe (e.g. Franks, 2005; Wolter, 2006; Altmeppen, 2010). The chapter draws on research conducted across the world to map how new technologies are transforming foreign coverage and some of the key factors that are contributing to declining attention to foreign news.

The role that journalists play in reporting war and conflict is the focus of Chapter 7. Over several centuries, wars and conflicts have dominated not only the geopolitics of international relations but have also engaged the attention of journalists and the news media. There is a growing body of research on media coverage of conflict, including perspectives on how the media can contribute to the peaceful resolution of such conflicts (e.g. Löffelholz, 2004; Wolfsfeld, 2004; Lynch & McGoldrick, 2005). Thus, peace journalism has been advanced as a new form of journalistic reporting that encourages and promotes a culture of peace. Indeed, Wolfsfeld (1997, p. 54) states that the press 'can either reinforce or deflate images of the enemy, spread optimism or pessimism about the chances for peace, strengthen or weaken the public's willingness to make compromises, and increase or decrease the legitimacy of the ruling government'. It is in this context that attention has been devoted to the performance of journalists, including the relationship between the media and governments during war, as well as the potential for the news media to make a difference through the 'peace journalism alternative' (Lynch & McGoldrick, 2005). This chapter explores these perspectives with respect to their global application. First, we examine the ways in which wars and conflicts have been reported by journalists in different cultural contexts. These include intra-national conflicts (examples include wars fought in Rwanda, Sri Lanka, Indonesia and in the Balkans), as well as regional wars and global conflicts. Wars within nations and regions have also taken on an ethnic dimension. We explore in this chapter the relationship between the media and governments in terms of influence, as the debate over the so-called CNN effect – especially in wartime – persists. Finally, we examine critically the theory of peace and conflict reporting and analyse its potential for success. This discussion is set against a background of numerous examples from across the globe.

In Chapter 8, we look at how contemporary journalism across the world is being challenged by commercial pressures spawned by technological changes that threaten to disrupt more traditional forms of journalism practice. McManus (2009, p. 219) defines commercialization of news as 'any action intended to boost profit that interferes with a journalist's or news organiza- tion's best effort to maximize public understanding of those issues and events that shape the community they claim to serve'. When media organizations place greater emphasis on their business interests rather than on the public interests, quality journalism suffers (Picard, 2004, p. 55). The crucial term in these conceptualizations which should help us to engage critically with the analysis of commercialization of journalism is the media's preference for profit over public service or good. Increasing commercialization of media raises questions about the role of media in democratic societies. Closely con- nected to this is the role of journalism as one of the elements of the public sphere. The chapter conceptualizes notions of the public sphere and citizen- ship, and focuses on the role that the mass media play against the background of threats posed to journalistic independence by market forces. The public sphere is one of the most important aspects of contemporary discourse on democracy and journalism. The media is seen in this context as reinforcing a public sphere and public discourse as being reinvented as media discourse. The public sphere is important for journalism across the world because it is within this sphere that citizens are furnished with information concerning public issues (Habermas, 1989). Unfortunately, the role of the media as a vehicle for dissemination of public issues is under assault by the forces of commercialization.

Research suggests that new technologies (e.g. the Internet, interactive mul- timedia systems, digital telecommunications and e-mail) have transformed journalism practices in various ways, such as faster access to news, more frequent news updates, live coverage of breaking news events, citizen involve- ment in news reporting, as well as greater quantity and diversity of news available to media audiences. Thus, the emergence of new technologies in journalism practice has challenged core assumptions about traditional news reporting and production, such as the notion that professional journalists have the exclusive right to set the public agenda and to define social reality (Deuze, 2005, p. 451). These issues are analysed in Chapter 9. Although new technologies have expanded the terrain of journalism and the global audience for news has increased in the same way that news consumers have multiple sources of news, these developments have not eliminated certain blemishes associated with online commentary and news reporting. In this chapter, we examine the strengths and weaknesses of technological changes in journalism, including how online report published in the form of commentary, analysis or news tends to blur the distinction between straight news and commentary. Rather than enhance journalism, this practice is seen to promote rumour and therefore undermines journalism because of lack of accountability, because of anonymity of contributors to online content and because of the inability to verify the accuracy of online reports in some circumstances (Fenton, 2010b, p. 10).

The general overview we present in this chapter shows that there is something for everyone in this book. Professional journalists, journalism academics and researchers, media organizations and news consumers, as well as students who have an interest in the role of the media and journalists in different societies will find this book a useful resource to enhance their knowledge about issues that underpin journalistic practices across the world. The arguments we advance throughout the book serve as our response to the gaps we identified in the literature on journalism training and practices in different cultures. We have focused on the past and contemporary issues in journalism that straddle the discipline. The major plank of our arguments is the central role that culture plays in the construction of journalistic practices across the globe. Thus, we see a global world in which existing media systems and journalistic practices are influenced by cultural differences.

CHAPTER 2

Evolving press theories and media models

Introduction

This chapter examines contemporary and past media models and theories of the press, as conceptualized variously by different scholars. The essence of the analyses presented here is to facilitate an understanding of the history of media systems and press theories and to examine the extent to which media systems explain or influence journalistic practices and the role of the media in different cultures. Distinct from previous analyses of media systems, this chapter goes beyond Western media models to explore other global perspectives, including media systems in non-western societies. It does this by highlighting the political, social, cultural and economic factors that influence journalistic practices in different societies. For example, many of the past approaches to classifying media systems were underpinned by political and economic factors, while they neglected larger cultural issues (Mowlana, 1997). While cultural approaches are examined in more depth in Chapter 3, we highlight briefly in this chapter the value of examining approaches that were overlooked in the past, which might be more appropriate for classifying non-western media systems. Furthermore, the chapter recognizes that technological changes have led to dramatic transformations in the meanings traditionally attached to concepts such as the press. In the age of the Internet, for example, does the word 'press' capture new forms of online journalism? Do some of the media models examined in this chapter still constitute an accurate representation of global press systems in the twenty-first century? In a globalized world, is there any reliable and universal schema for classifying media systems and press theories, and are such classifications still valid? The essence of the analysis conducted here is to advance new knowledge and understanding of international journalism and communication issues that inspire scholarly debate in the discipline.

Hanitzsch (2008) has identified four paradigms that capture past and present scholarly research adopted in mapping media systems across the world. The first conceptual framework which he labelled 'The US and the rest' marked the dominance of the United States in intellectual discourse in the 1950s and 1960s. This represented the period when seminal works such as *The Passing of Traditional Society* (Lerner, 1958) and *Four Theories of the Press* (Siebert et al., 1956) engaged the attention of communication and political science scholars. This period was marked by a lopsided focus on the United States and the portrayal of Western values and ideas as the models to which every nation should aspire. Thus, the West signified 'modernity' while the non-west was represented as societies held back by 'tradition' (Hanitzsch, 2008, pp. 113–14). The collapse of the modernization theories propounded by communication scholars such as Daniel Lerner, Wilbur Schramm, Lucian Pye and Everett Rogers signified the end of the paradigm that ignored the impact of culture on the socio-economic development of newly emerging nations.

The second conceptual framework identified by Hanitzsch (2008) – 'The North and the South' – covered the period of the 1970s when intellectual discussion at the United Nations Educational, Scientific and Cultural Organisation (UNESCO) was dominated by agitations for global media reforms that were expected to restructure the lopsided nature of media and information flows between the West and the rest. The debate was informed by calls from developing countries for a New World Information and Communication Order (NWICO). Concerns raised by developing countries during the NWICO debate included but were not limited to: developing countries' reliance on the news media of the West; the negative impact of Western media products (e.g. television entertainment programs such as movies, soap operas, dramas, etc.) on the culture and media audiences of developing countries; and Western media's preoccupation with reporting negative events in developing countries (Hachten, 1996). The mid-1980s marked the development of the third paradigm labelled by Hanitzsch as 'The West and the West'. The period saw comparative media studies that examined media systems in specific European and Western countries because of the similarities and comparative differences among the countries. One example of a major study conducted during the period was the widely acclaimed book by Hallin and Mancini (2004). The fourth and most recent paradigm, according to Hanitzsch, is 'The West and the Global'. During this period, academic and research interests focused on 'media systems on a truly global scale' (Hanitzsch, 2008, p. 114). In the context of the chronological frameworks examined by Hanitzsch, we start our analysis of media models and press theories by examining the oldest of the press classifications – *Four Theories of the Press*.

Four Theories of the Press:
An old map for a changing world?

The *Four Theories of the Press* (Siebert et al., 1956) was conceptualized at
the peak of the Cold War. Essentially, the book reflected the ideological
differences that separated capitalism from the Soviet communist system
(Soviet communism). In *Four Theories of the Press*, Siebert et al. presented
what they termed four basic frameworks for understanding the relationship
of the state to the media. These frameworks were '(1) the nature of man, (2)
the nature of society and of the state, (3) the relation of man to the state,
and (4)...the nature of knowledge and of truth' (Siebert, 1956a, p. 10). On
the basis of these frameworks, the authors presented four theories of the
press, namely the authoritarian, libertarian, social responsibility and Soviet
communist press theories. In the authoritarian theory, the press was used
to inform people what their rulers felt they should know and the policies the
rulers wanted the people to support. In its simplest form, the authoritarian
theory viewed the press as 'a servant of the state'. In this system, the press
was obliged to support the policies of the leadership. Private ownership of
the press was permitted but only through the grant of a 'special permit' that
'could be withdrawn any time the obligation to support the royal policies
was considered to have been dishonored' (Siebert et al., 1956, p. 3). In the
authoritarian system, the mass media were assigned specific roles and were
thus subjected to controls deemed essential for attainment of the goals of
the state.

The libertarian theory drew heavily from the philosophies of John Milton
and John Stuart Mill. In the libertarian system, the press served as a check
on government, a watchdog of society. The libertarian theory believed 'the
underlying purpose of the media was to help discover truth, to assist in the
process of solving political and social problems by presenting all manner of
evidence and opinion as the basis for decisions. The essential characteristic
of this process was its freedom from government controls or domination'
(Siebert, 1956b, p. 51). The social responsibility theory highlighted the obligations and responsibilities that the press owed to society. The theory underscored the relationship between press freedom and responsibility. In the old
Soviet communist system, the press was an instrument of the Communist
Party. In the communist press system, criticism of the Party leadership was
not tolerated. The communist press was therefore 'conceived to interpret the
doctrine, to carry out the policies of the working class or the militant party'
(Schramm, 1956, p. 110).

More than four decades since its publication, *Four Theories of the Press* continues to attract critical attention from communication and media scholars. The popularity of the book, its widespread appeal to audiences across cultures and its use as a basic text for the study of media and politics have been identified as its major strengths. Additionally, it has been commended for furnishing us with a map for tracing the development of the press since the discovery of the printing press, and for facilitating an understanding of the changing relationships of the press to politics and society, as well as their impact on social and political change (Nerone, 1995). Consequently, *Four Theories of the Press* has been hailed by scholars as the first major attempt to conceptualize theories of the press. However, the book has drawn intense criticisms for its ideological biases, its methodological weaknesses and its ethnocentric arguments (Nerone, 1995; Picard, 1982/1983).

Critique of *Four Theories of the Press*

Since the publication of *Four Theories of the Press* more than 55 years ago, the world has experienced significant transformations in many ways. Despite its theoretical and practical blemishes, *Four Theories of the Press* is still considered a relevant work because of its 'tremendous impact on teaching and thinking about freedom of the press' (Nerone, 1995, p. 1). Sparks (2000, pp. 36–7) argues that the two main press systems – the soviet communist system and the libertarian system – made scientific sense in highlighting the difference between the two ways in which the market shapes the media and the ways in which the state influences the media. Nordenstreng (2006, p. 35) believes that, at the peak of its popularity, the book made a significant contribution to the academic literature on the role of the press in society, by directing scholars' attention to the relationship between the press and society. He regards the book as important because it offered a 'method of contrasting different paradigms of press and society' that proved useful in the education of journalists (Nordenstreng, 2006, p. 35). A related argument noted that the appeal of the book was sustained by 'the long-standing need for a theory of state-press relations' (Picard, 1982/83, p. 26).

However, a number of scholars have also criticized the book. For example, Nerone (1995) insisted the book was steeped in ideological contestations, despite Siebert et al.'s claim that it was value-free. Nerone argued the book was loaded with the propaganda elements of the time – the cold war agenda of 'global expansion of U.S. model of privately owned for-profit media' (p. 8). In fact, Nerone unmasked the ideological cloak of one of the authors of the book – Wilbur Schramm – who wrote the chapter on the Soviet communist theory. Nerone suggested that Schramm was immensely educated in anti-communist propaganda and had indeed served in various capacities as consultant to the United States' defence force departments during and after the Second World War. This implied that leading officials of the US government and those who benefited through research grants were influenced by policy to shape the world according to the views of the United States. According to Nerone, it was in this context that the authors of the *Four Theories of the Press* tried to explain 'why media systems are what they are', and thus 'catalogued historical relations between media and the state' (p. 15).

Other critics claim the book inaccurately presented press systems which existed across the world because it ignored the media in emerging countries despite the growing influence of the Non-Aligned Movement and other pro-independence organizations at the time (Picard, 1982/83, p. 25). Not only did the book overlook the media systems in the developing world, but Hallin and Mancini (2004, p. 10) also argued that the book offered little by way of the sketchy analysis of European media systems. The emergence of newly independent nations in Africa, Latin America and South Asia, as well as the growing intervention of the state in mass communication in some European countries, reinforced the shortcomings of the *Four Theories of the Press* and the need to modify press concepts. As Picard (1982/83, p. 28) argued, press typologies 'must constantly be reevaluated to reflect the changing realities of the world'. Nordenstreng echoed a similar sentiment, stating that the development of the mass media after the Second World War required a re-assessment of the functions of the media (2006, p. 35). Hallin and Mancini (2004, p. 10) contend that developments in the world, the demise of the geopolitics of the North versus the South, shifting political and economic ties and alliances signal an urgent need to accord the *Four Theories of the Press* 'a decent burial and move on to the development of more sophisticated models based on real comparative analysis'.

Other attempts to modify press systems

The shortcomings of the *Four Theories of the Press* no doubt generated scholarly efforts to modify press systems or to conceptualize new ones in order to reflect the realities of global geopolitics and the expanding international media landscape. For example, Hachten (1981) proposed five concepts – authoritarian, Western, communist, revolutionary and developmental – to replace the *Four Theories of the Press* even though his models share some similarities with Siebert et al.'s (1956) press concepts. Picard (1982/83, p. 26) believes that Hachten's press concepts provided a more accurate representation of the world at the time, as well as a clearer understanding of the relationship between the state and the press. Nevertheless, Picard admitted that Hachten's authoritarian and communist concepts were replicated from the *Four Theories of the Press*. Additionally, he acknowledged that even the Western concept proposed by Hachten was no more than a new heading adopted from a mix of the libertarian and the social responsibility theories. This leaves us with two new (original) concepts developed by Hachten, namely the revolutionary and the developmental models. The developmental press model examined the role of the media in the socio-economic development of new nations. The revolutionary press concept refers to the use of the press for revolutionary purposes in order to overthrow existing political systems. Examples of this include the use of the photocopier by civil rights and pro-democracy groups to convey information to the world during the 1989 Tiananmen Square demonstrations in China, as well as the use of audio cassettes during the Iranian revolution which overthrew the regime of the Shah of Iran in 1979.

In the mid-1990s, Hachten (1996) revised his press concepts and included two additional models – the democratic socialist and the democratic participant models. The key elements of the democratic socialist model were the advancement of greater diversity of views, and economic subsidies for weaker media which are aimed to sustain media pluralism. Lambeth (1995, p. 13) observed that the democratic socialist model was premised on the notion that 'governments have a responsibility to actively promote not only press freedom but citizen access and diversity of political expression'. This model of the media is common in Scandinavian countries such as Sweden, Norway and Denmark.

Other attempts at classifying media systems include Martin and Chaudhary's (1983) global media analysis which divided media systems into Western, Communist and Third World models. One of the criticisms against Martin and Chaudhary's media analysis is the failure to recognize the differences that underline the media systems in different countries and contexts within such broad areas as Western countries. Altschull (1995) also proposed three media models – market, communitarian and advancing. The market model was Altschull's response to criticisms of *Four Theories of the Press* which underplayed the influence of economics (market forces) on journalistic practices in capitalist North American and Western European states. Altschull also argued that the communitarian media model was proposed rather than the communist system in order to reduce the negativism associated with the Cold War era communist ideology. The communitarian model, he argued, was a more acceptable representation of those entities in which greater accent is given to the wellbeing of the society rather than to individual members. Another scholar who explored press theories and media models is John Merrill whose *Global Journalism* text (1983, 1995) is regarded as standard reading among journalism and communication students and teachers (see also de Beer & Merrill, 2004). Several scholars (e.g. Hallin & Mancini, 2004) have identified a major weakness in attempts to produce a global and homogeneous media system that fails to recognize cultural, political and economic differences that influence journalistic practices in different countries. In the sections that follow, we explore some of the conceptualizations of media systems that have been made in various regions of the world in order to show the variety that exists globally.

North American and Western European models

We start our analysis of more recent media systems by examining Hallin and Mancini's (2004) work which offers a theoretical basis for analysing media systems in Western Europe and North America. In their book, Hallin and Mancini developed three models which they named the Liberal Model (applicable mostly to Britain, Ireland and North America), the Democratic Corporatist Model (noticeable in northern continental Europe) and the Polarized Pluralist Model (applicable to the Mediterranean countries of southern Europe). The characteristics of these models are explored in the following paragraphs. Hallin and Mancini state that the main feature of the Liberal Model is the influence of market forces and the predominance of commercial media. The Democratic Corporatist Model is marked by the mutually beneficial relationship that exists between commercial media and media that are tied to social and political groups. This model also features 'a relatively active but legally limited role of the state' (2004, p. 11). The Polarized Pluralist Model is marked by a mix of weaker commercial media and more active interplay of party politics and the state.

As a starting point of their analysis, Hallin and Mancini (2004) propose four criteria for comparing media systems in Western Europe and North America. These are:

(1) the development of media markets, with particular emphasis on the strong or weak development of a mass circulation press; (2) political parallelism; that is, the degree and nature of the links between the media and political parties or, more broadly, the extent to which the media system reflects the major political

divisions in society; (3) the development of journalistic professionalism; and (4) the degree and nature of state intervention in media system. (p. 21)

Hallin and Mancini (2004, p. 22) argue that the chief distinguishing element among media systems is the level of 'the development of the mass circulation press'. The difference in mass circulation newspapers does not refer only to mere numbers but also relates to 'the nature of the newspaper, its relation to its audience and its role in the wider process of social and political communication' (p. 22). For example, while newspapers in southern Europe tend to target a small, educated and influential metropolitan audience, newspapers in northern Europe and North America are oriented towards a mass audience that is not necessarily entrenched in political activities.

In terms of professional roles, Hallin and Mancini (2004, p. 27) contend that one of the distinguishing elements among media systems is that while media in some countries are affiliated to political groups and parties, other media do not have such links. Thus, Hallin and Mancini argue that journalism, as practised in every part of the globe, is never neutral. They also draw a parallel between public broadcasting systems and the political system in each country. They identify four essential models for the administration of public broadcasting, namely: the government model (in which the government is directly involved in the control of broadcasting institutions); the professional model (which argues that broadcasting should be administered by professional journalists in order to protect broadcasting institutions from political interference and control); the parliamentary or proportional representation model (in which control of broadcasting is divided among political organizations on the basis of proportional representation); and the civic or 'corporatist' model which relates to the parliamentary model in that control of public service broadcasting is divided among various social and political entities (pp. 30–1). The civic or corporatist model differs from the parliamentary model because control is also extended to other important groups such as 'trade unions, business associations, religious organizations, ethnic associations, and the like' (p. 31). The authors point out that the four models of broadcasting are by no means mutually perfect. Some media systems combine or draw on some of the elements inherent in other models.

Hallin and Mancini's three media models

In the analysis of factors that define the relationship between media and political systems in North America and Western Europe, Hallin and Mancini

(2004, p. 69) identify three models along which discussion can be focused. They note that the development of the media systems was influenced by their geographical region of dominance and distinctive political systems that define the relationship between the media and political institutions. However, they caution that although they have grouped countries along various bands, the countries are not in general homogeneous. For example, although the United States and Britain are grouped as countries with liberal media traditions, there are significant differences between them. In the following paragraphs, we outline the three models in some detail.

The Mediterranean or Polarized Pluralist Model is typified by a small but influential press marked by the late arrival or institutionalization of the ethos of press freedom, as well as the late emergence of the commercial media. In this system, newspapers have a weak financial foundation and are subsequently in need of financial support; the print media tends to carry content rich in political life; the press has a 'tradition of commentary-oriented or advocacy journalism' (2004, p. 73). Another element includes control of the media by outside influences such as political parties, politicians, social movement organizations and economic forces. Within the Mediterranean media model, public broadcasting adopts the elements that characterize government or parliamentary models. Here, professionalization of journalism is not as strongly developed as is the case in the other models. Hence, in this media model, the 'state plays a large role as an owner, regulator, and funder of media, though its capacity to regulate effectively is often limited' (p. 73). These elements underpin the 'high degree of ideological diversity and conflict that characterizes the Southern European countries and which in turn is rooted in delayed development of liberal institutions' (pp. 73–4).

The North/Central European or Democratic Corporatist Model is distinguished by the early development of the culture of press freedom and the emergence of the newspaper industry, as well as high newspaper circulation. This media system has a solid record of political party-affiliated press, including other forms of media that are tied closely to social organizations. This party-affiliated press existed together with the commercial press for most decades of the twentieth century. The Democratic Corporatist Model, according to Hallin and Mancini, is also marked by commentary-oriented form of journalism, which is often combined with 'objective' reporting and the journalism that is oriented towards information provision. This model is also characterized by a high degree of journalistic professionalism, as well as a high level of official management and operation. In this model, as Hallin and Mancini (p. 74) describe it, 'Media are seen to a significant extent as social institutions for which the state has responsibility, and press freedom coexists with relatively strong state support for and regulation of media.' This model features public broadcasting systems that are parliamentary in nature. In this system, political parties and other social groups are involved in the control and administration of broadcasting. Hallin and Mancini point out that in the Democratic Corporatist Model, powerful commercial media industries frequently coexist with politically oriented media (p. 74).

The North Atlantic or Liberal Model which has similarities with the Democratic Corporatist Model is typified by the early emergence of the canons of press freedom and the development of the mass circulation press. In this model, commercial newspapers constitute a dominant force and the professionalization of journalism is deemed to be quite strong even though it lacks the kind of official organization that distinguishes the countries that constitute the Democratic Corporatist Model. One feature of the North Atlantic or Liberal Model is the influence of commercial pressures (market forces) on journalistic independence. Here, the practice of journalism is information-oriented although, in Britain, journalists tend to be more commentary-oriented. According to Hallin and Mancini, the state has a limited role in this media system, especially in the United States, Canada and Ireland. Professionalism underpins public broadcasting and broadcast regulation in this model. This ensures greater protection of journalists from political control. These characteristics suggest that liberal traditions developed quite early in the United States, Britain, Canada and Ireland, the countries that constitute the North Atlantic or Liberal Model (Hallin & Mancini, 2004).

Hallin and Mancini reinforce the argument that although North American and Western European countries share a number of characteristics, there are fundamental differences that exist not only within each media model but also across the three models. For example, 'in the Liberal countries the media are closer to the world of business, and further from the world of politics' (p. 76). However, in the Polarized Pluralist systems, the media are more powerfully entrenched in politics while in the Democratic Corporatist societies, the media are strongly tied to political and economic forces.

Critique of Hallin and Mancini's book

The three media models presented by Hallin and Mancini are relevant because they provide us with an organizing framework for analysing the media in North American and Western European countries. They also provide insights that are important for exploring the historical relationship (or lack thereof) between Western media models and media systems in other cultures. Can our knowledge of media systems around the globe be enhanced or diminished by an understanding of the three Western models presented by Hallin and Mancini? The answer is both yes and no. Although Hallin and Mancini's models are steeped in historical, political and economic relationships among North American and Western European countries and how those relationships define the different media systems, the frameworks they offer provide useful insights into how the media systems relate and differ. Their approaches also suggest various routes that researchers exploring global media systems might wish to take.

In terms of historical relationships, there is at least one way through which we can connect the Western European models to the origins of the press systems elsewhere. The fact that European powers influenced the development of the press in their colonies in Latin America, Africa and the Asia-Pacific region means we can find some similarities to European models. For example, Hallin and Papathanassopoulos (2002) point to common characteristics among southern European media and Latin American media, which may have their roots in the Spanish and Portuguese colonial history. Similarly, colonial powers such as Britain, France, Belgium, the Netherlands, Italy and Germany during the twentieth century influenced the nature of the media that emerged in their African colonies. We can therefore draw some historical links between European models and the systems of mass media that emerged in former colonies after independence.

Nevertheless, Hallin and Mancini's work suffers from some fundamental weaknesses such as the tendency to underplay the importance and history of the media systems in non-western societies such as Africa, Latin America, the Middle East and Asia. Implicit in Hallin and Mancini's work, as well as in Siebert et al.'s (1956) *Four Theories of the Press*, is the assumption that analysis of non-western media systems should be based on the frameworks that underline Western media systems. For example, in the opening chapter of their book, Hallin and Mancini make the point that the 'Anglo-American or Liberal media is typically taken as the norm against which other media systems are measured' (2004, p. 38), despite conceding that the North American and Western European media models do not necessarily fit media systems in other cultures. By suggesting that their focus on the media models of North America and Western Europe was informed by the predominance of the Western media models and their influence over the development of other media systems, Hallin and Mancini (p. 6) imply that the North American and Western European media systems are preeminent media systems which should serve as models for media systems in non-western countries.

If indeed there are variations within the North American and Western European media, there must be differences and similarities in non-western media systems. Media systems and models, whether at regional or continental levels of assessment, are not homogeneous. Differences in historical, legal, cultural, political, economic and religious frameworks influence the diverse nature of journalistic practices in Western and non-western countries. McQuail (1994, p. 133) makes this point clearly: 'In most countries, in any case, the media do not constitute any single "system", with a single purpose or philosophy, but are composed of many separate, overlapping, often inconsistent elements, with appropriate differences of normative expectation and actual regulation.' Elsewhere, Mancini (2005, p. 77) acknowledges that an exclusive European model of journalism does not exist owing to fundamental differences that define the media models in European countries. Nevertheless, he appears to commit the same error of universalizing the discourse on media systems when he contends that 'the Anglo-American model of journalism, with all its professional implications, seems to stand out as the only universal model' (2005, p. 78). Yet, there are media systems in non-western cultures that are not distinctively Anglo-American in terms of journalism practice and professional orientation. Typical examples can be found in the Arab world (Amin, 2002; Ayish, 2002; Mellor, 2005, 2008; Pintak & Ginges, 2008; Sakr, 2005). In the next section, we explore the history, characteristics and nature of the media systems of Africa.

Media systems in Africa

Campbell (2003) uses four typologies – Vanguard, Subservient, Reinforcing Change Agent and Clandestine press systems – to classify the African press and the role the press plays at different times in history. He acknowledges that these 'cannot define the press in every African state in every era... But the typologies are valuable nonetheless in illuminating and clarifying the multiple functions of newspapers in African societies over time' (Campbell, 2003, p. 32). The vanguard press underlines how pro-independent newspapers led the struggle for political and economic liberation of Africa. However, following the attainment of political freedom, emerging African leaders advocated a new role for the press – a press that serves as a 'servant of the state' or a press that mobilizes the population for socio-economic development. Press subservience in Africa is widely regarded as an essential element of 'Development Journalism', the brand of journalism that promotes 'positive news' and advocates collaboration between the state and the media.

While there exists a vast literature on development journalism, many scholars have different understandings of the concept itself. Altschull (1995, p. 231), for example, cautions that the concept is hard to define essentially because of the nature of its origins. Nevertheless, Aggarwala (1979, p. 181) defines development journalism as 'the use of all journalistic skills to report development processes in an interesting fashion'. One perspective sees development journalism as a form of journalism practised in developing societies where the media are expected to serve as instruments for nation building and as facilitators of national socio-economic development through provision of information that contributes to a reduction in hunger, illiteracy and poverty (Hachten, 1981, 1996; Altschull, 1995, pp. 230–1). The concept of development journalism received greater attention among communication scholars during the debate over a NWICO which took place at the UNESCO in the 1970s and up to the early 1980s. During the debate, leaders of developing countries criticized Western news media for their preoccupation with negative events in developing countries. They also argued that foreign news flow was quantitatively and qualitatively weighted in favour of the West (see Hachten, 1996). In this context, developing countries called for development journalism practice that recognizes 'positive' news and developments in their societies. Advocates of development journalism argue that, rather than serve as a critical watchdog of society against abuses by government officials, the media should assist the government to promote national unity.

Founded on the same principles as development communication, development journalism advocates the belief that journalists should serve as agents of social change and development in the societies in which they operate. Development journalism represents an alternative view of the role of journalists in developing countries, contrary to the dominant Western understanding of the critical and adversarial relationship that should exist between the media and government. As Romano (1998, p. 64) explained, while objectivity is the key operating term in Western journalistic practice, such a term is suppressed or underplayed in the form of non-adversarial journalism that is common in developing countries.

Critics of development journalism assert that the media must serve as an independent watchdog of society rather than as a mouthpiece of the state. In the context of Africa, Campbell (2003, p. 37) argues that the concept of development journalism 'was little more than a guise for strict state control of newspapers and of the broadcast media'. Altschull (1995, p. 236) shares a similar view, describing development journalism as a 'smokescreen' that permits 'dictators to subject their press to iron controls and strict censorship'.

Campbell (2003) also describes another press role in Africa as that of a reinforcing change agent in which the African press was expected to champion political reforms and to serve as a catalyst for change. The clandestine press, which has its roots in anti-colonial struggles, is similar to what Hachten (1996) refers to as the underground press or what is also referred to as 'guerrilla journalism' in Nigeria in the 1990s (see Olorunyomi, 1998). It is the kind of underground journalism that resists authority, and engages in robust and constructive criticism of military dictators and political leaders.

The historical context, professional practices and the role of the African press differ quite markedly from the North American and Western European media models, not withstanding that Nyamnjoh (2005) feels that the African journalism system is a replication of the Western liberal democracy model. Shaw (2009, p. 493) disagrees with Nyamnjoh and argues that there are different traditions of journalism practice in Africa which are determined by particular periods in history. He argues, for example, that prior to the introduction of colonial rule, there was a unique form of African journalism that 'took the form of oral discourse, using communication norms informed by oral tradition and folk culture with communal storytellers (griots), musicians, poets and dancers playing the role of the modern-day journalist' (Shaw, 2009, p. 493). Shaw notes that it is the 'African world view largely based on group solidarity and belonging that informs the oral discourse style of journalism unique to pre-colonial Africa' (p. 493). However, during the colonial period, the African press was influenced by classical liberal democratic traditions of the press which served as a watchdog and an advocate of freedom of expression – both of which helped to uncover the abuses committed by the colonial administrators.

The watchdog role of the press in colonial Africa set the tone for pro-independence campaigns. Shaw identified the watchdog role of the African press during colonial rule as a common element in Anglo-American journalism (p. 498), although some of the partisan newspapers in Britain and the United States were more strongly attached to political parties than the African press. All these suggest that the role of the African press differed significantly during each historical epoch, namely the pre-colonial, colonial and postcolonial times. However, what is missing from the frameworks analysed here is a discussion on the forms of media ownership and how they affect media performance. There are two basic forms of media ownership in Africa – government-owned and controlled media and the privately owned, profit-oriented media. Both forms of ownership carry consequences for the type of journalism practised in the continent. Rønning (2005, p. 178) has noted how the relationship between government-owned media and privately owned commercial press has affected the nature of journalism practice in Africa.

> At the moment, it seems as if in many African countries there is a situation where the official media maintain an over-close and uncritical relationship with government, while the independent press often has a tendency to be sensationalist and rumour mongering.

Other scholars have also analysed African media systems from different perspectives. For example, in her book – *Mass Media in Sub-Saharan Africa* – Bourgault (1995) argues that the key attributes of the African media are rooted in Africa's oral traditions. She states that 'mass media in sub-Saharan Africa have all been affected to varying degrees by three factors: the precolonial legacy of the oral tradition, the presence of an alienated managerial class, and the domination of modern African societies by systems of political patronage' (Bourgault, 1995, pp. xiii–xiv). In the book, she also discusses the influence that political, social, economic, historical and cultural forces have had in framing Africa's media landscape, particularly media systems in Anglophone and Francophone Africa. In a more recent edited volume, Orgeret and Rønning (2009) examine the role of the media in Africa, with particular focus on political, social and economic development of the continent, including the role of new technologies as drivers of socio-political change. The next section examines the Latin American media systems to explore their relationships (if any) with the North American and Western European media models.

Latin American media systems

The media situation in Latin America has been influenced significantly by the dynamics of the economy and the nature of politics in the region. As Waisbord (2000) argued, the state and market forces strongly influenced the press system in Latin America. He states that although North America and Western Europe may have had major influences on the development of broadcasting and the press in South America, it would be misleading to propose that the media systems that eventually developed in the region were direct transplants of the Western models. The varying relationships between the media, the state and market forces have been attributed to the variations in the Latin American media systems. Thus, in South America, 'The liberal ideology of the US press could not effectively serve as the organizing principle, given that newspaper owners were interested in cultivating close-knit relations with government officials and that press economics were anchored in the state' (Waisbord, 2000, p. 50). However, Herscovitz (2004, pp. 73–4) notes that, in regard to newspapers, editors in Latin America 'had access to European and American journalistic standards at different points in the evolution of newspapers' development in the region'. For example, American influence over Brazilian journalism was cultivated through sponsored visits and training programmes that enabled Brazilian journalists to visit the United States. The effect was that, 'When they came back, many of these journalists sought the application of elements of the American style to Brazilian press' (Herscovitz, 2004, p. 74). Hallin and Papathanassopoulos (2002) also identified common elements that shaped the media systems of southern Europe and those of Latin America. The defining characteristics include 'low levels of newspaper circulation, a tradition of advocacy reporting, instrumentalization of privately-owned media, politicization of public broadcasting and broadcast regulation, and limited development of journalism as an autonomous profession' (2002, pp. 176–7). There is the notion that the similarities in the media systems of southern Europe and Latin America occurred because in both regions 'conflict between liberal democratic and authoritarian traditions continued through most of the 20th century' (p. 175). The authors observe that in Latin America as in the southern European states, the media are controlled by private businesses that tend to use their media corporations to achieve overt and covert political objectives (p. 177). For example, 'In Brazil, instrumentalization is most evident in the case of the regional media: regional newspapers and broadcasting companies are typically owned by local oligarchs who use them to solidify their political control' (p. 179).

Waisbord identified diverse factors that helped to construct the South American media models. These include the strong ties between commercial interests and the state, the formulation of newspapers as political ventures rather than profit-oriented businesses, state monopoly of critical resources that constitute the bedrock of press economics, the dominant role of government advertising as the chief source of income for media, state ownership of big businesses prior to privatization in the 1990s, state control of banks and the modalities for issuing of loans to businesses, as well as state influence over foreign exchange rates, taxes and charges that are required for the importation of raw material and the technologies for production of newspapers (Waisbord, 2000, p. 51). As Waisbord explained, it was the strength of the economic power of the state that tied the operations of the media closely to the apron strings of the government. In a situation of unequal relationship, it was not surprising that media owners had to cultivate the friendship of state officials in order to remain in business. While the critical or confrontational press was subdued through refusal of licence renewal applications and denial of favourable exchange rates for importation of raw material and equipment, Waisbord notes that these anti-press freedom strategies did not eliminate occasional criticisms of state officials.

In general, the absence of the liberal traditions of objective journalism and the failure of the press to serve as the watchdog of society over government abuses in South American countries could be attributed to the absence of a powerful 'cultural-political push to depoliticize the press, to downplay partisan allegiances, and to follow the canon of objective reporting' (Waisbord, 2000, p. 52). Authoritarian rule which dominated Latin American countries in the 1960s and 1970s also contributed to the evolution of the prevailing media systems (Waisbord, 2000). For example, with the exception of Venezuela and Colombia, all of South America was ruled by military dictators (2000, p. 54). In Brazil in particular, military rule lasted for 22 years, from 1964 to 1986 (Herscovitz, 2004, p. 72). Just as the media sided with state officials prior to military dictatorship, the South American media also supported military dictators by playing down human rights abuses and violations of press freedom and freedom of citizens to express themselves. Waisbord (2000, p. 54) cites specific instances in Chile where the *El Mercurio* newspaper openly backed the 1973 coup and the despotic rule of Augusto Pinochet; in Brazil where the press consented to state censorship while the *Globo* television network took on the role of the government defender; and in Argentina where the media acted as the official mouthpiece of the government in the 1982 war with Britain over the ownership of the Falkland Islands and where the media also overlooked serious crimes committed by state officials. In Colombia of the 1990s, however, a different system prevailed. Journalism in that country was deemed to be particularly risky because of the fear of what might happen if journalists exposed drug traffickers, guerrilla forces and the activities of other underground groups (Miralles, 2010, p. 136). The risky nature of Colombian journalism thus induced fear in journalists and led to self-censorship.

The end of authoritarian rule in much of South America and the emergence of liberal democracy produced journalistic practices that are at variance with the previous models. Porto and Hallin (2009) note that the processes of democratization that swept through the region in the past three decades, even if one-sided, contributed not only to the abandonment of military dictatorship and the entrenchment of a culture of democracy but also heralded radical changes in political and economic systems. However, these changes had their drawbacks such as 'economic recession, hyperinflation, and the adoption of neoliberal policies, with significant consequences to all spheres of society, including the mass media' (Porto & Hallin, 2009, p. 291).

The growth of democracy in Latin America meant that journalists were able to expose corruption and human rights abuses compared to their performance in the previous era of authoritarian rule. Journalists also enjoyed relatively greater levels of freedom than was previously the case. As Waisbord (2000, p. 58) notes, the entrenchment of liberal democracies in the region has 'opened room for reporting on subjects such as official corruption and human rights violations which were shunned in the past ...' However, even in the growing atmosphere of press freedom in South America, the point has been made that journalists in the region experienced different levels of freedom and were able to practise advocacy journalism only to a certain degree. Waisbord makes the point that, although governments in the region may not control the media directly as was the case in the past, Latin American media are still not free from government controls, including government monopoly over economic resources that are essential for media operation.

In the next section, we examine the Arab and Middle East media systems to understand how cultural, religious and political forces helped to influence existing journalistic practices in the region.

Arab and Middle East media systems

There are divergent views about how to categorize the media systems in the Arab world, including the Middle East. While some scholars draw on the social responsibility model to analyse the Arab and Middle East media systems (Hamada, 1993, cited in Mellor, 2005, p. 50), others describe the Arab media through the lens of development theory (Abu Zeid, 2000, cited in Mellor, 2005, p. 50). This model perceives the Arab media as an agent of socio-economic development. And yet a third model examines the Arab media through the theory of dependency (Abdel Rahman, 1983, cited in Mellor, 2005, p. 50). This model views the Arab media as products of decades of colonial and despotic rule that has left the media dependent on foreign media.

Arguably the most contested classifications of the Arab media were proposed by Rugh (2004). Rugh categorized Arab press into four systems, namely: mobilization; loyal; diverse; and transitional. Rugh's classifications have been criticized for a range of reasons, including the ambiguity in the categories used in describing the region's press systems, as well as the failure of the classifications to reflect changes in the Arab media that began in the 1990s

(Mellor, 2005, p. 51). Arab and Middle Eastern scholars have also challenged the philosophical, theoretical and practical assumptions that underline Rugh's categorizations.

The mobilization model identifies the media as an instrument used by the regimes in Syria, Libya and Sudan to mobilize the population towards the achievement of the governments' goals. However, according to Rugh, the press in loyalist systems enjoys a certain degree of freedom, including private ownership of the press. Despite this climate of freedom, the central governments in Saudi Arabia, Oman, Palestine, Bahrain, Qatar and the United Arab Emirates still apply a measure of indirect control over the press. Indirect government control means that press owners still pledge allegiance to the government. Under this arrangement, press owners and their businesses avoid publication of material that could offend government officials. According to Rugh, the diverse press in the Arab world enjoys greater freedom from government control and the publication of news and material that reflects different views in societies such as Kuwait, Yemen, Iraq and Lebanon. The press in the transitional system is marked by lack of clarity about the direction in which it is headed, as well as lack of awareness about its movement to a different system. Countries that reflect this system are Algeria, Jordan, Egypt and Tunisia. So, Rugh's classifications depict (in terms of ownership structure) a press that is in private hands in the Loyalist and Diverse systems but under government control in the Mobilization model, and also under mixed control in the Transitional system.

Rugh's typology of the Arab press has received severe criticisms from scholars within and outside the region. One criticism is that Rugh created the impression of a uniform or homogeneous media system in the Arab world. Another criticism points to the lack of a solid theoretical foundation on which the typology was formulated (Mellor, 2005, p. 52). And yet another criticism is that there are elements in one press system that could be found in other systems, thus blurring the line of distinction that separates one press system from another. Mellor (p. 53) also contends that Rugh's classifications of the Arab press systems reflect traditional Western models in which the political system is associated with press systems such as totalitarian, communist and social responsibility models. The key flaw in these Western models is their failure to recognize non-western media systems (p. 53). A major weakness in Rugh's classifications of the Arab press is that he 'uses one primary variable, namely ownership, to categorize the Arab press into four main categories: mobilized, loyalist, diverse, and transitional' (Mellor, 2005, p. 72). However, as several scholars have pointed out, the mode of press ownership may have little or no impact on the contents of the press. Al Jazeera is cited as an example of media which is funded by the Emir of Qatar but still classified as a 'commercial' television channel (2005, pp. 72–3). Questions have also been raised about the level of loyalty served by media in those countries whose media system has been classified as loyal. As Mellor queried:

> if the loyalist media outlets aim to preserve the status quo and enforce existing policies and traditions, then how can we explain the paradoxical situation where wealthy Arabs, particularly Saudi businessmen, finance satellite channels that largely depend on beautiful young hostesses to attract the audience (Al Kadry & Harb, 2002), or on certain types of entertainment programs that serve the same purpose.... (2005, p. 73)

As evidence of the failure of Rugh's typology to reflect the changing landscape of Arab journalism, Pintak and Ginges (2008, p. 197) point out that at the onset of the twenty-first century, many Arab journalists believed their mission was to champion political and social changes in the region, to represent their region and the Muslim world, and not to identify themselves with specific Arab states. More fundamentally, Arab journalists of the twenty-first century 'see political reform, human rights, poverty, and education as the most important issues facing the region; and while protective of the Arab people, Arab culture, and religion, they are not overtly anti-American' (Pintak & Ginges, 2008, p. 197). As an indication of the difficulty of categorizing Arab media, Pintak and Ginges (2008, p. 194) note how the establishment of Al Jazeera television in 1996 sparked an upsurge in the establishment of free-to-air Arab satellite channels, 'in the growing aspiration for independence on the part of print journalists across the region, and in the rise of bloggers, who are spearheading a newly aggressive form of reporting'. Surely, technological changes in journalism have transformed the nature of the media and modes of journalism practice across the Arab world.

Ayish (2002, p. 138) believes the rise of satellite television in the region has 'brought to Arab homes not only a wider range of program choices but also new public affairs genres that seem to shape television journalism practices on Arab world television'. However, it has been suggested that the emergence of commercial satellite television operating in tandem with government-owned television helped to engender not only 'a pan-Arab public sphere' featuring diverse news programs but also the rise of citizen deliberation on the political process (Ayish, 2002, p. 139). Khouri (2001) disagrees with this view, arguing instead that the arrival of satellite television may be having unintended impacts on Arab society, such as the installation of authoritarian regimes in the region rather than the promotion of a democratic culture and transparent leadership. Nevertheless, scholars are divided on the impact that satellite television is having on political systems and freedom of expression in the region (e.g. al-Kasim, 1999; Sakr, 2005, p. 147; Mellor, 2008, p. 481). Mellor (2008) illustrates one way through which Arab satellite television has had an impact on journalism practice in the region. Arab journalists are held up as popular folk heroes and heroines 'for their bravery in reporting from the heart of violence, for example, the Iraq War or the Palestinian *intifada*. They have become the new "heroes" who have endured harassment, murder, and arrest in their truth-seeking mission' (Mellor, 2008, pp. 475–6). The next section examines the media situation in China.

Media transformations in China

Political developments in China, in particular the dominant influence of communist ideology in the country have profoundly affected the media system that existed in China at particular periods in history. The history of China's media marks the story of an evolving media system that experienced remarkable transformations at different times – from a strictly controlled Party organ to a media that combined elements of free market principles with propaganda role of the media. China's media emerged from strict Communist Party controls during the leadership of Mao Zedong up to 1978 when Deng Xiaoping replaced Mao as Communist Party leader. Deng's policies, while still retaining elements of communist party propaganda in the media, ushered in an era of greater freedom for Chinese media. Thus, the economic and media reforms that kicked in from the late 1970s and into the 1980s saw the emergence of privately owned press that enjoyed market expansion, editorial and financial independence, and the freedom to expose corruption and to criticize failed state policies (de Burgh, 2000; Yong, 2000).

During the reign of Mao Zedong, Chinese news media served as propaganda tools of the Chinese Communist Party (CCP). The media were required to perform specific roles and were heavily subsidized because no commercial advertising was allowed. Journalists were regarded first as employees of the state rather than professional journalists beholden to their professional values and canons of the industry. However, the changes in the Chinese media, brought about by the atmosphere of freedom, were so strong that by 1979 the media were able to 'criticize aspects of official behavior and to expose official malpractice; programmes giving space for ordinary people to voice their opinions and human interest stories appeared' (de Burgh, 2000, p. 551; see also Sun, 1996).

Historically, the emergence of Maoism as a political philosophy has been traced to the conditions faced by the CCP in the 1930s and 1940s (Huang, 2002). According to Huang, from 1945 to the death of Mao in September 1976, the CCP's official philosophy was deemed to be heavy on extreme dedication to voluntarism, revolutionary nationalism, class struggle and populism (2002, p. 45). One of the main characteristics of Maoist media philosophy was the strong belief in the power of the mass propaganda role of the media. Essentially, Mao and his followers believed the mass media should be used to spread the Party's doctrines (Huang, 2002, p. 67). Specifically, under Mao, there was no such thing as press freedom. Press criticism was not tolerated and so too was bad news. As Mao argued, 'if we do 10 things and nine are bad, and they are published in the press, then we will certainly perish' (Mao, 1959, cited in Huang, 2002, p. 74). Huang (2002) identified certain key features of the media during Mao's regime. For example, the Party and the state tightly controlled the Chinese news media and there was a great deal of self-censorship by journalists. The media were also anti-West in their coverage of Western news events. Furthermore, Western news media were banned in China. For instance, during the Cultural Revolution, people were not allowed to listen to foreign radio broadcasts. Maoist media philosophy was also characterized by anti-commercialism (Huang, 2002, pp. 75–81). 'Under the strictly centrally-controlled and planned economy, the news media's budgets, circulation, and the sizes of staff were all controlled by the central or local governments' (2002, p. 81).

When Deng Xiaoping succeeded Mao in 1978, he set about institutionalizing major reforms that transformed the political and economic systems, as well as journalistic practices (Sun, 1996; Chengju, 2001). For example, major Western news agencies such as the Associated Press (AP) and the United Press International (UPI) were allowed to set up bureaus in Beijing in 1979. Other major US newspapers such as *The New York Times*, the *Washington Post* and the *Los Angeles Times* were allowed to establish offices in China, something that was never allowed during the time of Mao (Huang, 2002, p. 136). As Huang explained, 'while propaganda still remained largely the dominant content, the news media and journalists also began to pay more attention to news and propaganda-free materials – human interest stories, reports on disasters, accidents, and crimes, entertainment features, and so on' (2002, p. 137). Most of the media reforms introduced by Deng Xiaoping in the late 1970s and early to mid-1980s have been retained by his successors, thus underlying the impact that market reforms have had on Chinese journalism post-Mao (Chengju, 2001).

Beyond China, some scholars have critically examined the role of the media in countries such as India (see Rajan, 2005, 2007; Vilanilam, 2005) although such scholarly efforts did not exclusively dwell on the media systems in the country or in the region.

Conclusion

This chapter has analysed systematically and critically past and contemporary media models and press systems. The media systems include the *Four Theories of the Press* (Siebert et al., 1956), as well as other scholarly attempts to modify media models and press concepts such as Hachten's (1996) media classifications (authoritarian, Western, communist, revolutionary, developmental, democratic socialist and democratic participant), Martin and Chaudhary's (1983) Western, communist and Third World models, and Altschull's (1995) market, communitarian and advancing media models. These classifications underline scholarly attempts to rectify the inadequacies that were identified in previous media models and press systems. Whether the evolving press theories and media models have adequately addressed the flaws inherent in the *Four Theories of the Press* remains a subject of academic debate.

However, this chapter argued that past attempts at formulating media models and press systems had tended to be predominantly Western in orientation and ethnocentric in scope, narrow in terms of depth and lacking in analytic rigour. A unique feature of this chapter therefore is the analysis of non-western media systems that highlighted the political, social, cultural and economic factors that underpin journalistic practices in different regions. The chapter also examined the more recent North American and Western European media systems (Hallin & Mancini, 2004) that have been hailed because they offered an organizing framework for analysing media systems in the two regions and also for exploring the historical relationship and differences between Western media models and media systems in other cultures. For example, Western European models are seen to have influenced the media systems in parts of Latin America, Africa and the Asia-Pacific region, thus providing some historical links between European models and the systems of mass media that emerged in former colonies after independence. Hallin and Papathanassopoulos (2002) also point to common characteristics among southern European media and Latin American media, which may have their roots in the Spanish and Portuguese colonial history.

The chapter also analysed the media systems in Africa, Latin America, the Arab world and the Middle East, as well as media transformations in China. This is by no means an exhaustive list of the media systems that encompass the world of journalism but they reflect the different characteristics of media across different political, economic and cultural platforms. Analysis of various media systems suggests that significant differences and similarities exist across the world. In continental Europe, for example, there are major differences that distinguish the media in Mediterranean (southern) Europe from the media in Northern Europe. Although Western Europe and the United States share certain democratic and cultural traditions, the media systems in both regions are far from homogeneous. Although much of Africa was colonized by European powers and although colonial rule influenced the origins of African media, there are still differences in the media systems of Africa and Europe. More significantly, analysis of media models and press systems presented in this chapter shows how different journalistic norms in various regions of the world are shaped by different cultural practices and political experiences, as well as different economic forces. The underlying message is that media systems across the world are more heterogeneous than they are homogeneous, even if there are traces of similarities in the systems that exist in some parts of the world.

DISCUSSION QUESTIONS

1. Summarize the main differences between the various models discussed in the *Four Theories of the Press,* and, using current examples, discuss whether your own country's media system still fits any of the classifications.

2. How do the three media models presented by Hallin and Mancini (2004) in their book relate and/or differ? Discuss these in light of scholarly critiques of the book.

3. Outline and discuss the four schema used by Campbell (2003) to classify the African press. What are the merits and drawbacks of his classifications?

4. Explain how politics and big business played a significant role in shaping the Latin American media landscape before, during and after the era of military dictatorship.

5. Discuss how the advent of satellite television transformed the profile of Arab journalists and the process of democratization in the Middle East.

CHAPTER 3

Journalistic practices and role perceptions

Introduction

Arguments about why some events transform into news and others do not have dominated journalism and communication research interest for quite some time. There exists a considerable body of knowledge of how journalism is practised across the world. This knowledge relates to observations of journalistic work and routines, journalists' professional values, as well as their views and backgrounds. Increasingly, scholarly focus has been on comparing practices across cultures, as researchers have been concerned with the way journalism is practised in various forms globally. However, attention to comparative journalism studies does not have a long history, and, until recent decades, much of the literature considered the Anglo-Saxon journalism model as the blueprint for the globe, neglecting other types of journalism. In fact, as German journalism scholar Frank Esser has pointed out, some of the previous analyses of journalism have been ethnocentric in nature: 'In mass communication research, some Anglo-Saxon scholars seem to believe that organizational structures and routines in newspaper offices are the same everywhere. There are, however, fundamental differences between countries, although from just looking at the final product one would hardly assume it' (Esser, 1998, p. 376).

This chapter examines research on journalism practices, in particular journalists' role perceptions and their professional values in order to determine the various types of journalism that exist in diverse regions of the world. Much of this literature is based around surveys that examined differences and similarities in journalists' professional views. This chapter includes an examination of influences on journalistic practices across individual, organizational, media system and cultural levels. In particular, the chapter focuses on how culture influences journalism practices, and examines arguments for

37

regional approaches that emanated from a belief that journalism works best if it reflects local cultural values. Many of these regional models emerged from a resistance to imported Western models which local journalists did not see as applicable to their cultural circumstances. We examine these models and propose a variety of frameworks through which we can approach such comparisons, such as established models from cross-cultural psychology and anthropology.

Journalistic decision-making

Every day, journalists across the globe make decisions about which of the multitude of events that happen around them deserve to be selected or rejected as news stories. The basis on which such decisions are made is important because there is some evidence that media coverage reflects social reality through which audiences experience the world (Berger & Luckmann, 1966; Adoni & Mane, 1984).

Scholarly interest in how events become news has its origins in the work of David Manning White (1950) who conducted the first of the so-called gate-keeper studies. Nowadays, gatekeeping is typically understood as 'the process by which billions of messages that are available in the world get cut down and transformed into the hundreds of messages that reach a given person on a given day' (Shoemaker, 1991, p. 1). This notion was strongly influenced by White's study of a US wire editor (a man he called Mr Gates) at work. White's work had its origins in a concept that social psychologist Kurt Lewin (1947, 1951) termed 'gatekeeping' some years earlier. Lewin had used this term to refer to the way in which food reached a family's dinner table, passing through various gates at which decisions about its inclusion or rejection were made. In a concise overview of his work, Shoemaker and Vos (2009b, p. 76) point out how Lewin's study concluded that 'not everyone is equally important in making food selection choices, and he showed how influencing the person who orders or shops for food could change the food habits of the entire family'. Drawing on his food analogy, Lewin (1947, p. 145) explained that news flowed through 'certain communication channels', and that certain areas within the communication channels operated as 'gates'. According to Lewin,

> Gate sections are governed either by impartial rules or by 'gatekeepers'. In the latter case, an individual or group is 'in power' for making the decision between 'in' or 'out'. Understanding the functioning of the gate becomes equivalent then to understanding the factors which determine the decisions of the gate keepers

and changing the social process means influencing or replacing the gate keeper. (1947, p. 145)

White (1950) was fascinated by Lewin's references to gatekeepers and how various gates determined the selection of news (For an in-depth historical background of White's involvement in gatekeeping studies, see Reese & Ballinger, 2001.) He subsequently examined the processes of decision-making adopted by 'Mr Gates' at the wire desk of the *Peoria Star* in the mid-Western United States, in what has since become an influential study in journalism (White, 1950). White asked the wire editor to note the reasons for rejecting various news items (which constituted 90 per cent of all the news items received during the one-week period) and subsequently analysed them. A majority of the reasons related to technical aspects of journalism, such as lack of space, poor writing and other style aspects. Yet, a few also related to more individual perceptions, with Mr Gates noting 'B.S.' or 'propaganda' in a few cases, and overall around a third related to Mr Gates' personal reasons. White argued that Mr Gates' reasons for selecting and rejecting news showed 'how highly subjective, how reliant upon value-judgments based on the gatekeeper's own set of experiences, attitudes and expectations the communication of "news" really is' (White, 1950, p. 386). The study has its shortcomings because instead of looking at the wider structures and multiple gates within an organization, White merely focused on one individual's gatekeeping role. Nevertheless, as Shoemaker and Vos (2009b, p. 78) note, White's 'study encouraged many communication researchers to look at selection decisions in news'.

Other studies progressively identified a wider variety of influences which, over time, have led to a complicated set of influences on journalistic decision-making. Gieber (1956), for instance, found wire editors were also influenced by their perceptions of their community and readers, the traditions of their newspaper and the news policies of their superiors. Technical aspects were also influential, such as deadlines, production requirements and competing news items – factors he called a 'straightjacket of mechanical details' (1956, p. 175). Breed (1955) also identified how journalists quickly learned the rules of their own organization through a socialization process that taught them the unwritten rules or policies of their news organization. Breed's study in particular highlighted the powerful influence that an organization can have over what becomes news. Rather than individual reporters engaging in news making decisions based on their own individual biases, Breed argued that news was the outcome of what powerful members of an organization decided.

Over the past 50 years, there have been numerous analyses of journalists and their gatekeeping roles. These studies have significantly enhanced our understanding of the complex and large number of influences on news making. Shoemaker's (1991, pp. 70–5; also Shoemaker & Reese, 1996) model, which takes a more holistic approach to the factors that influence gatekeepers' decisions, has since become one of the most influential. In her three interrelated gatekeeping models, Shoemaker argued that not only were gatekeepers influenced by their own life experiences and the organizational characteristics and communication routines, but the news organization itself was also embedded in social system ideology and culture. Thus, the journalists working at a newspaper's foreign desk, for example, ought to be studied with all three influences in mind: their personal history and character; their organization; as well as the political, social, economic and cultural systems in which they operate. In one of the most widely cited studies of gatekeeping, Shoemaker and Reese (1996) theorize further about five levels of influence which they believe exist on a continuum from micro to macro. At the lowest level is the individual, already identified by White (1950). This includes the individual's personal biases, backgrounds, professional views and attitudes. Above this level, Shoemaker and Reese identify media routines, which refer to the set of journalistic practices and techniques such as news values.

There exists a vast body of knowledge about news values, much of which was inspired by Norwegian researchers Galtung and Ruge's (1965) seminal study that analysed the way in which four Norwegian newspapers covered three international crises in Congo, Cuba and Cyprus. The study focussed on eight general news factors – Frequency, Threshold, Unambiguity, Meaningfulness, Consonance, Unexpectedness, Continuity, Composition – as well as four culturally determined news factors – Reference to Elite Nations, Reference to Elite People, Reference to Persons and Reference to Something Negative. The authors argued that an event was more likely to become news the more it satisfied the above criteria (selection). Once the news event had been selected, those factors that made it newsworthy were accentuated (distortion). Others have since attempted to update and refine Galtung and Ruge's original list, most notably Harcup and O'Neill (2001) who examined day-to-day coverage in three British newspapers, arguing that this would give a more representative picture, rather than looking exclusively at foreign news coverage, as Galtung and Ruge had done. Based on their study, Harcup and O'Neill developed 10 news values dealing with: the power elite; celebrity; entertainment; surprise; bad news; good news; magnitude; relevance; whether it was a follow-up; and, lastly, whether it reflected a newspaper's agenda. Such studies have not been without criticisms, most pointedly the argument that examinations of the content of newspapers do not allow conclusions to be made about news selection processes (Hjavard, 2002). Another criticism was that Galtung and Ruge used hard-to-define categories (Harcup & O'Neill, 2001). Nevertheless, the study by Galtung and Ruge serves as the most influential explanation of news values (McQuail, 1994, p. 270), with a large number of researchers adopting its framework and for the most part investigating or replicating Galtung and Ruge's arguments, albeit with some modifications.

Returning to Shoemaker and Reese's (1996) model, the media routines' level is followed by the organizational level, which relates to the internal goals and structures of the organization. This level echoes Breed's (1955) earlier work, and generally refers to such influences as ownership of news organizations. At the next higher level, Shoemaker and Reese locate extra-media influences, namely such outside forces as social institutions, technological aspects and the economic environment in which journalists operate. The fifth and highest level addresses the impact of the social system, or culture (see also Shoemaker & Vos (2009a) for an up-to-date account of gatekeeping theory). Other attempts at classifying the influences on journalistic decision-making have yielded broadly similar models, even if they sometimes vary in terms of the number of levels they identify (see, e.g., Ettema et al., 1987; McQuail, 2005; Preston, 2009). Nevertheless, Hanitzsch et al. (2010, p. 7) point out that 'the conceptual overlap between these models is not particularly overwhelming. Although they contain, by and large, similar sources of influence, they often place them on different levels. The only exception is the individual level, on which all reviewed models agree'.

Koponen (2003, p. 155) has pointed out that journalists do make their own decisions but those decisions are guided by the larger forces surrounding the journalists in their organization as well as the wider social and political systems. Therefore, the selection of news could be regarded as a result of a combination of different selection criteria that apply in a different mix depending on a situation that changes not only from country to country and media organization to media organization but also from one hour to the next (Koponen, 2003, p. 156). A hierarchy could therefore also be problematic, as the relative influence of the various levels may vary from time to time.

Most of the attempts at classifying the different levels of influences have been conducted within nations rather than analysed from a comparative approach. One recent attempt, however, examined the influences on journalism as perceived by 1700 journalists in 17 countries around the globe, including Australia, Austria, Brazil, Bulgaria, Chile, China, Egypt, Germany, Indonesia, Israel, Romania, Russia, Spain, Switzerland, Turkey, Uganda and the United States (Hanitzsch et al., 2010). Based on an analysis of the extent to which journalists in those countries perceived 21 different kinds of influences as important in their work, the study identified six dimensions. These consisted of political, economic, organizational, procedural, professional and reference group influences. Remarkably, the dimensions were the same in all the countries studied. More important, the various levels of influence were not seen to be equally important but followed the same order. The most important types of influence as perceived by journalists were those that stemmed from professional and procedural factors. *Procedural influences* included 'the various operational constraints faced by the journalists in their everyday work' (Hanitzsch et al., 2010, p. 15) such as deadlines and the availability of resources. *Professional influences*, on the other hand, 'refer to the policies, conventions, and customs of the profession in general and, specifically, the newsrooms for which the journalists work. These cultural conventions mostly pertain to what is commonly believed to be good and acceptable practice in journalism' (Hanitzsch et al., 2010, p. 15). Pressures from within the newsroom, such as supervisors and editors, but also from the wider organizational environment (management and owners) constitute the dimension of *organizational influences*. A type of influence that previous gatekeeping research had not explicitly identified as a distinct dimension was the existence of *reference groups*. This includes the immediate surroundings of a journalist in terms of their friends, acquaintances and family but also professional influences such as audiences, colleagues in other media and competing news organizations. As Hanitzsch et al. (2010, p. 15) argue, 'these are the groups and institutions journalists look at, be it for the purpose of monitoring competitors or as a means of self-ascertainment'. The final two types of influence refer to pressures on journalistic work: political and economic factors. These have received much attention in the literature. Among *political influences*, Hanitzsch et al. (2010) identified government officials, politicians, censorship, as well as business people. Noting that the inclusion of business people in political factors may be surprising, the authors explain that this type of group often has an interest in economic policymaking, and therefore may be seen as a more political influence. Further, 'in many, especially Asian and Latin American countries, political and business elites are strongly interlinked, which makes it hard for the journalists to clearly distinguish among them' (Hanitzsch et al., 2010, p. 15). Included in *economic influences* were those that were more likely to have a direct impact on journalists, such as organizations' profit expectations, advertisers' needs, the implications of market and audience research, as well as the needs of advertisers. The influence of market forces on journalism practice is explored in detail in Chapter 8.

The fact that journalists did not see the six dimensions as equally influential in their work demonstrated that there was a clear hierarchy 'in which organizational, professional, and procedural influences are seen to be the most powerful limits to the journalists' work' (Hanitzsch et al., 2010, p. 17). On the other hand, political and economic influences, which many scholars have seen as more important than individual influences, were perceived to be much less important by the surveyed journalists. In trying to explain this discrepancy, Hanitzsch et al. noted:

> This does not mean that political and economic influences are trivial. Quite to the contrary, it points to the possibility that these factors might actually be more powerful than the journalists' perceptions of their effects suggest. The impact of political and economic factors may be less noticeable under the circumstances of routine news work, mostly because their significance is masked by organizational and procedural influences that have a stronger grip on the journalists' everyday practice. Furthermore, journalists might tend to consciously negate political and, even more so, economic influences as part of a professional ideology according to which journalism is supposed to operate independently of political and economic interests. (Hanitzsch et al., 2010, p. 17)

The literature on the factors that influence journalistic practices around the world is important to keep in mind when we examine the way news workers think about their job and how they practise it. In addition, the roles of gate-keepers are changing rapidly because of the impact of new technologies and the emergence of participatory journalism around the world (Singer, 1997). We will discuss the impact of new technologies on journalism in more detail in Chapter 9. The following section provides an overview of what we know about journalists' professional views in various regions of the world. This particularly relates to the question whether there is such a thing as global journalism. As we will see, there are similarities across cultures but at the same time important differences persist.

Journalists' professional views around the world

Journalists' perceptions of their roles have been examined over a number of decades, beginning in the United States with Cohen's (1963, p. 20) typology that differentiated between journalists who saw themselves as either neutral observers of, and those who viewed themselves as participants in, the political process. Janowitz's (1975, pp. 618–19) seminal study saw journalists assuming somewhat similar roles but which he termed gatekeepers (those who placed emphasis on objective reporting and non-involvement in the news process) or advocates (who believed it was important to be partisan and actively advocate certain values). Still in the United States, Weaver and Wilhoit (1996, pp. 137–9), following their survey of American journalists, distinguished between four types of roles, which they termed the 'interpretive/investigative', 'disseminator', 'adversarial' and 'populist mobilizer' functions of journalism. In the interpretive function, to which most journalists subscribe, three roles are important: the investigation of government claims, analysis and interpretation of complex problems and the discussion of public policies in a timely way. The disseminator function, the second most popular role which was also supported by just over half the respondents, consists of a desire to get information to the public quickly and avoid stories with unverifiable facts. In the adversary function, journalists are constantly sceptical of public officials as well as business interests, while populist mobilizers considered it important to develop interests of the public, provide entertainment, set the political agenda and let ordinary people express their views. This last perspective, however, was upheld strongly by only 6 per cent of the journalists surveyed.

While these early studies were mainly conducted within a US context, a number of comparative approaches in other parts of the world have emerged in recent decades. For example, a comparison of German and British journalism found a strong tendency in German journalism to follow 'the traditional role of a species of political and intellectual career, which tends to place a lot of value on opinion and less on news' (Köcher, 1986, p. 43). This was supported by a finding which showed that 42 per cent of German journalists and only 14 per cent of British journalists categorized themselves as 'intellectuals' (Köcher, 1986, p. 50). According to her analysis, British journalists could be seen as 'bloodhounds', based on their predominantly adversarial stance. Recent evidence, however, suggests that the intellectual approach may be slowly on the way out in Germany (Weischenberg et al., 2006). Nevertheless, Patterson and Donsbach (1996, p. 465) found in their study of journalists in the United Kingdom, United States, Germany, Italy and Sweden that the German media system was the most partisan, while the US and British systems were the least partisan. Differences, in particular between German and Anglo-Saxon approaches, went deeper than simply disagreements on professional functions, however. In a comparative study of national news cultures in the Netherlands, Germany, Britain, Australia and the United States, Deuze (2002) noted that approach to work marked a major difference between the Dutch and German practices of journalism and the Anglo-American way. In Anglo-Saxon countries, journalists are tied to a certain function, with clearly distinct titles for news writing (reporter) and layout and selecting (sub-editor and section editor) (Deuze, 2002). In Dutch and German news organizations, however, journalists approach their work more holistically, combining news writing, selection and layout into one position, known in Germany as *redakteur*. Esser (1998, p. 378) noted that while 'you need almost a dozen job labels to describe the members of a British newsroom, all German members call themselves *redakteur* (i.e. editor or desk worker)'. In addition, while in the Netherlands and Germany there was at least a subset of journalists who defined journalism's watchdog role as 'pro-people' rather than 'anti-government', Deuze (2002, p. 142) found that Australian and British journalists rated the adversary role highly, which, he believed, suggested a Commonwealth tradition in journalism.

Increasingly, researchers have also gathered evidence about journalists' role perceptions from non-western countries. A first large-scale comparative study in this regard was Weaver's (1998a) edited volume, which reported results of journalists surveyed in 21 countries and territories around the world. The one role perception that appeared to receive support from journalists across the board was related to a primary function of news journalism: getting information to the public was considered very important in most countries included in the study. Some agreement also existed in regard to providing access to the public to express themselves. However, Weaver (1998b, p. 478) noted that, 'beyond these roles, there is much disagreement over how important it is to provide entertainment, to report accurately and objectively, to provide analysis of complex issues and problems, and to be a watchdog on government'. Being a watchdog, for example, was mainly considered very important in Western countries such as Australia, Britain and Finland, while countries with a shorter history of democratic government, such as Taiwan, Algeria and Chile, did not see this role as so important. There were no clear trends, however, with Chinese journalists ranking the watchdog role higher than their French and Canadian counterparts, and German and Algerian journalists exhibiting similar level of support for this role. Of course, as Weaver (1998b, p. 479) pointed out, 'what journalists in a survey say is sometimes inconsistent with what they do in daily practice', and we need to keep in mind that research into role perceptions tends to look at ideal-typical views. Providing analysis of complex problems was seen as very important in Finland and Britain, with Taiwanese and French journalists least likely to support it. Providing entertainment was regarded as less important in Canada and France, while it was seen as relatively important in Germany and Chile.

Strong disagreements also existed in terms of the extent to which journalists thought it justifiable to use questionable reporting methods. These differences, Weaver (1998b) believed, were most likely traceable to respective cultural norms, as opposed to differences in role perceptions, which were more likely to be influenced by political systems. For example, only 9 per cent of Canadian journalists thought it justifiable to pay for secret information, while 65 per cent of British and 62 per cent of Finnish journalists thought it was. Claiming to be someone else was justifiable for 63 per cent of respondents in Brazil and 58 per cent in Chile but only for 7 per cent in Canada. Badgering or harassing news sources was a concern for German journalists, of whom only 12 per cent thought it was justifiable, compared to 84 per cent in Hong Kong and 82 per cent in France. A vast majority of journalists in Britain, Brazil and the United States thought it was justifiable to use business documents without permission, but only 26 per cent of Taiwanese journalists thought so.

A study of Chinese, Taiwanese and US journalists also found similarities and differences in the way they perceived the importance of information, interpretation and entertainment roles (Zhu et al., 1997). The role of information provider was considered the most popular across the three countries, with entertainment the least popular, although opinions about entertainment were the most diverse. The interpretation function was also not highly valued by US and Taiwanese journalists, but was very popular among those from mainland China. In trying to find causal factors for these role perceptions at individual, organizational and societal levels, Zhu et al. (1997, p. 93) found 'clear-cut evidence that societal factors have much stronger effects than organizational factors, which in turn have stronger effects than individual factors on views about media professionalism'.

The surveys published in Weaver's (1998a) edited collection have since spawned numerous other surveys around the globe, including in non-western countries and regions such as in the Arab world (Pintak & Ginges, 2008), Bangladesh (Ramaprasad & Rahman, 2006), Brazil (Herscovitz, 2004), Egypt (Ramaprasad & Hamdy, 2006), Indonesia (Hanitzsch, 2005), Nepal (Ramaprasad & Kelly, 2003), Tanzania (Ramaprasad, 2001) and Uganda (Mwesige, 2004). Pintak and Ginges' (2008) survey of 601 journalists in 14 Arab countries showed that many of them subscribed to an active role in trying to bring change. Role perceptions of 'encouraging political reform' and 'using news for social good' were rated as most important by 75 and 60 per cent, respectively. Educating the public also received strong support, with 66 per cent of respondents rating it very highly and 40 per cent strongly supported a need to be objective in reporting. Thus, Pintak and Ginges (2008, p. 218) argued that 'the primary mission of Arab journalism (...) is that of fostering political and social change in the Arab world, with a secondary role of defending the Arab/Muslim people and values against outside interference'. This finding also coincides somewhat with a survey of Egyptian journalists which found that supporting Arabism and Arab values was the most important role dimension for this group (Ramaprasad & Hamdy, 2006). In particular, supporting the cause of the Palestinians was ranked as the role perception that received the highest support. The second- and third-most important dimensions as perceived by journalists in Egypt related to sustaining democracy (including typical watchdog functions of the press), as well as the entertainment role. Importantly, however, when asked how often they were able to perform these roles, sustaining democracy function was rated last, while support for Arabism was ranked first.

In her study of 402 Brazilian journalists, Herscovitz (2004) identified three types of role perceptions – the interpretive, adversary and disseminator functions. The disseminator role was considered the most important, followed by the interpreter and finally the adversarial role. While there was some similarity to American journalists in that the adversary role was the least valued of the three in both countries, Herscovitz suggested that considerable differences between American and Brazilian journalists still existed due to strongly divergent emphases on this role in the two countries. In addition, questionable or controversial practices generally received higher tolerance from Brazilian journalists, which she believed was 'in line with their level of general distrust in political and social institutions in Brazil' (2004, p. 84).

In Tanzania, Ramaprasad (2001) found a duality of views among journalists who rated western journalistic functions such as accuracy, analysis, investigation and entertainment highly, while also exhibiting somewhat unique role perceptions that related specifically to national development in the Tanzanian context. The most important role was the information/analysis dimension, followed by the entertainment and educator functions. While the national development function was ranked the lowest, it still received above average support. It included items such as the need to portray a positive image of the country, promote the strength and unity of communities, and to actively support government national development programs. Such findings, Ramaprasad (2001, p. 551) argued, echoed the results of a study in nearby Kenya which showed that journalists there also placed importance on communitarian roles of the media (Pauli, 1999). In Uganda, journalists held similar views to those of Tanzanian journalists, in terms of typical western functions of information, analysis/interpretation and investigation of official claims (Mwesige, 2004). The populist mobilizer role also received strong support. Of course, Mwesige warned that 'some of the values that Ugandan journalists endorsed are not necessarily reflected in what they produce. For example, much of the information on government-owned radio and television stations remains "protocol news" about the activities of the President and government ministers' (2004, p. 87). Mwesige believes that 'a western conceptualisation of journalism is taking hold in the rest of the world, at least in so far as it provides information and entertainment, investigates claims by government and gives ordinary people a voice' (2004, p. 92).

In Asia, Hanitzsch's (2005) survey of Indonesian journalists found the neutral disseminator role was most highly regarded, demonstrating once more similarities to other journalists around the world. Comparing them to other Asian journalists, Hanitzsch found Indonesian journalists were somewhat similar to their counterparts in Taiwan, as both groups appeared to place less emphasis on the watchdog and adversarial roles. Ramaprasad and Kelly's (2003) survey of Nepalese journalists was similar in terms of broadly identifying the role dimensions Ramaprasad (2001) found in her earlier work in Tanzania, with a similar hierarchy:

> For both, the factor that captured an adversary media role in terms of investigating government claims and providing ordinary people a voice in public affairs was the most important, followed by education of citizens and entertainment roles at about the same level of importance. The least important function in both samples was the national development role. (Ramaprasad & Kelly, 2003, p. 309)

Similarly, in Bangladesh, Ramaprasad and Rahman (2006) identified a predilection among journalists for libertarian role definitions, such as evaluation, analysis and education, thus exhibiting a number of traits that had been found in Western democracies with free press traditions. However, there were also two major differences. First, Bangladeshi journalists rated the importance of libertarian roles as much more important than how frequently they said they practised them, pointing to the restrictive environment of developing countries where a long history of press freedom is lacking and criticisms of policies and practices equally absent. Second, Bangladeshi journalists valued development journalism functions, though they did not rank them as highly as libertarian ones. Nevertheless, even here 'national development reporting does not appear to be deeply institutionalised in Bangladeshi journalism because of lack of an explicitly stated government policy for print media and journalists' own primary view of the press as a political instrument' (Ramaprasad & Rahman, 2006, p. 163).

Theoretical frameworks to analyse role perceptions

At the conceptual level, Donsbach and Patterson (2004, pp. 265–6) used existing studies as well as their own fieldwork to distinguish journalistic role perceptions in two major ways. One referred to the passive-active dimension, while another related to the neutral-advocate dimension. Along these, they argued, journalists could be located and compared cross-nationally. More recently, Hanitzsch (2007a) argued that one could actually identify seven dimensions along which journalism cultures could be distinguished globally. These were:

- *Interventionism* which is the extent to which journalists believe they should intervene in the news process. Interventionist journalists are involved, socially committed, assertive and motivated, while detached journalists are uninvolved and dedicated to objectivity and neutrality.
- *Power distance* which refers to journalists' position in regard to where power is located in society. Journalists can be seen on a continuum with an adversary pole on one hand and a loyal pole on another.
- *Market orientation* relates to whether journalists see their role as providing information that is in the public interest, or whether they are only interested in news that will reach the widest audience.
- *Objectivism* refers to the extent to which journalists believe that an objective truth exists 'out there'.
- *Empiricism* is concerned with aspects of how truth claims can be justified. This can be done, on one end of the continuum, by the use of empirical evidence and, on the other end, through opinion and analysis.
- *Relativism* 'focuses on the extent to which individuals base their personal moral philosophies on universal ethical rules' (Hanitzsch, 2007a, p. 378).
- *Idealism*, on the other hand, is concerned with the consequences of the responses to ethical dilemmas. Idealistic journalists believe that consequences should always be obtained through the 'right' action, while others might see the goal as more important than their actions, thus justifying harm to others as long as the desired result is achieved.

The seven constituents formed three dimensions, namely institutional roles (interventionism, power distance and market orientation), epistemologies (objectivism and empiricism) and ethical ideologies (relativism and idealism) (Hanitzsch, 2007a). The dimensions were applied in the recent cross-cultural project – *Worlds of Journalism* – which surveyed journalists in 18 countries across the globe (Hanitzsch et al., 2011). The study found that there were some important similarities in terms of some role perceptions but also significant differences in terms of others. Role perceptions that appeared to be valued highly in the vast majority of countries were those that were 'characterized by detachment and non-involvement. Being a watchdog of the government and, to a lesser extent, business elites, as well as providing political information do also belong to the functions of journalism that have universal appeal' (Hanitzsch et al., 2011). Further, there were similarities in terms of epistemological orientations. Here, journalists around the globe thought personal beliefs should not influence reporting. They further displayed a strong commitment to neutrality and impartiality, as well as an awareness of the importance of reliability and factualness of information. Thus, the notion of journalism as a detached watchdog that provides mainly political information based on facts seems to be popular across the globe (Hanitzsch et al., 2011).

However, Hanitzsch et al.'s study also identified some important differences in the way journalists viewed their roles. Significantly, the extent to which journalists should intervene in society depended on the country in which journalists operated. This view, linked to traditional concepts of development journalism (see Chapter 2), was 'much more endorsed among journalists in developing societies and transitional contexts' than in Western countries (Hanitzsch et al., 2011). There were also significant discrepancies as to the extent to which journalists thought it was important to be objective, as well as the need to separate facts from opinion. Interestingly, the study found that US journalists showed a tendency to move away from the objectivity paradigm, which has historically been associated with the US model of journalism. This, the authors point out, adds further weight to Weaver et al.'s (2007) results from their national survey of US journalists, which concluded on a similar note. 'As a consequence, the United States might no longer be seen as the epitome of an "objective" journalism' (Hanitzsch et al., 2011). Other differences were noted in relation to ethics, where 'non-western journalists tend to approve of the idea of contextual and situational ethical decision-making and the application of individual standards more than their colleagues in the West' (Hanitzsch et al., 2011). Conducting a cluster analysis of the results of the study, Hanitzsch (2011) was able to identify four main types of professional milieus, which he termed detached watchdog, populist disseminator, critical change agent and opportunist facilitator. The detached watchdog milieu clearly dominated in most Western countries. In non-western countries, however, there was a tendency for more journalists to belong to the opportunist facilitator (who are more likely to support official policies and convey a positive image of political and business leadership) and critical change agent milieus (who are critical of government and business elites, but also emphasize the need to advocate social change, influence public opinion and set the political agenda).

As we can see from the multitude of studies on the professional views of journalists around the globe, there appear to be some important aspects of journalism that are valued universally, while at the same time significant differences remain in some respects. Some of the differences relate to dissimilarities in political and economic structures of the media systems that were discussed in Chapter 2. There is, however, a cultural dimension to some of the differences, an issue that has received increasing attention lately. Some scholars as well as politicians have called for a journalism that is more attuned to the cultural values of their own regions. The following section discusses these largely normative ideas. The section will be followed by an analysis of a framework based on cultural values which is designed to facilitate an understanding of how journalism is practised in different ways across the globe.

Normative models of regional values in journalism

Traditionally, development communication scholars such as Everett Rogers, Wilbur Schramm, Daniel Lerner and Lucian Pye had advocated the diffusion of Western models of journalism in order to modernize traditional societies. However, in a substantial shift, this field has in recent decades moved away from North American or ethnocentric views towards pluralistic approaches and evolutionary changes. This perspective promotes appreciation of local conditions rather than looking down at them. Within many nonwestern countries there have been similar developments aimed at reasserting cultural authority over journalism, and in a sense promoting a journalism that recognizes diverse cultural practices and values.

One particularly well-known debate over culturally appropriate journalism models has been over whether Asian news media should adhere to Asian values (see Xu, 2005, for an in-depth discussion of this debate). The argument for a journalism that recognizes Asian values is related to ideas about Asian society propagated most prominently by the Singaporean and Malaysian governments under Lee Kuan Yew and Mahathir Mohamad respectively during the late 1980s and the 1990s. As Massey and Chang (2002, p. 992) noted, the premise of this argument was that 'the modern, economically strong Asian society is best built on a foundation of traditional Eastern beliefs, not transplanted Western values'. As an extension of this logic, the school of thought that favours an Asian values' approach to journalism similarly believed it was necessary to ground the paradigm in the core beliefs of Asian societies. This included values such as respect for authority, group dynamics and an emphasis on communalism (collectivism) rather than a focus on individualistic values. These were supposed to lead to a new type of journalism, significantly different from that of the West (Xu, 2005). A major stumbling block for implementation of this perspective lies in the fact that some Asian cultures differ widely from one another. To complicate matters further, the Asian values approach was widely perceived as an excuse for restricting press freedom (Xu, 2005). Some observers argued that the Singaporean and Malaysian governments in particular had a vested interest in using these selected values for their own advantage, to curb media criticism and to use the press as a tool to advance the interests of the governments. In a study of Asian values in journalism, Massey and Chang (2002) examined the frequency of stories that took into account key Asian values such as harmony and supportiveness. They found that the two values were particularly evident in domestic news reporting and were concentrated in the Southeast Asian countries of Singapore, Malaysia and Brunei, countries that also had restrictive press systems. Yet, they also found that 'the Asian values of harmony and supportiveness emerged as neither convincingly pan-Asia nor even uniformly Southeast Asian journalistic norms' (Massey & Chang, 2002, p. 999). In relation to the coincidence (in their results) that Asian values were dominant in countries with a restrictive press environment, the researchers argued that this could have been based on two potential reasons. First, it could be that the controlled media systems were responsible. Second, 'it could be that Asian values appear in the journalism of Singapore, Malaysia, and Brunei because the political leadership promotes them as beneficial to national development, and journalists conceive of themselves as the government's nation-building partners' (2002, p. 999).

The argument that journalistic practice should reflect local conditions has also been made in Africa. Here, there has been a repeated push for an Afrocentric approach based on the perceived inadequacies of the dominant Western-style journalism that was exported to the continent during colonial times. The push for a journalism based on African values was made forcefully and prominently by scholars such as the late Francis Kasoma (1996, p. 93), who argued that 'the individualism and divisionism that permeate the practice of journalism in Africa today should be discarded since they are not only unAfrican but also professionally unhealthy'. Kasoma believed that imported journalism models from the West were inadequate for the African context mainly because they were based on individual ideals rather than on a collective approach. He saw African journalists as having 'discarded the mutual counselling and correction of African communal living' (Kasoma, 1996, p. 101), and that regaining these should be paramount for the profession on the continent.

The calls for Afrocentric approaches have been somewhat haphazard and lacking of any wider concerted academic effort (Fourie, 2008). Similar to the developments in Asia, the African approach has been subjected to criticisms, most notably from renowned South African media scholar Keyan Tomaselli (2003, p. 428), who warned of the dangers of deifying essentialistic African approaches. In a critique reminiscent of those of the Asian approach, he makes a key point against adoption of any one African approach because 'embedded in this definitional conflation and essentialistic thinking is the utterly reductive assumption that the 54 African countries, and myriad array of cultures, religions and languages, can be prescriptively reduced to homogeneous sets of continent-wide social and cultural "African values"' (p. 428). He cautions that such approaches may run the risk of being adopted too easily for the purpose of 'authoritarianism and regressive nationalism' (p. 436). In addition, Shaw (2009) believes that modern African journalism is not as pure a replica of the Western model as some commentators may have argued. He adduced evidence that suggests that some aspects of journalistic practices that predated colonial times have managed to survive until today.

Nevertheless, a number of scholars have explored the possibilities of an African approach to journalism, based essentially on the tradition of *ubuntuism* (see, e.g., Blankenberg, 1999; Christians, 2004; Wasserman & de Beer, 2004; Fourie, 2008). *Ubuntuism* is essentially a community-focussed approach which can be understood as

> a social philosophy, a collective African consciousness, a way of being, a code of ethics and behaviour deeply embedded in African culture. It is the capacity in African culture to express compassion, reciprocity, dignity, harmony and humanity in the interest of building and maintaining a community with justice and mutual caring. (Fourie, 2008, p. 62)

Fourie argues that objectivity may not be important or even necessary in *ubuntu* journalism, as the philosophy does not provide for the journalist to serve as a spectator; rather, he or she is always defined through group relations and membership of the community. Thus, 'active involvement and dialogue with the community rather than detachment in the name of objectivity and neutrality may be required' (Fourie, 2008, p. 65). Fourie is also wary of the potential negative implications of the misuse of such an approach for ideological and political purposes. His framework for *ubuntu* journalism thus remains a tentative step towards further evaluation of the concept.

Calls for an indigenous-oriented restructuring of journalism also echo in other regions of the world such as the Pacific Islands. Here, Rooney et al. (2004) argue in their case study of Papua New Guinean media that the Western-influenced journalism training and Western style of reporting could not simply be transplanted into Papua New Guinean society, which has different societal needs from those countries in the West. Papoutsaki and Sharp (2006) note that much of the journalism training in PNG has been conducted by Western educators, and even though there have been recent efforts to train local staff, this training was performed in the West, further reinforcing Western practices. Robie notes in his surveys of Papua New Guinean and Fijian journalists increasing calls for a reclaiming of Pacific images which have become necessary because of the perception that dominant news media in the area are Western, which 'have failed to seriously take Pacific and indigenous cultures and their world views into account' (Robie, 2004, p. 249). According to Papoutsaki and Sharp (2006), students in the Pacific hold the view that 'confrontational style' of journalism is not appropriate for PNG, where a more collaborative model is seen as more appropriate. In fact, the issue of a Pacific identity at large has been discussed on a wider theoretical scale in the Pacific region for some time. As far back as 1993, Epeli Hau'ofa had argued for a new direction in theoretical and practical thinking in the region, towards a 'Pacifc Way', which would more accurately reflect the region's needs (Hau'ofa, 1993).

Relevance of comparative research to cultural values

Comparisons of cultural values and how they impact on people's lives in a variety of contexts have been well-established and documented in the field of cross-cultural psychology but they have rarely found application in the study of journalism. Culture has invariably been defined in a number of ways, ranging from the broad perspective (culture is everything) to the narrow (cultural institutions such as the opera). In cross-cultural psychology, cultural orientations are discussed with reference to two general levels of analysis. At the level of the individual, cultural values which are embraced by people are referred to as 'deeply rooted, abstract motivations that guide, justify and explain attitudes, norms, opinions and actions' (Schwartz, 2007, p. 169). At the societal level, culture is understood as 'the rich complex of meanings, beliefs, practices, symbols, norms and values prevalent among people in a society' (Schwartz, 2004, p. 43). Scholars have found a variety of value systems which differentiate between instrumental and terminal values (Rokeach, 1973), 'social axioms' (Leung & Bond, 2004), as well as traditional vs secular values, on one hand, and survival and self-expression values, on the other (Inglehart, 1997). This section draws on the work conducted by two prominent scholars in the field, Geert Hofstede and

Shalom Schwartz, as their work has had the biggest impact on this area of scholarship.

Following extensive surveys of work-related values around the world, Hofstede (1980, 2001) identified five independent dimensions along which dominant value systems could be ordered. These dimensions are:

- *power distance* (the extent to which the less powerful members of institutions and organizations accept and expect that power is distributed unequally);
- *uncertainty avoidance* (the degree to which a society can deal with uncertainty, i.e. whether a member of a culture is comfortable or uncomfortable in a new and unknown situation);
- *individualism* (in individualist countries, there are only loose ties between individuals and everyone primarily looks after themselves and their immediate family. While in collectivist societies, individuals are part of very strong and cohesive groups, such as extended families with dozens of members who protect them in exchange for unconditional loyalty);
- *masculinity* (the degree to which masculine or feminine values dominate a society);
- *long-term orientation* (which relates more to virtues rather than truth, a main concern for the uncertainty dimension. High long-term orientation countries are usually associated with values such as thrift and perseverance, while short-term orientation cultures exhibit respect for tradition and the fulfilment of social obligations).

Hofstede's work has not been without criticisms, much of them directed at the methodology, which surveyed workers in Western multinational corporations. McSweeney (2002), for example, argued that Hofstede generalized about national cultures on the basis of a few questionnaires administered to employees of IBM subsidiaries in some countries. McSweeney doubted that IBM employees in one country could be representative of a whole culture. Other criticisms have included the lack of surveys of Arab and African countries, as well as implicit claims of regional cultural clusters (Servaes, 2002). Yet, as Hofstede and Hofstede (2005) point out, a number of follow-up studies have investigated the original framework, with many lending support particularly to the individualism dimension.

A more recent approach to comparing cultural values has been developed by the Israeli cross-cultural psychologist Shalom Schwartz (2004), who differentiates between two levels of analysis, the individual level and the cultural level. Based on 210 samples of teachers and students in more than 67 countries, Schwartz (2004, p. 174) postulates that, at the individual level, the following value dimensions can be identified:

- *power* (related to an individual's social status and prestige, control or dominance over people and resources);
- *achievement* (personal success according to social standards);
- *hedonism* (pleasure or sensuous gratification for one's self);
- *stimulation* (excitement, novelty and challenge in life);
- *self-direction* (independence of thought and action);
- *universalism* (understanding, appreciation, tolerance and protection for the welfare of all people and for nature);
- *benevolence* (preservation and enhancement of the welfare of people with whom one is in frequent personal contact);
- *tradition* (respect for, commitment to and acceptance of the customs and ideas that traditional culture or religion provide for the self);
- *conformity* (restraint of actions, inclinations and impulses likely to upset or harm others and violate social expectations or norms);
- *security* (safety, harmony and stability of society, of relationships, and of self).

Schwartz (2004, p. 175) locates these dimensions on a circular arrangement, representing what he calls a 'motivational continuum'. According to this model, values which are close to one another on the circle are similar in their underlying motivations but those situated further away from one another represent antagonism. In even broader terms, Schwartz argues that we can make out four higher-order values: *openness to change* (encompassing self-direction and stimulation values, emphasizing independent action, thought and readiness for new experiences) is contrary to a *conservation* dimension (including security, conformity and traditional values, emphasizing self-restriction, order and resistance to change). Similarly, we can discern a *self-enhancement* dimension (power and achievement, emphasizing self-interest) which opposes *self-transcendence* (universalism and benevolence values, emphasizing concern for the welfare and interests of others).

At the cultural level, Schwartz (2004, pp. 140–1) identifies seven cultural value orientations which form three broader dimensions that reflect the way societies cope with basic issues and problems:

- *Intellectual autonomy* (referring to broad-mindedness, curiosity and creativity);
- *Affective autonomy* (pleasure, exciting life and varied life);

- *Embeddedness* (social order, respect for tradition, security, obedience and wisdom);
- *Egalitarianism* (equality, social justice, responsibility, help and honesty);
- *Hierarchy* (social power, authority, humility and wealth);
- *Harmony* (world at peace, unity with nature and protecting the environment); and
- *Mastery* (ambition, success, daring and competence).

One of the three dimensions examines whether people are autonomous or embedded in their groups, and differentiates between Embeddedness on one hand and Affective and Intellectual Autonomy on the other. The second societal subject is to guarantee that people behave in a responsible manner that preserves the social fabric. The dimension that deals with this issue stretches between Egalitarianism and Hierarchy. The third societal issue is to regulate how people manage their relations to the natural and social world. There are two ideal-typical cultural responses to this problem: Harmony vs Mastery.

Applying values research to comparative journalism practice

While relatively few studies have examined the link between cultural values and journalism, there is some evidence that such work can be useful in explaining differences in journalistic practice. Most of the existing studies that employed the concept of cultural values focused on the work of Hofstede. For example, a comparison of the ways in which German and Australian newspapers report death in foreign news showed that a number of Hofstede's dimensions could be seen as influential (Hanusch, 2008a). The study found that differences in visual treatment of death, language conventions and ethical codes could be traced to differences between Australia and Germany along the value dimensions of uncertainty-avoidance and individualism. German journalists' code of ethics was far more complex and prescriptive than the Australian journalists' code of ethics. These differences could be related to the countries' scores on Hofstede's uncertainty avoidance dimensions, which rank Germany as strong uncertainty-avoiding and Australia as weak uncertainty-avoiding. The individualism dimensions could be seen as partially responsible for differences in considering issues of the human dignity of foreign dead. While German journalists, ranked only as slightly individualistic, considered collective interests in their use of graphic photos, Australian journalists generally showed fewer such concerns, in line with Australian culture being ranked as strongly individualistic.

In his framework for the study of journalism culture, Hanitzsch (2007a) also acknowledges the usefulness of some of Hofstede's work, in particular the power distance dimension. Hanitzsch argues that an important dimension of journalistic culture is related to journalists' attitude towards power. He notes that in most Western democracies, journalists follow the adversarial tradition of the press. Acting as the 'Fourth Estate' or 'watchdogs', journalists see themselves as independent critics of established authorities. In other countries, Hanitzsch (2007a) notes, an adversarial stance may conflict with values of consensus and harmony (e.g. Asian countries), yet criticism is still possible in a covert form. On the low end of the power distance scale, however, there are journalists who perceive themselves as loyal to those in power and remain uncritical, thus serving as a mouthpiece for the government.

In a study of how news stories about the Internet in China were framed in Hong Kong, Singapore, the United States and the United Kingdom, Zhou (2008) found that the dimension of long- versus short-term orientation was a significant factor in determining most types of news frames. Applying Hofstede's work to framing theory, Zhou found a complexity of dimensions at work, with often two dimensions significantly determining one news frame, lending further strength to the argument that Hofstede's five dimensions are inherently inter-related and operate concurrently. Zhou (2008) found that results on the salience of issues and the use of news frames between Singapore and Hong Kong on the one hand and the United States and the United Kingdom on the other could be attributed to differences in long-term orientation. The two Western countries reported predominantly on the controversial issue of Internet control and censorship in mainland China, while the two Asian countries focussed more on e-commerce and Internet diffusion in China. Zhou explained that, as people in short-term orientation countries believed there were clear guidelines on good and evil, they might focus more on problems in a given system. On the other hand, people in long-term orientation countries such as Hong Kong and Singapore perceive the differences between good and evil as indistinct. Hence, they do not have a strong desire to correct social injustice. 'Therefore, journalists in such a society might have switched their attention to the pragmatic practices with long-term benefits, such as Internet use and Internet business' (Zhou, 2008, p. 131).

Kim and Kelly (2008) analysed news and feature photographs in 10 elite American and Korean newspapers and argued that the significant differences between the style of photojournalism in both countries could be put down to the individualism/collectivism dimension. They argued that American photojournalists relied on 'their own individual interpretations, observe and document their subjects as individuals, and focus on distinctive individual personalities. This interpretative approach to visual reporting depends on individual creativity' (2008, p. 171). In contrast, Korean newspapers tended to focus more on the group in their photojournalism, and relied on mere description rather than interpretation. 'Korean photojournalists adhere more strictly to their societal responsibilities. They are part of a larger group, either the journalistic community as a whole or their particular news organization. They act according to the group's interest rather than according to their own interpretations' (2008, p. 171).

Other studies have found cultural values to be a useful tool for the analysis of journalism practices. Chang and Massey's (2010) survey of work motivation among Taiwanese and US journalists, for example, showed significant variations in job satisfaction in line with differences along the individualism-collectivism dimension. Winfield et al. also compared Chinese and Japanese press systems and argued that collectivist values played an important role in those press systems. They noted that despite the differences that exist between the two systems on the surface (e.g. differences in ownership regulations), 'the concepts of group harmony, collectivism and the place of the individual within the group explain similar aspects of both press systems at the beginning of the twenty-first century' (Winfield et al., 2000, p. 347).

The *Worlds of Journalism* project also presents some evidence of the relationship between cultural values and journalists' professional views (Hanusch, 2010a). The study found a significant correlation between the individualism/collectivism dimension and interventionist approaches to journalism. Journalists from collectivist cultures were thus much more likely to value role perceptions such as 'setting the political agenda', 'influencing public opinion' and 'advocating for social change' than their counterparts in individualist cultures. Those whose cultures ranked high on the power distance dimensions were also more likely to value the role perceptions of 'influencing public opinion' and 'advocating for social change', as well as 'supporting official policies' – a role perception that was also associated with collectivist cultures. When explored against Schwartz's cultural value dimensions, interventionist role perceptions were negatively correlated with Affective and Intellectual Autonomy, and positively correlated with Embeddedness. This indicates that there is a link between journalists supporting interventionist roles in countries that are more hierarchical and tradition-oriented. Further links exist with the role perception of 'supporting official policies'. Here, countries that rank low on autonomy are more likely to value this view, which is also cherished in hierarchical societies. Nevertheless, while there exist important relationships between these role perceptions and Hofstede's, as well as Schwartz's dimensions, there are also significant links in regard to the extent to which countries ranked on press freedom scales and their economic power as measured by gross domestic product (Hanusch, 2010a). This points to a more complex picture.

The studies discussed here suggest that the use of cultural value systems (based on either Hofstede or Schwartz) can be valuable in exploring and explaining differences in how journalism is practised across the world. Of course, they can never serve as the only frameworks to explain differences in journalism practices across cultures. In fact, as Weaver (1998b, p. 478) noted, similarities and differences among journalists surveyed in his edited collection were 'not neatly classifiable along some of the more common political or cultural dimensions', suggesting that 'journalism education and professional socialization are not necessarily a function of politics or dominant ideology'. At the same time, however, he admits that cultural norms and political values do play some role in influencing journalists' professional views and ethical beliefs. As we discussed previously, journalism practice is influenced at various levels, and how journalists make their decisions is always a complex mix of factors, which can range from individual biases to organizational pressures to more opaque influences on the societal level. We need to be mindful of these influences whenever we compare journalistic practices across cultures.

Conclusion

Decision-making processes in journalism are affected by a range of factors. While early gatekeeping studies had placed a lot of emphases on the way in which individual biases affect news selection, more recent approaches have begun to take into account a much more complex and multilevel structure. More precisely, newsmaking is now seen to be affected by individual, procedural, professional, organizational, extra-media, as well as societal or cultural factors, that make up an intricate web of influences. And while journalists tend to be more aware of lower levels of influence, such as the procedural and professional demands of the job, higher level factors such as the political and economic systems as well as national cultures still play a measurable and perhaps even more important role.

Nevertheless, there are some similarities across cultures that allow us to speak of a limited number of global aspects of journalism. For example, as Hanitzsch et al. (2011) have shown, detachment, non-involvement and watchdog functions were supported in the vast majority of the countries in which they surveyed journalists. In other respects, however, there were considerable differences, such as the degree to which journalists believed they could be objective, and the extent to which they pursued goals in line with ideals of development journalism. Individual studies from across the globe are reasonably in line with these assessments, with studies across Africa and Asia, in particular, showing that the development role is more pronounced there than in the West. See Chapter 2 for a detailed discussion on development journalism.

Further, this chapter detailed ways in which cultural values can influence journalistic practices and role perceptions. Past comparative approaches to journalism studies have often tended to neglect the dimension of culture as a factor, perhaps because of the difficulty of measuring it. Instead, political and economic influences have generally been highlighted, most probably because of their impact on the historical development of journalism in the West. Yet, if we apply the discussion on cultural values to differences in journalistic practices, it becomes clear that culture is very often an important variable. A discussion of studies that have deployed cultural values in examining differences in journalistic practices around the world has demonstrated that culture is still at the core of factors that drive many differences in journalism practices.

DISCUSSION QUESTIONS

1. Explain and discuss the five hierarchical levels of influence outlined in Shoemaker and Reese's (1996) theory of gatekeeping, taking into special account the impact of new technologies.
2. Review the arguments for and against employing cultural values in journalism (as outlined in the Asian values' debate and proposals for *Ubuntu* journalism in Africa or a 'Pacific Way' in the Pacific Islands) and discuss whether and how these can be aligned with traditional concepts of journalism as the fourth estate.
3. Examine Hanitzsch's (2007a) dimensions of journalism culture and outline how these apply in the context of your home country.
4. Referring to available literature and drawing on your own ideas, make a list of specific factors that influence journalism practice, using broad headings of political, economic, cultural, technological and legal influences.
5. Using Hofstede's (2001) classification of cultural values, examine how cultural values might impact on journalism practices in your own country.

CHAPTER 4

Journalism education around the world

Introduction

The way in which journalists are trained and educated is invariably related to the quality of journalism around the world. Over the past couple of decades, a lively debate has arisen over how best to achieve high quality in journalism education. Until recently, journalists in most countries learned their skills on the job once they completed secondary education. However, in recent years, there has been a clear trend towards university education for journalists in many countries in the West, but also increasingly in non-western countries. Yet, as this chapter demonstrates, there exists a multitude of national variations in terms of the approaches to journalism education around the world. As Nordenstreng (2009, p. 513), an authority on journalism education, has pointed out in the conclusions to a recent volume about journalism education in 33 European countries, even within a continent such as Europe 'the situation of journalism education seems to be quite specific to each country'. In fact, he notes, the models of journalism education do not fall nicely into the patterns that Hallin and Mancini (2004) outlined in their analysis of media systems, which we discussed in Chapter 2.

Journalism education is seen as such an important undertaking because it has the potential to shape future journalists' practices, role perceptions and understanding of ethics, among other things. For example, Gaunt (1992, p. 1) believes that 'journalism training perpetuates or modifies professional practices and moulds the perceptions journalists have of the role and function of the media'. This influence has been at the core of concerns worldwide over what curricula or training methods are most appropriate for journalists. The debates, while somewhat similar across the globe, have almost always been localized in the sense that they were led within specific social, cultural, and national – and essentially ideological – environments of individual countries.

This chapter reviews the current state of journalism education around the world and takes into account the diverse cultural, political and economic environments. To set the scene, we examine the history of journalism education in order to better understand how and why journalists are trained in different ways in different countries. The chapter then discusses some of the tensions that exist in journalism education globally, in particular the arguments for and against on-the-job and university-only models. Subsequently, we review in-depth existing training systems in individual regions of the world in order to provide a sound overview of journalism education globally. By doing so, we hope to shed light on the benefit of journalism education models that are specific to individual cultures rather than Western-developed models which may not necessarily apply in other contexts.

A brief history of journalism education in a global context

Up until the late nineteenth century, journalism education was a little discussed topic. Journalists entered the profession simply through 'doing' journalism, mostly in the form of an apprenticeship. Weaver (2003) notes that journalists such as Benjamin Franklin began as apprentices, while others honed their writing skills first through a general education in the liberal arts at private universities. The idea that journalists should be educated more formally only emerged between the 1870s and 1920s, according to Weaver (2003). In this context, General Robert E. Lee, who introduced scholarships in journalism in 1869, is generally held up as the leader in global journalism education (Weaver, 2003; Medsger, 2005). Individual courses began to slowly spring up around the country, but it would take almost 40 years for the first university to dedicate a department to the education of journalists. In 1908, Walter Williams, a newspaper journalist, started what is commonly regarded as the world's oldest journalism school at the University of Missouri (Weaver, 2003). The objective of the school was to both 'improve the minds of journalists and to improve the image of journalism' (Medsger, 2005, p. 206). Other universities quickly followed Missouri's example, with Indiana University establishing its school in 1911 and the University of Wisconsin in 1912. That was also the year Columbia University finally relented and accepted newspaper baron Joseph Pulitzer's endowment to form a school of journalism (Medsger, 2005). Yet, the education of journalists and improvement of newspapers were not the principal objectives; the men involved in these early moves rather saw journalism education as an instrument. 'The larger goal to which they aspired was to produce a more informed citizenry through better journalism' (Medsger, 2005, p. 208).

The United States was not the only country to take journalism education seriously and establish university departments, however, even though it undoubtedly has had the biggest influence on the discipline (Josephi, 2009). A desire for a more formalized education of journalists also began to take hold in Europe, where the first school of journalism was established in Paris in 1899 (Charon, 2003), although it took another 25 years for a second school to be founded, this time in Lille. As Charon (2003, p. 142) points out, the major emphasis in journalism education in France was on aspects of style, which continues to this day in the tradition of the country's comparatively more literary tradition of journalism. In Germany, there was growing concern towards the end of the nineteenth century that, with the increasing numbers of journalists required due to the growth in newspaper sections, the proportion of academic graduates had fallen considerably. Hence, the year 1899 saw the establishment of a short-lived journalism school in Berlin, and in 1916 the Institut für Zeitungskunde (Institute for the Science of the Press) was established at the University of Leipzig (Fröhlich & Holtz-Bacha, 2003c). University education for journalists was only seen as preparatory training, however, and graduates were still required to undertake an apprenticeship. The objective was 'to guarantee research on a subject deemed relevant that was until then only studied incidentally and unsystematically, and to provide for some basic knowledge for journalists, supplementing their practical training at the publishing houses' (Fröhlich & Holtz-Bacha, 2003c, p. 190). In Eastern Europe, journalism courses were first taught at university in a more formal way in 1928, at the Free School of Political Science in Prague (Hiebert & Gross, 2003). In Britain, however, the development was contrary to the other major powers of Europe. Esser (2003) notes that, except for a two-year diploma in journalism at King's College in London, which lasted from 1922 to 1939, the dominant view in the industry was that journalism had to be learnt on the job. This approach became more formalized through the establishment of the National Council for the Training of Journalists, but day-release courses and, later, one-year courses at universities needed decades to take a hold (Esser, 2003).

The establishment of the American model of journalism education in the early years of the twentieth century, coupled with United States' growing influence around the world over the ensuing decades, also led to the establishment of formal schools of journalism outside of Europe and North America. A number of schools which followed the Missouri model emerged in Republican China during the 1920s and 1930s. First, Peking University introduced a journalism curriculum in 1918, and then in 1921 the Christian St John's University established the country's first journalism department, to be followed in 1924 by Yenching University in Beijing (Volz & Lee, 2009). The move was so successful that most other universities quickly followed suit, so that in 1937 journalism departments had been established in 26 of the 32 public and private universities in China, all having some connection to the United States. Volz and Lee (2009, p. 726) believe that the success of the American model was in great part due to 'America's official neo-colonial ideology, proclaiming democratic values and an open-door policy in China'. This was in stark contrast to the heavy-handed control exercised by the British up until then (Volz & Lee, 2009). Journalism education was also introduced in India during the 1920s, although it was not until sometime around 1938–40 when the first diploma course in journalism was introduced at Aligarh University in the country's north (Karan, 2001). Soon, the model was adopted elsewhere, and tertiary education in journalism began to take hold at many other universities around the country.

In Australia, the idea that journalism education should be more formalized also began to attract a lively debate when first introduced in 1912 (Sheridan Burns, 2001). Again the American approach of providing specialized practical and theoretical training in universities was the dominant one. Yet the idea was also fought strongly by some people, with the view that journalists are born not made persisting to this day in Australia (Sheridan Burns, 2001). Following years of debate over the pros and cons of journalism education at universities, the first diploma course was eventually established at the University of Queensland in 1921. Nevertheless, it took until 1989 for the first chair in journalism to be appointed (Kirkpatrick, 1996). The situation in nearby New Zealand was somewhat different, in that a vocational model persisted, and tertiary journalism education only began to take hold in the 1970s (Boyd-Bell, 2007). In the Pacific Islands, many of which are in Australia and New Zealand's spheres of influence, journalism education was introduced in the 1970s in Papua New Guinea, with the state-run University of Papua New Guinea offering a course in 1975 and the Catholic Divine Word University introducing subjects in journalism in 1979. The regional University of the South Pacific in Fiji did not begin its courses in journalism until 1994 (Robie, 2001; Rooney, 2003).

On the African continent, education specific to journalism arrived only after the Second World War and the resultant processes of decolonization. Once again it was the US model of journalism education that a majority of countries adopted. The American University in Cairo had imported it in 1935, and the first journalism programme was established in Ghana in 1958, with Nigeria following suit in the early 1960s. Both programmes were established with considerable aid from the United States. Murphy and Scotton (1987) report that Eastern Nigerian political leader and editor of the *West African Pilot*, Nnamdi Azikiwe, felt the British model of a university was too academic and the American vocational orientation suited Africa's needs better. The model, supported with the help of UNESCO, quickly spread around the region, so that by 1970, Algeria, Cameroon, Ethiopia, Kenya, Nigeria, Senegal and Zaire (now Congo) had established journalism programmes in universities (Murphy & Scotton, 1987, p. 15). The 1960s were also a time when journalism education became popular in South African universities. Botha and de Beer (2007) note that the first departments of journalism were set up at the Afrikaans-language universities, with Potchefstroom University making a start in 1959, and others following suit in the 1970s. English-language universities followed in the 1980s, with Botha and de Beer (2007, p. 200) commenting that this was perhaps due to 'an elitist academic view of journalism as something "the study and research of which do not belong at universities"'. In other African countries, however, journalism education arrived very late. Skjerdal and Ngugi (2007) note that Rwanda did not have a journalism school until 1996, when the School of Journalism and Communication at the National University of Rwanda at Butare established its programme. In the same year, University of Swaziland (Uniswa) began offering the first diploma in journalism in Swaziland (Rooney, 2007).

The roots of journalism education in Latin America can be traced back as far as the 1930s, when the first schools opened in Argentina, Brazil and Mexico. Argentina is typically cited as the first country to establish such a school, when the Circulo de Periodistas (Circle of Journalists) of La Plata decided to create a journalism school in 1933, which was opened on 27 April 1934 (Knudson, 1987). The school was later incorporated into the University of La Plata, with studies including specifics of the job (such as journalistic techniques), cultural aspects (history, sociology, law, demography), as well as practical features (English, editing, typographical art and graphics). The school also provided its students with practical experience by way of its small in-house newspaper internship (Knudson, 1987, p. 22). The first journalism school in Brazil was established only one month after that in Argentina, when the Instituto Grafico was established on 25 May 1934. Mexico followed in 1936, when its first school of journalism was founded at the Universidad Femenina de Mexico (Knudson, 1987). Interestingly, this school almost exclusively taught women, which, according to Ferreira and Tillson (2000, p. 62) 'underscored the low esteem for the craft'. While the 'big three' countries of Latin America led the way in journalism education in the 1930s, it would take until after the Second World War for most other countries in the region to establish such programmes. Venezuela and Cuba made their first moves by establishing schools during the war years, in 1941 and 1942, respectively (Ferreira & Tillson, 2000). Ecuador, Colombia and Peru followed in 1945, while Chile did so in 1947. In Central America, the Central American School of Journalism began operating in Guatemala in 1952. Uruguay, Costa Rica, El Salvador and the Dominican Republic began journalism education around 1959 (Knudson, 1987).

The spread of the US model of journalism education to many parts of the world, which has been in line with US-led aid efforts, has arguably contributed to the presence of typically Anglo-Saxon journalism practices in non-western countries, a point we discussed in detail in chapters 2 and 3. Yet, increasingly, these countries are also trying to develop their own models in order to advance approaches to journalism that reflect local cultures. In the following section, we review the current state of journalism education around the globe. We see six major strands that dominate discussions about journalism education across the globe:

- The growth in journalism education, which is evident everywhere;
- Tension over whether journalism education should focus on teaching mainly theory or practice dominates in a large number of contexts;
- Controversy also exists in terms of the licensing of journalists;
- Concerns in developing countries over imported educational models from the West;
- A shortage of resources and technological infrastructure in many developing contexts; and
- In authoritarian countries, as well as others that are emerging from former authoritarian regimes, debate exists as to the amount of state ideology that affects journalism education.

Growth in journalism education

Increasing numbers of journalists around the world have had at least some exposure to university education, even if it was not specifically in journalism. In his review of a number of studies of journalists in 21 countries around the world, Weaver (1998b) found considerable variation between countries in terms of the percentage of university-educated journalists. The highest percentage of university graduates existed in the United States, Korea, Spain, Chile and Ecuador, with all of them reporting that at least 80 per cent of journalists surveyed held a degree. In contrast, Australia, Finland and Mexico all reported figures of less than 40 per cent. Yet, in terms of the percentage of university graduates who had majored in journalism, only three countries – Spain, Brazil and Chile – reported figures of more than 50 per cent. Most countries, according to Weaver (1998b), reported percentages of just under 40 per cent of graduates who had majored in journalism. Recent years have seen an accelerated growth in journalism education at universities, with the recent *Worlds of Journalism* study, which surveyed journalists in 18 countries around the world, reporting results that appear to show a marked increase in university-educated journalists in different parts of the world (Hanitzsch et al., 2011). The analysis shows that of the total number of 1800 journalists, 83 per cent held some kind of university degree, with no country scoring below 50 per cent. Even taking into account the fact that Hanitzsch et al.'s study was conducted with samples of only 100 journalists in each country, it demonstrates a trend towards a more university-oriented journalism education.

Africa in particular is currently experiencing somewhat of a boom in journalism education. While previously many journalists went overseas to Europe or North America for journalism training, increasing numbers are being trained in their own countries (McCurdy & Power, 2007). The growth has been phenomenal, considering that while Nordenstreng and Boafo (1988) had identified 36 journalism institutions in the field during the mid-1980s, roughly twenty years later there were almost 200 journalism schools (Berger, 2007). Due to the popularity of journalism education in the continent, there has, however, also been a rapid increase in substandard training schools for journalism, which have led some countries, like Nigeria, to introduce an accreditation process for journalism schools (UNESCO, 2008). In Asia, journalism education in India has, after a slow start, seen an exponential increase in the number of journalism schools since the 1990s. Rao (2009) notes that, during 2007–8, nearly one dozen journalism schools were opened in metropolitan areas around the country. She points out that, in contrast to many Western countries where the number of journalism graduates easily exceeds the number of entry positions, the reverse is the case on the subcontinent. Xu et al. (2002) have also noted the significant expansion of journalism education in China in recent years.

The growth of the media industries in Europe in the 1960s went hand in hand with a strong growth in journalism education institutions across the continent. Nordenstreng (2009) reports that there are more than 100 organizations which offer journalism education or training in Britain, almost 200 institutions in Germany, 80 in Poland and 60 in France. In Spain, there are more than 17,000 students enrolled in journalism programmes. Yet, while the growth of journalism education has been across Europe, there still exists considerable heterogeneity in terms of the actual educational models, making it difficult to even identify groupings of countries (Nordenstreng, 2009). In Britain, the traditional approach of on-the-job training was a dominant one for a longer time than elsewhere, with an industry that was negative of formalized training at universities persisting until the 1970s. Since then, however, British 'journalism education and training has undergone a quite extraordinary transformation' (Bromley, 2009, p. 49). While in 1957 the proportion of university-educated journalists was 'negligible' (Delano, 2000, p. 267), the number skyrocketed to 95 per cent in 2002 (Phillips, 2005). This represents quite a transformation, particularly as there had been quite a strong opposition to university-educated journalists in the industry. In 1975, the National Council for the Training of Journalists (NCTJ), one of the main accreditation bodies, believed that no graduate 'would readily accept the canon of the popular press' (NCTJ cited in Delano, 2000, p. 267). In 2008, the NCTJ accredited 70 journalism courses in 40 institutions – including 22 universities – in Britain (Bromley, 2009). In total, there were 38 universities in 2006 which offered journalism as a single subject first degree (Sanders et al., 2008).

Weibull (2009) notes that in most of the countries that belong to Hallin and Mancini's (2004) Democratic Corporatist model – essentially Northern Europe, the Benelux countries (Belgium, the Netherlands and Luxembourg), as well as the German-speaking countries – journalism education began to expand rapidly in the 1960s, in connection with the unprecedented expansion of the media and the growing perception of journalism as a profession. While originally journalism training was installed by journalist unions, these were taken over by public education in most countries eventually, and university education now constitutes the major form of journalism training there, even though a multitude of alternative pathways exists (Weibull, 2009). In North America, journalism education today is well established within universities, situated mostly in a social sciences context (Weaver, 2003). It has proven so popular that at the turn of the millennium, there were 462 degree-granting programmes in the field of journalism and mass communication in the US (Weaver, 2003). As a result, news organizations have also placed emphasis on hiring new journalists who hold journalism or mass communication degrees, with both newspapers and television stations reporting around 90 per cent of new recruits as having studied some form of journalism, though only half have usually studied it as a major (Weaver et al., 2007).

Tensions between practice and theory

The debate around whether to teach the theory or practice of journalism features in many countries. While we will delve deeper into these tensions later in the chapter, we will here limit our discussion in this section to the kinds of debates that exist in various corners of the globe. In Africa, the debate over theory and practice appears to depend on whether each country's individual situation should determine what is more appropriate and urgent (Banda et al., 2007; McCurdy & Power, 2007). One of the most prominent debates in the United States is still over the type of curriculum that journalism students should be exposed to, with a perennial debate over the extent of a purely professional skills-based education as opposed to a liberal arts degree. Macdonald (2006) argues that in recent years there has been a renewed shift towards the professional model which would go beyond basic skills training and instil in aspiring journalists a sense of journalism as a profession that pursues a public service ideal. We discuss this notion in more depth later in the chapter.

In Latin America, journalism education can be divided into two historical periods, which are marked by the establishment of CIESPAL (*Cientro Internacional de Estudios Superiores de Periodismo para América Latina* – International Centre of Higher Journalism Studies for Latin America). Ferreira and Tillson (2000) note that, prior to the establishment of this journalism training and education institute in 1960, and even during its early years, there was a relatively strong emphasis on skills training. From the mid-1970s, however, educational approaches began to shift towards a more scholarly direction, which stressed 'social communication' and neo-Marxist critical approaches. This new focus believed it was important that journalists 'needed to be made socially aware of the region's experiences with poverty, dictatorships, foreign exploitation and other social problems' (Ferreira & Tillson, 2000, p. 65). Towards the end of the Cold War, however, CIESPAL began to temper its radical policies and journalism education returned to a skills-based emphasis once more. In some places, this change has been so complete that 'some critics fear that universities have embraced skills training too strongly and that efforts to instil students with a concern for social values have been abandoned' (Ferreira & Tillson, 2000, p. 75).

Australia has witnessed in recent years a clear move from a mostly apprenticeship-based system to an increasingly university-dominated approach to journalism education, as evidenced by the persistent increase in the number of journalists with university degrees (Hanusch, 2008b). While journalism used to be learnt on the job in Australia, the dominant career path today is for students to complete a three-year undergraduate degree. This is usually followed by a one-year paid traineeship at a media company. Yet, despite the success of the tertiary model, journalism education has also been dogged by a steady debate between the values of vocationally-oriented versus theory-oriented approaches. This debate came to the fore particularly in the late 1990s, during a lengthy and fiery debate between journalism educators and cultural studies' scholars (for an overview of the debate, see Turner, 2000). This tension was borne out by the fact that journalism education in Australia 'has evolved out of competing Anglo-European and American paradigms – generally framed as a culturist/positivist divide – and now includes a sprawling variety of course titles, job descriptions, and range of discipline areas drawn on' (Deuze, 2004, p. 133). Thus, there still exists an ongoing unresolved tension in journalism education in Australia, as well as in New Zealand. On the one hand, the media industry demands graduates who are job-ready and can quickly fit into a working newsroom, while on the other hand the university environment 'demands a more intellectual and scholarly approach from journalism educators' (Hirst, 2010, p. 87).

In Germany, the path into journalism usually leads through a mix of university education and vocational training by way of a so-called *Volontariat* (traineeship). Fröhlich and Holtz-Bacha (2009) note that during the 1970s, journalism programmes were established at universities in Munich, Dortmund and Hohenheim, using a model that combined a traditional university degree with outside practical training. This was also the start of the new discipline of journalism, which 'provided a theoretical basis for journalism education and the profession in general' (Fröhlich & Holtz-Bacha, 2009, p. 143). A process of expansion and differentiation began in the 1990s, leading to a situation in which 'almost 200 universities, universities of applied sciences, academies, journalism schools, associations and foundations engage in some kind of journalism education' (Fröhlich & Holtz-Bacha, 2009, p. 143). Like in other countries, university graduates now represent the majority of journalists, with the latest national survey identifying 69 per cent of journalists as having graduated from a university, although only 14 per cent actually studied journalism specifically (Weischenberg et al., 2006). Thus, the most common way into journalism is the completion of internships and particularly the so-called *Volontariat* (traineeship) once the person has graduated from university. The *Volontariat*, which can be compared with trainee and cadetships in other countries, consists of a two-year (or 15–18 months for degree holders) training programme that is conducted in-house at media companies (Fröhlich & Holtz-Bacha, 2009).

In southern Europe, formal education in journalism developed late compared to Western Europe. Papathanassopoulos (2009) notes that for a long time, one only became a reporter by way of political, family and friendship connections and even then only through on-the-job training, owing to a situation where journalists often acted as political advocates in line with the political parallelism that defines Hallin and Mancini's (2004) Mediterranean model. Journalism schools existed in many countries in southern Europe, and in Italy for example it is still the only way to enter the industry (Agostini, 2009). The common path into journalism is now to undertake a general degree at university, followed by two years at one of the 22 registered journalism schools around the country. Thus, the theoretical knowledge that is gained in university is supplemented at journalism schools with the vocational skills needed for working in a news organization (Agostini, 2009).

The divide between theory and practice orientations has been somewhat less pronounced in Asian communication programmes. Chan (1996) has pointed out that the relatively recent development of research efforts in Asian universities has allowed predominantly practice-oriented journalism schools to be held in high regard. 'Thanks to the glamour of the media and the general acceptance of professional skills, communication schools in Asia are in general more readily accepted by university colleagues and society at large' (p. 23). In India, the dire need in the media industry for job-ready graduates has also brought about a change in curricula. While previously university education in journalism was almost exclusively theoretically focused, Karan (2001) has noted a significant shift to include more skills-based training to meet industry needs. See also Rajan (2005) for current debates and issues relating to Indian journalism and journalism education.

Licensing of journalists

Debates about journalism education in Latin America have been dominated by the issue of licensing of journalists, which relates to the so-called *colegio* system. *Colegios* are organizations that, as some argue, essentially license journalists because they require them 'to have a degree from a recognized domestic university in order to practice' (Ferreira & Tillson, 2000). Many commentators, particularly from the United States and also from regional publishers and press associations, strongly criticized the *colegio* system as endangering freedom of the press. However, as Knudson (1996) has pointed out, the universities and many journalists who argued for the creation of *colegios* claimed they would professionalize journalism around the region. As a by-product, restricting the number of available journalists also meant that journalists' salaries were raised considerably and marked a move away from the previously 'humiliating economic dependency on (journalists') news sources' (Knudson, 1996, p. 886). Knudson also notes that before the establishment of *colegios*, journalists were not recognized as professionals and were not entitled to a number of benefits. Ferreira and Tillson (2000) point out that much of the debate over *colegios* was affected by Cold War rhetoric and, as Knudson (1996) notes, was wound up in the wider ideological battles over press freedom as expressed in the UNESCO debates over a New World Information and Communication Order. Communist and developing nations advocated for the establishment of *colegios*, which reinforced 'the view among media professionals and American journalists and educators that *colegios* posed a threat to press freedom' (Ferreira & Tillson, 2000, p. 63). Yet Knudson (1996, p. 885) argues that far from threatening press freedom, *colegios* actually have a record of strongly defending it, as demonstrated in their opposition to dictatorships in the region. Since the end of the Cold War, the debate has subsided and the number of countries with *colegios* increased from 8 in 1973 to 13 in 1993, with Knudson (1996) noting that increasingly even US commentators are at least presenting the case for *colegios* when they discuss the issue.

The debate over licensing of journalists is not restricted to Latin America, however. Journalists have been licensed for quite some time in France and Italy, where a national accreditation body oversees registration (Agostini, 2009). In Australia, the pros and cons of at least accrediting journalism programmes have been discussed from time to time; in New Zealand this is already the case (Green, 2005). The debate over the merits and drawbacks of licensing journalists has also polarized Nigerian journalists and the public following the introduction of a bill in parliament. The bill is entitled 'An Act to Provide for the Repeal of the Nigerian Press Council Act 1992 and Establish the Nigerian Press and Practice of Journalism Council'. While the Nigerian Guild of Editors perceives the bill as pointless and as an attempt to license journalists, many members of the House of Representatives argue the bill would improve journalism practice in the country (Iriekpen, 2009).

Concerns over imported media models

In chapters 2 and 3 we discussed the concern in many non-western countries over imported media models from the West. This tension also exists in relation to journalism education. In Africa, for example, a persistent topic of debate has been the dependence on Western donors for training programmes, and the reliance on Western trainers and textbooks that went with it. Nordenstreng et al. (1998) noted in a survey of the use of textbooks that Africa in particular was still extremely reliant on textbooks that had been published in the United States (in Anglophone Africa) and Europe (mainly in Francophone Africa). Only 6 per cent of textbooks in Anglophone, and 8 per cent in Francophone countries had been published in the region. Still, at least 20 per cent of textbooks in Anglophone Africa had some regional relevance, while in Francophone Africa that was only the case in 8 per cent (Nordenstreng et al., 1998). The dependence on Western donors and non-governmental organizations was also highlighted as a problem in interviews with African journalism educators (McCurdy & Power, 2007). A major concern, according to many of these educators, was that it was too formulaic and 'often failed to reflect or dovetail with the domestic realities of those being trained' (McCurdy & Power, 2007, p. 133). One of the main complaints, which relates to the debates on African values in journalism discussed in Chapter 3, was the need to adapt the training to local cultural sensitivities. Language could also be an issue because even though most countries in Africa speak either English or French, many journalists also have to work in local dialects or regional languages. For example, a dean at an Ethiopian university said he was reliant on English textbooks because there were none in the local language. This presented a problem particularly because of the subject matter: 'At the present, I am teaching editing – the subject matter. The book is in English. The materials for editing should also be in Amharic because most of the journalists are expected to work in Amharic' (cited in McGurdy & Power, 2007, p. 134). Owing to the relatively recent emergence of journalism training on the continent, many countries also have to contend with the difficulties of attracting qualified and experienced journalism trainers. This has led to a reliance on expatriate teachers from North America and Europe in many places (Skjerdal & Ngugi, 2007; McCurdy & Power, 2007).

Nevertheless, the recent years of fast growth in media organizations in many African countries, coupled with the spread of journalism education on the continent, imply that nowadays most researchers in the field see the future being determined within African contexts by Africans rather than the previously imposed models of Western aid organizations. McCurdy and Power (2007), for example, have called for such an African approach, arguing that

> there is a need to question the everyday, assumed and accepted practices of African journalism. It then needs to be asked how these observations and insights can contribute towards and open discussion around the need for Africans to develop their own approach to journalism and how this can be done. Such an undertaking must only come from within Africa. While support from

non-African donors and NGOs would no doubt be welcome, the agenda must be driven by those on the ground. (McCurdy & Power, 2007, p. 145)

Similarly, Botha and de Beer (2007, p. 205) see an emergence of African ideas and debates, and believe that 'unlike in the past, when answers were mostly sought within the context of the North (read the English speaking world), the questions and answers now seem to be embedded in the folds of the continent'. Indeed, first moves are underway to identify who could take the lead in this respect, with a UNESCO-commissioned report by Berger and Matras (2007) identifying 12 potential centres of excellence in journalism training on the continent, covering Uganda, Kenya, Nigeria, South Africa, Namibia, Mozambique, Senegal, Cameroon and Morocco.

In the Pacific Islands, an interesting debate has emerged as to the ideological context within which journalism was being taught. Rooney et al. (2004) argued in their case study of Papua New Guinean media, for example, that the Western-influenced journalism training and Western style of reporting could not simply be transplanted into a society such as Papua New Guinea (PNG). Development models that emerged in other developing countries around the world therefore also played a role in the Pacific, as our discussion of this issue in Chapter 3 has shown. In this context, Rooney (2003, pp. 88–9) lauded the 'commitment to social justice and the need to provide voice for the voiceless' at PNG's Divine Word University, and agreed that a promising curriculum was being created. However, he also warned that the next step in journalism education would have to 'move learning beyond the acquisition of knowledge to include intellectual skills, analysis, synthesis, evaluation and problem solving, all within a PNG context' (p. 89).

A shortage of resources

Many journalism schools in less developed countries are affected by a lack of resources for their programmes. In Africa there is a constant need for and dependency on external funding for journalism training. Skjerdal and Ngugi (2007) report that in Eastern Africa, many universities' journalism programmes use technology that is inferior by far to that used in major media organizations of these countries. Universities can therefore only inadequately prepare graduates for technological aspects of their work. Hume relates the situation in Nigeria, where at one polytechnic 'the journalism studies program has two first-generation Macintosh computers that cannot be used because there is no electricity. There is nothing on the dean's desk to type on. There is no water even to flush the toilet' (2007, p. 7). The desperate need for improved infrastructure was also highlighted during a meeting of African journalism educators in 2008 (UNESCO, 2008). In many universities on the continent, staff and students lack basic access to computers and the Internet, thus making education for a technology-focused profession like journalism difficult. If students do not have access to the kind of equipment they will encounter in the newsroom, it will make their transition from university to industry very difficult.

Some Central Asian republics face similar problems. Gross and Kenny (2008) have argued that among the most pressing problems in Uzbekistan, as well as in Tajikistan and Turkmenistan are educators' lack of familiarity with digital information-delivery systems as well as a related lack of access to new technologies. In Kyrgyzstan and Kazakhstan, however, Gross and Kenny (p. 55) see some well-run journalism schools that boast 'well-run facilities and up-to-date, US-style curricula that are computer-driven and housed in institutions that allow for optimum learning'.

Clashes between state ideology and journalism education

In many authoritarian countries, as well as countries recently emerging from authoritarian rule, journalism curricula face a clash of priorities over ideological instruction and demands of a market-driven journalism. In Chinese journalism education this is most evident, where there is an obvious tension between communist state ideology and market demands. Xu et al. (2002) have pointed out that the sweeping reforms in the People's Republic over the past 20 to 30 years have created significant clashes between political orientation and economic imperatives. Noting the rapid rise in the number of journalism schools around the country in recent years, they find that 'in the short span of a few decades, journalism education in China has evolved into a mixed creature with Chinese educational mentality expressed in Russian-style operation built on an American foundation' (p. 65). In practical terms, this has meant a return to many aspects of the US-style education that was dominant in journalism schools before the Cultural Revolution (Volz & Lee, 2009). Yet, the significant expansion of journalism education in China in recent times has not yet been able to bring it to the level of Western countries in terms of professionalism, infrastructure provision and staff competence (Xu et al., 2002).

Journalism education in Vietnam has a much shorter history than in many other countries, with the first dedicated journalism schools in the country only opening in the early 1990s (Dinh, 2004). As a result of the political structure of Vietnam, the primary focus of journalism education has been on communist ideology and party politics, a fact that has been bemoaned by commentators (Dinh, 2004; Nguyen, 2006). In a practical sense, the fact that journalism graduates are usually indoctrinated in ideology rather than journalistic skills means that employers do not hold them in high regard. In fact, 'they lag behind reality with a bulk of outdated knowledge and are seldom ready to meet the requirement of the job market' (Nguyen, 2006).

In Central Asia, many former Soviet republics are finding it difficult to adjust their journalism programmes at a time when autocratic regimes still rule most of the countries in the region. In Uzbekistan, Shafer and Freedman (2003) found that academics were sufficiently familiar with media theories but lacked expertise in skills such as 'gathering information, interviewing, balancing sources, distancing from the power structure, writing news clearly and effectively, maintaining independence, engaging in the watchdog role and maintaining reader interest' (2003, p. 102). Freedman (2007) notes that, at least in Kyrgyzstan, Soviet-style teaching methods still dominate the curriculum, which focuses heavily on the teaching of theory rather than practical training (Freedman, 2007). As a result, news organizations are finding it difficult to hire graduates who have the necessary skill set to work as journalists.

Journalism education in Eastern Europe under communism was 'defined as political education and coupled with propagandistic techniques to be applied both in print and broadcast media' (Gross, cited in Jakubowicz, 2009, p. 349). As a result, some argue that the biggest challenge for the new journalism programmes emerging in the area is to overcome low professional and ethical standards, lack of resources and corruption, despite the considerable sums of money spent by Western European and North American countries on media development (Jakubowicz, 2009, pp. 349–50). Education also does not necessarily occur only at universities, with many countries offering it through post-secondary journalism schools and other training programmes. A particular concern for many in the field is the divide between practice and theory and conflicting beliefs in terms of what should be taught. As a result, Jakubowicz (2009, p. 355) argues, 'journalism education has made some, but limited contribution to shaping a new understanding of the professional role and definition of journalism, and to raising the professional skills of journalists'.

Integrating approaches to journalism education

Despite the existence of a plethora of studies documenting the ways in which journalists are educated around the world, as the overview presented here has shown, there exist surprisingly few theoretical models that have tried to integrate what is going on across the globe. Gaunt (1992) argued nearly 20 years ago that while journalism practices and media systems differ considerably across the globe, the education of journalists was also faced with similar challenges: 'Whatever the geographic area or socio-political context, journalism educators and media professionals have had to come to terms with the same problems' (p. 2). One more conceptually-oriented overview was provided by Deuze (2006), who, based on the work done by Gaunt (1992) as well as Fröhlich and Holtz-Bacha (2003a), argued that we can differentiate between the following five distinct types or models of journalism education worldwide.

(a) The first, and increasingly the dominant mode of education, is the training at schools and institutes located at universities. This is the main mode of training in the United States, Canada, Finland, Sweden, Spain, South Korea, Egypt, Kenya, Argentina, the Gulf States and, more recently, Australia and Britain.
(b) The second type of education comprises of the mixed systems of both stand-alone schools and university-level training (as found in France, Germany, Ireland, Portugal, India, Indonesia, China, Brazil, Nigeria, Turkey and South Africa).
(c) The third type, according to Deuze, is journalism education in stand-alone schools, as seen in the Netherlands, Denmark, Norway and Italy, although Fröhlich and Holtz-Bacha (2003b) note the latter is moving more and more towards the first group.
(d) The fourth type represents primarily on-the-job training through apprenticeships, the previously most dominant form of journalism education in Australia and the United Kingdom, but still practised in Austria and Japan.
(e) A fifth type, Deuze argues, is a mix of all of the above, and is evident in countries in Eastern Europe, North and Central Africa and the Middle East.

Warning that 'one should not reduce regional and local complexities too much', Deuze (2006, p. 22) argues that 'the literature does suggest most if not all systems of journalism education are moving towards the first or second model, indicating increasing levels of professionalization, formalization and standardization worldwide'. However, he warns that this is not meant as 'a claim to singularity or universality as an inescapable byproduct of globalization' (pp. 22–3), even though recent trends support his assessment. Fröhlich and Holtz-Bach (2003b, pp. 319–20) believe that 'the most powerful influences for journalism education are the factors of the societal sphere or the system including the historical and the cultural background of a country, as well as the media structure with its normative and economic background variables'. Yet there do not seem to be any clear predictors of whether a country adopts one type of education model or another. The above categories cut across a large number of continents as well as media models, as well as other cultural, political and economic variables. Considering that former French colonies have tended to adopt a French system of journalism education and former British colonies show distinct traits of the British system (e.g. the Nigerian Broadcasting Corporation adopting the BBC model in its early years), we can see how a culture's history and media system can impact on journalism education. The US model has been popular around the world not through colonization but mainly through the expansion of US interest by way of aid programmes. As we discussed in chapters 2 and 3, these imported models of journalism (and by extension journalism education) have led to much disquiet in many countries in Africa, Asia and Oceania because of their overreliance on Western models of thinking. As the proponents of these approaches have argued, such strategies are necessary, in terms of the curriculum, in order to take account of local cultural conditions. As the discussion of journalists' role perceptions in Chapter 3 demonstrated, journalists in developing countries tend to emphasize somewhat different roles from their Western counterparts, at least in some respects.

In order to provide an analytical framework for the examination of journalism education, Deuze (2006) has proposed 10 categories which can be seen as steps following on from one another. These categories include, as a first step, *motivation*, that is, the question of why journalism education is necessary. A second category refers to *paradigm*, which relates to the major ideas that guide the education of journalists, followed by a description of a *mission* as the third step. A fourth point is the *orientation*, that is, 'on what aspect (or aspects) of journalism is the education based (such as: the media, genres, or functions of journalism in society)?' (Deuze, 2006, p. 23). Next follows a step where the *direction* is clarified, that is, the characteristics that journalism graduates should ideally have. A sixth category, according to Deuze, is concerned with *contextualization*, which refers to the social context of journalism education. This is followed by the question of *education*, and whether it is seen as a socializing or individualizing agent. One of the major points of debate in journalism education is listed at number eight in Deuze's framework. It refers to the question of the *curriculum* and what the best balance is between practical and contextual knowledge. Category nine refers to the *pedagogical method* with which journalism is taught, and finally, the framework is also concerned with the way in which journalism education is *managed and organized* (p. 23). Deuze believes that the concept of journalism needs to be re-examined in order to be able to determine what it should be. This, he argues, needs to be done consistently in the context of 'community' because it means 'that any conceptualisation of journalism must always be framed in terms of journalism and society, as it then can be situated in particular technological, economical, political and social contexts' (p. 30). Further, Deuze believes that journalism education needs to be taken seriously as a field of study in order to 'empirically document the impact of the different choices available within and between the distinct categories as outlined' (p. 30).

Debates over university-based journalism education

As Deuze (2006) points out, the topic of curriculum has attracted the most attention from scholars, and it remains one of the most contentious issues in journalism education today. Journalism education at universities has always been characterized by an 'industry-academic dichotomy' (Reese & Cohen, 2000, p. 217) between media industry demands for job-ready graduates and academy demands for a more theory-centred education. This is very much a global phenomenon, with various scholars from around the world describing the relationship as 'not a bed of roses' (Stephenson, 1997, p. 23) or a 'dialogue of the deaf' (Dennis, 1988, p. 4). The predicament that educators thus have to deal with is whether it is possible to align those diverging demands and how that alignment can take place. As Skinner et al. have pointed out,

> journalism education is the servant of two masters. On the one hand, journalism educators seek to satisfy the demands of news organizations by providing a steady stream of graduates ready for the newsroom. On the other hand, journalism schools are asked to meet the standards of university administrators who perceive post-secondary education as something more than vocational training. (2001, p. 344)

The important question then is: how can university educators equip journalism graduates with the necessary job skills but also include a wider critical awareness of the journalistic environment that should be part and parcel of a university degree?

First, we need to consider that one of the primary reasons for the creation of formal journalism programmes at universities was to professionalize journalism, and to give it the added credibility that comes with such a process. Professions generally consist of at least four elements: a body of knowledge, a public service ideal, an ethical framework and a core set of skills (Reese & Cohen, 2000, p. 217). Yet, journalism is 'quite different from the traditional learned professions such as medicine that carry significant judgemental autonomy for the practitioner and impose barriers to entry' (Reese & Cohen, 2000, p. 217). In particular, the fact that many media organizations are privately-owned and journalists employed at these organizations are therefore first and foremost in the service of that organization's owner, rather than the public, complicates the ideal of professionalism significantly. The result of the complex conceptualization of professionalism in journalism education thus is often reduced to what Reese and Cohen (2000, p. 217) call 'vocationalism to the extent that it involves learning by emulation'. Skinner et al. (2001, p. 345) also criticize such pure vocational approaches, arguing that they lack an understanding that 'news production is, in fact, the convergence of theory and practice, and that any attempt to provide fair, balanced and accurate depictions of events involves much more than a simple presentation of "the facts"'.

In the United States, Carey (2000) lamented that journalism had not found a home in the humanities and was taught on models that had existed for almost 50 years. 'Journalism is surrounded now by many more well-conceived and well-taught courses in history, law, ethics, and similar subjects. However, the central subject matter, journalism, has not been found but merely displaced to the margin' (Carey, 2000, p. 14). de Burgh (2003) calls for a move away from mere vocational approaches, arguing that, while perhaps favoured by the industry, a society needed more from its journalists. 'In order to perform their functions journalists need an education which enables them to put themselves and their society in perspective; find out anything and question everything. Motor skills yes, but also the intellectual confidence which comes from knowledge' (de Burgh, 2003, p. 110). Adam (2001) has argued along similar lines in his outline of a curriculum that could return to the basis of Pulitzer's vision for journalism education more than 100 years ago. These views have come largely in response to a widely held view of journalism as a profession in crisis in a neo-liberal environment. Yet, Macdonald (2006) believes that such a liberal arts-based model would merely place the onus on individual journalists to be professionals when they actually must work in a news environment that may not allow them to pursue such ideals. She believes that such a proposal 'does not adequately address the organisational, structural and economic roots of the professional crisis' (Macdonald, 2006, p. 760).

Australian journalism educator Kerry Green (2005) argues that there is a need to look at society rather than the separate needs of either industry or academy. He notes that only one-third of graduates ever enter into the mainstream media, and wonders whether journalism educators have failed to challenge students for too long. 'Behind many of the ideas in question is the assumption that journalism education has for too long contented itself with replicating journalism, rather than working to broaden, deepen and invigorate journalism' (Green, 2005, p. 188). He makes three suggestions for how the gap between industry and academy can be bridged: 'first, journalism education must institute a form of accreditation; second, professionals must become more familiar with journalism courses and what they offer; and third, universities must show they value the professional skills of staff members by acknowledging the benefit of newsroom refresher courses' (p. 192). Skinner et al. (2001) similarly argue for an integration of theory and practice rather than teaching the two together.

> We advocate a more holistic approach which posits journalism as an institutional practice of representation with its own historical, political, economic and cultural conditions of existence. What this means to the journalism curriculum is that students require not only a particular skill set and broad social knowledge, but they also need to understand how journalism participates in the production and circulation of meaning in our society. (p. 342)

In order to achieve that end, they provide a number of examples, such as the need for students to look more closely at language in order to understand the different connotations certain words can evoke. Other suggestions include writing news from different cultural perspectives and utilizing journalistic methods (e.g. interviews and photographs) in academic research. However, they acknowledge that it would be necessary to (1) re-orient course curriculums to ensure courses had common elements running through them, and (2) heal divides between theory and practice from an administrative level (Skinner et al., 2001). Consequently, they believe the introduction of a curriculum that is based on critical communication studies 'offers students a means of bridging the practical and abstract components of course work and provides journalism as a method with a sound epistemological basis' (2001, p. 357).

It would seem logical that future curricula in journalism need to take account of both practice and theory, and try to satisfy the sometimes divergent demands of industry and academia as best they can. The future of journalism practice depends on university education in its effort to attain the public's trust. In public opinion surveys, journalists are regularly ranked below other professions in terms of credibility (Barnett, 2008), and some still believe that ongoing professionalization can restore public faith in journalism. In very practical terms, of course, media organizations benefit from having their journalists educated in universities because they are able to save a considerable amount of money from not having to train them themselves, or at least to only conduct minimal training. At the same time, the popularity of journalism and consequent large enrolments in journalism courses at universities around the world also present an opportunity for universities in an increasingly market-driven higher education environment, at least in Anglo-Saxon countries. It would thus not be in universities' interests to remain steadfast in demanding purely theory-based approaches. A healthy mix of both practical education that is grounded in theory and which educates rather than trains budding journalists will therefore be in the valuable service of society at large. After all, both universities and media organizations aspire to public service ideals and better-educated journalists are in the public interest.

A global curriculum

The rapid pace of globalization, increasing contact between cultures around the globe and the similarities in the problems facing journalism education worldwide have in recent years inspired movements towards a truly global approach that could set normative expectations or goals for a global journalism curriculum. In its collection of model curricula for journalism education, which were gathered from around the world, UNESCO (2007) defined the purpose of journalism education in a comprehensive fashion:

> A journalism education should teach students how to identify news and recognize the story in a complex field of fact and opinion, how to conduct journalistic research, and how to write for, illustrate, edit and produce material for various media formats (newspapers and magazines, radio and television, and online and multimedia operations) and for their particular audiences. It should give them the knowledge and training to reflect on journalism ethics and best practices in journalism, and on the role of journalism in society, the history of journalism, media law, and the political economy of media (including ownership, organization and competition). (...) It should ensure that they develop – or that they have as a prerequisite – the linguistic ability necessary for journalistic work in their country, including, where this is required, the ability to work in local indigenous or vernacular languages. It should prepare them to adapt to

technological developments and other changes in the news media. (UNESCO, 2007, p. 6)

The increasingly global approaches led to the establishment of the World Journalism Education Council (WJEC) in 2007. The council represents 29 academic associations of journalism education from all six continents, and its purpose is to 'provide a common space for journalism educators from around the world and to focus on issues that are universal in the field' (WJEC, 2010). There have been two conferences, one in Singapore in 2007 and another in South Africa in 2010. At its first conference, the member associations adopted the first-ever Declaration of Universal Principles of Journalism Education, which refers to 11 important principles that should be observed around the world (WJEC, 2007). Some of the principles state that:

- At the heart of journalism education is a balance of conceptual, philosophical and skills-based content. While it is also interdisciplinary, journalism education is an academic field in its own right with a distinctive body of knowledge and theory.
- Journalism is a field appropriate for university study from undergraduate to postgraduate levels. Journalism programmes offer a full range of academic degrees including bachelors, masters and Doctor of Philosophy degrees as well as certificate, specialized and mid-career training.
- Journalism educators should be a blend of academics and practitioners; it is important that educators have experience working as journalists.
- Journalism curriculum includes a variety of skills courses and the study of journalism ethics, history, media structures/institutions at national and international level, critical analysis of media content and journalism as a profession. It includes coursework on the social, political and cultural role of media in society and sometimes includes coursework dealing with media management and economics. In some countries, journalism education includes allied fields like public relations, advertising, and broadcast production. ('Principles of Journalism Education', World Journalism Education Council, 2007)

Conclusion

This chapter examined the development and current reach of institutionalized journalism education around the world. The origins of journalism education are mostly located in the United States, but some European countries began educating journalists more formally at least around the same time, if not even a little earlier. Of course the fact that journalism education is seen to have originated in the United States can be explained by the dominance of US scholarship in journalism and journalism education. But it is also due to the enormous popularity the US model has found around the globe. Much of this popularity has been attributed to aid programmes that were often motivated by a desire to advance US influence in developing regions and a desire to install stable democratic systems. On the other hand, as discussions of journalism education in Europe have shown, it is difficult to divide the world in terms of approaches to journalism education. Nordenstreng (2009) points out that within Europe, there are distinct and significant differences between individual countries that barely allow arguing about any groupings based on geography or politics. Hallin and Mancini (2004) made a similar argument in regard to media systems in general, as was discussed in Chapter 2. Once more it seems that specific cultural conditions play an important role.

Journalism education has proved immensely popular across the globe. Recent decades have seen a phenomenal uptake in many countries, and recent evidence from journalist surveys shows that in many countries university-educated journalists are in the majority. It may not always be the case that they studied journalism-specific courses at university but the fact that they possess a tertiary education certainly marks an important break from previous models. Even in Britain, for a long time a bastion of on-the-job training, students are now flocking to university courses in journalism. Of course different countries have different challenges. While in many Western countries the main battles take place primarily over the amount of practice or theory-related courses, authoritarian countries such as China must contend with finding a balance between commercially motivated journalism that takes on Western characteristics and the demands of a one-party state ideology. In many developing countries, a lack of technological infrastructure presents fundamental barriers to improving journalism education.

Nevertheless, despite the varied nature of journalism education around the world, there have been renewed attempts in recent years to lay a foundation for a universal approach, based on efforts initiated by UNESCO. Largely, they are concentrated around notions of professionalism, and most notably a combination of theory and practice in curricula, in order to produce journalists who possess the required skills to undertake professional work and who are also capable of reflecting on their own work and the profession at large. This combination is necessary to ensure the best possible outcomes for journalism education that would be in the interest of societies and the profession across the globe.

DISCUSSION QUESTIONS

1. Trace the history of journalism education in your own country and identify the model it followed. Do you think the current model is suitable to the realities of your country in the twenty-first century?
2. Summarize the six major strands that dominated discussions about journalism education as outlined in this chapter.
3. Discuss the pros and cons of theory- as well as practice-focused curricula in journalism education.
4. Review UNESCO's (2007) model curricula for journalism education (available on the Internet) and discuss how useful and effective such a model is in your local context.
5. Discuss key arguments for and against exporting journalism education models from developed to developing countries.

CHAPTER 5

Gender in journalism

Introduction

While journalism traditionally developed as a male-dominated industry, increasing female participation in the workforce particularly in the
developed world has led to a growing presence of women in journalism.
In fact, when it comes to journalism education, women easily constitute
the majority. Yet, within the profession, there are still some considerable
differences in terms of gender roles. In this chapter, we focus on the role
gender plays in news production processes around the world. Newspaper
journalism was clearly gendered in the early years of the twentieth century, with certain positions and areas of coverage designated specifically
for men and women. Most of the changes that took place in the last few
decades or so, particularly through the increasing presence of women on
screen, conceal a permanent differentiation in assigning roles. Women
are usually given, for the most part, news stories about fashion, entertainment and culture, while men normally cover political, economic,
financial and sport stories (Lont, 1995; McRobbie, 1996; Robinson,
2005). When women make the news, Gallagher (2010) writes, it is often
in conventionally stereotyped ways – as celebrities, victims of crime, or
in clearly 'woman-centred' stories that are usually marginal to the main
news agenda.

As this chapter demonstrates, the trend, at least in the developed world,
appears to be towards some form of gender balance in terms of the number
of practising journalists. In fact, in some areas of journalism, women are in
the majority in some countries. However, there are still clear and distinct
differences in the roles that women and men occupy within the profession.
Fröhlich (2007, p. 163) notes that, as international studies have shown, 'an
overwhelming majority of women journalists worldwide agreed that women
journalists face professional barriers that their male colleagues do not and
that the top obstacle for women in management is continually proving their

87

...ilities to colleagues and supervisors'. Thus, when it comes to symbolic power in the field, as evidenced by the number of women in senior editorial positions, gender balance is still far from being a reality. A noticeable 'glass ceiling' still prevails. This chapter thus provides an overview of gender in journalism around the world.

A further interesting aspect of research, however, is not just how many women are in journalism but also the way in which they carry out their job. Do women practise journalism in significantly different ways from men, or do they appropriate the news values developed by men over centuries? As we highlight in this chapter, there is some evidence to suggest that some women, in an attempt to become 'one of the boys' and to be accepted as serious news reporters, adopt mainstream values. However, some researchers have also pointed to a general softening of news values in line with increasing participation of women in journalism.

The history of women in journalism

Gender, as Massey (1998) argues, has not figured prominently in the general literature on international journalism. Journalism, historically speaking, evolved as a male-dominated profession. Thus, male dominance in the media was unchallenged until the early years of the twentieth century. It was not as though women were not successful in journalism before the advent of the twentieth century. Indeed, some women featured quite prominently during the development of the press in the United States, such as Mary Katherine Goddard, who managed the first newspaper in Baltimore, the *Baltimore Journal*, during the American Revolution (Kitch, 2002). In the nineteenth century, women such as Margaret Fuller, Anne Royall and Sarah Josepha Hale were only some of the prominent journalists of their time. Yet, they were the exception to the rule. By and large, women were invisible in what was a truly male-dominated profession for quite some considerable time. In the United States, there were only 288 female journalists among the 12,308 journalists counted during the 1880 census, a mere 2.3 per cent. By 1900, their number had risen to 7.3 per cent, which more than doubled again in the ensuing 20 years, when women made up 16.8 per cent of journalists. It took another 30 years for that percentage to double yet again, up to 32 per cent in 1950 (Chamber et al., 2004, p. 15). In Britain, Delano (2003) notes that in the 1950s the proportion of women working in British newspapers was a mere 1 woman for every 16 men, while in magazines the ratio was much higher at 1:3.

While women were predominantly writing about domestic issues at the end of the nineteenth century, some publishers, most notably Joseph Pulitzer and Randolph William Hearst, used them as 'stunt reporters' who would go undercover and report sensational stories on crime and social issues (Kitch, 2002, p. 90). Most famous among those was Elizabeth Jane Cochrane, better known under her pseudonym of Nellie Bly. Bly is perhaps most famous for a ground-breaking assignment she undertook shortly after joining Pulitzer's *New York World* newspaper. She faked insanity in order to go undercover to report on the inhumane conditions in an asylum for the mentally insane. Her story caused outrage among New Yorkers and led to considerable improvements in the treatment of insane people. The concept of Bly's undercover assignment was so successful it found many imitators in the popular press of the late nineteenth century, leading Lutes (2002, p. 220) to argue that these women 'were the first newspaperwomen to move, as a group, from the women's pages to the front page, from society news into political and criminal news'. This move, Lutes believes, may also have played a role in defining male reactions to women reporters.

> The stunt reporters' popularity may even have inspired a misogynist backlash against women's growing presence in newsrooms. The aggressive masculinity of the dogged city reporter – so often cited as proof of women's marginal status – can also be read as a reaction against a perceived threat from women who had begun to write the news themselves. Undoubtedly, the figure of the manly reporter was a significant player in the explosive gender politics of turn-of-the-century news writing. That gritty masculine figure, however, arose in tandem with newspaperwomen, and the girl stunt reporter offered a particularly brash counterpoint. (Lutes, 2002, p. 219)

As Kitch (2002) argues, opportunities for women journalists during the first half of the twentieth century still depended heavily on what was happening to men. When jobs were scarce during the Great Depression, women's numbers remained stagnant, while during the Second World War they expanded, only to contract again after the end of the war, when the men returned home. Such trends reinforce the notion that despite some improvements for women journalists, what happened in the industry was still predominantly decided by men. It has also been the case in more recent times. In this respect, Chambers et al. (2004, p. 15) have argued that despite the relative growth of women in journalism, they 'occupied a subordinated "ghetto status" at least until the turn of the twentieth century and, in many respects, beyond that period'. When rationalizations in East German journalism around the time of reunification led to a 30 per cent loss of jobs there, women were the worst affected group: Their share of the workforce fell drastically from a majority of 60 per cent to a minority of 38 per cent (Lünenborg, 1993).

The historical development towards inclusion of more women in journalism was similar in other developed countries. For example, in Sweden, the start of the twentieth century saw a clear divide between men and women in newspaper journalism. Women were predominantly responsible for looking after the women's pages and columns, but were also, due to their high-level of education and command of foreign languages, involved in rewriting news stories from the foreign press (Djerf-Pierre, 2007). Other areas, such as party press, political and opinion-leading journalism, however, remained the domain of men. This separation of job profiles is likely to be an explanation for the lack of animosity between men and women in those early days, as Djerf-Pierre (2007, p. 87) notes that many women said they did not feel hindered in their pursuit, and that male colleagues were both friendly and helpful. Nevertheless, just as was the case in other developed countries, women only made up 11 per cent of all Swedish journalists in 1914, and even in 1970 that number had only risen to 20 per cent overall.

The increase in female journalists is generally attributed to the rise of a growing female audience in journalism. Kitch (2002, p. 88) argued that the increasing visibility of female journalists signalled a 'growing importance of female newspaper readers during an era when rising literacy, a growing middle class and industrialisation changed the pattern of women's lives'. Whitt (2008) also points out that newspaper editors during the 1950s and 1960s tried to attract female readers in order to open new markets and thus established women's pages. As the men at the top of these organizations knew little about what women wanted, employing more female journalists became a necessity. Yet, while from the 1960s and 1970s we saw a marked increase in women's participation levels in journalism, concurrent with achievements in other professions, recent studies suggest that the percentage of female journalists may be reaching a certain limit, at least in some countries. Periodical surveys conducted in the United States, for example, put the percentage of women in news journalism consistently at around one-third of the overall number of journalists, a number that has not changed significantly since the 1980s (Weaver & Wilhoit, 1986, 1996; Weaver et al., 2007).

Such developments have prompted many scholars to argue that despite the progress that had been made, women are still significantly disadvantaged. Gallagher (2001), for example, believes that while there are more women in journalism, external factors mean that fact alone has not made an impact on news content. Thus, she argues that 'the fundamental patterns of media representation that preoccupied the women's movement of the 1970s remain relatively intact thirty years later' (2001, p. 4). The limitations that women encountered are often referred to as the'glass ceiling', a term that, according to the US Department of Labor, is used to refer to 'those artificial barriers based on attitudinal and organisational bias, that prevent qualified individuals from advancing upward in their organisation into management level positions' (in Robinson, 2008, p. 82). Robinson believes that such a definition is too broad to be useful, and she advocates examining 'the specific behaviours, practices, and attitudes that females encounter in their attempts to reach the top' (2008, p. 82).

A crucial figure that is often cited in this context is the 30 per cent mark (Gallagher, 1981; Robinson, 2008; Rush, 2004). Robinson (2008, p. 82) believes that this number appears to be some kind of tipping point, 'suggesting that at this point a minority can change the operating rules by making strategic deals with the majority'. In a similar vein, Rush et al. (1982; Rush, 1989, 2004) put forward the hypothesis of R^3, the Ratio of Recurrent and Reinforced Residuum, which relates to the limitation on women 'in symbolic representation, occupational status and salary levels' (Rush, 2004, p. 264). Rush's formula, which resides around a proportion of females to males between one-quarter vs three-quarters and one-third vs two-thirds, 'effectively reveals that women's participation in the business and academic world of communications has been determined by an unwritten rule that keeps them either in low-status positions not desired by men and/or in a minority percentage across the ranks' (Rush et al., 2005, p. 240). The one-third mark has received relatively strong support from international empirical research, carried out by scholars such as Gallagher (1981, 1995), as well as in Weaver's (1998a) edited collection of surveys of journalists around the world. In the following section, we investigate the situation of female journalists around the globe more closely, using some of the published surveys about the representation of women among the journalistic workforce, as well as case studies from a number of regions. In doing so, our main focus, in the first instance, is to examine the representation of women in numbers, before moving on to take a more in-depth look at some of the practices and values within journalism that limit the involvement of women.

Representation of women in journalism

Where women work in various media platforms depends on the type of medium in most cases. International studies of the representation of women in journalism tell us that, worldwide, women are more likely to be employed in magazines and television than in newspapers, and are much more likely to cover soft news beats than hard news (Fröhlich, 2007; Gallagher, 2010). Perhaps the most-researched world regions in journalism and gender issues have been North America and Europe, mainly because they represent the sites of the dominant part of the global research community, but also because it is in those regions that the women's rights movements had their most immediate impact in the 1960s and 1970s. In the United States, for example, the regular surveys conducted every 10 years under the guidance of David Weaver (Weaver & Wilhoit, 1986, 1996; Weaver et al., 2007) have provided some useful insights into the representation and role perceptions of women in American journalism. Most significantly, the studies have shown that since the 1980s the proportion of female journalists has stagnated, ranging from 33.8 per cent in 1982 to 34 per cent in 1992 and 33 per cent in 2002, giving strong support to the R^3 hypothesis posited by Rush et al. (1982). The percentage of female journalists also varied depending on the type of medium in which they worked. The largest proportion of women were employed in news magazines (43.5%), while female journalists made up 37.4 per cent in television, 33 per cent in daily newspapers and only 21.9 per cent in radio (Weaver et al., 2007). Women were also still behind men when it came to salaries. Weaver et al. (2007) noted that the median salary of $37,731 represented around 81 per cent of men's median salary. This percentage was the same as Weaver and Wilhoit (1996) found 10 years earlier but still an improvement compared to 1982 when it was 71 per cent. Again there was some variance, with men and women who had fewer than 15 years of experience in journalism attracting comparable median salaries, while the largest gap existed among older journalists, that is those with 20 or more years experience (Weaver et al., 2007).

At the various editorial levels, the gender gap in American journalism is still the most obvious. Robinson (2008) reports that only 0.8 per cent of American newspaper editors-in-chief are female. At the level of editor, they also make up less than 1 per cent each in large and medium circulation newspapers but 14 per cent in small circulation dailies. Canada fairs slightly better when it comes to female representation in executive positions, according to Robinson (2008). Here, the proportion of female editors-in-chief reaches 10 per cent, with an average of 27 per cent at the editor level, and between 10 and 45 per cent at managing editor level, depending on circulation. In terms of the raw number of newspaper and television journalists, Robinson and Saint-Jean (1998) note that the print industry sees considerably fewer women, who make up only 28 per cent of journalists in Canadian dailies but 37 per cent of television journalists. Women's success at the executive level is also more pronounced in television, with women filling 18 per cent of all top executive producer positions, and 30 per cent of the next two levels, which are news directors and desk heads. Here, Robinson argued that women were beginning to make up a sizeable minority. 'Canadian females in television management have reached the one-third level at which they can begin to strategize and influence the majority, and thus play an effective managerial role' (Robinson, 2008, p. 84).

In their collection of surveys about women journalists in the United States, Canada, the Netherlands, Italy, Germany, Austria, Britain, Finland, France and Israel, Fröhlich and Lafky (2008) note that with the exception of Finland, journalism is still a male-dominated profession in all these Western countries. This was despite the fact that women have been in the majority in many of these countries' journalism schools for some time. Further, evidence of an entrenched glass-ceiling still persists: 'Female heads of departments, managing editors, or editors-in-chief are still the exception, and this is even true for countries where women make up at least a third of the profession (Fröhlich & Lafky, 2008, p. 3). Reaching the 30 per cent mark may thus not make such a big impact, after all. In fact, Fröhlich and Lafky find evidence that 'the communications sector is still a refuge for gender-based differentiation and discrimination' (p. 3).

In Sweden, considered nowadays as somewhat of a bastion for women's rights, the first gender-based statistics in 1978 revealed that women made up only 29 per cent of the journalistic workforce. Female journalists outnumbered their male colleagues only in magazines (53%), while they were in a clear minority (20%) in the tabloid press. Most significantly, only 9 per cent of senior staff, such as managers and editors, were women (Djerf-Pierre, 2007). By 2005, however, female participation in journalism had increased significantly; women had reached almost parity at 48 per cent. Female journalists were in the majority in magazines but also in public service broadcasting. Even in metropolitan newspapers, where 16 years earlier they had only made up 25 per cent of journalists, women now constituted 48 per cent (Djerf-Pierre, 2007). Yet, despite such advances, the glass ceiling remained relatively firmly in place even in Sweden, with three out of four executive positions still held by men. Nevertheless, Rush et al. (2005) believe that the only serious challenges to the R^3 hypothesis seem to come from Nordic countries, as well as the Baltic countries and Central and Eastern Europe.

In one of the first attempts to examine the status of women in journalism around the world in a comparative fashion, Gallagher (1995) reported a shift in gender patterns in media employment in the majority of countries studied.

She argued that the common trend was that female journalists were on the increase, and in some countries, such as New Zealand and the Nordic States, had almost achieved gender balance. Nevertheless, the lack of women in executive positions was still glaringly apparent everywhere, prompting Gallagher (1995, p. 2) to state that 'in most parts of the globe, the world of the media is still very much a man's world'. This was evidenced by her finding that of all the 43 countries in the study, only in Estonia and Lithuania did women actually outnumber men. In addition, in most countries the female participation rate was lower than their participation rate in the general work force. Countries with the highest proportion of female journalists included those in the Baltic states, Central and Eastern Europe, as well as the Nordic states. In southern Africa, the numbers varied considerably between individual countries, with Botswana and Lesotho reaching 46 and 42 per cent of women in media employment, while Malawi and Mozambique only registered 12 and 16 per cent respectively. The countries of Western Europe exhibited a relatively coherent picture, with an average of 35 per cent for the region. Latin America reached an average of only 25 per cent of female journalists, while India and Japan displayed extremely low levels of female participation, with women making up only 12 and 8 per cent of all journalists in those countries, respectively.

Yet, when it came to executive positions, Gallagher's (1995) data showed quite striking evidence of male domination. Of the 239 organizations in her study, only 8, or 3 per cent, were headed by women, with a further eight organizations having female deputy directors. Most of these, however, were small organizations in Latin America. At the top three levels of management, Gallagher (1995) found that women's average share was less than 20 per cent in all media and all regions except for broadcasting in Latin America. The lowest percentages were found in southern Africa and in the three Asian countries included in the study – India, Malaysia and Japan. The total average across all organizations was a mere 12 per cent across the top three levels of management, with only 9 per cent at the top level. Nevertheless, it is important to note that Gallagher's study was conducted more than 15 years ago. It is possible that the trend may have changed, even if slightly.

Weaver's (1998a) edited collection of surveys conducted in 19 countries and territories showed similarly low levels of women's participation in journalism. The overall average across all countries was 33 per cent, exactly the limit hypothesized by Rush et al. (1982). However, once more regional variations showed that women had made considerable progress in some countries, while they were still left behind in others. The regional results were somewhat similar to those found by Gallagher (1995), with Finland showing the highest proportion of female journalists (49%), followed by New Zealand (45%), both countries with relatively successful women's rights movements. On the other hand, women made up only 14 per cent of journalists in Korea, although their proportion was roughly one-third in the other Asian countries included in the study, namely China, Hong Kong and Taiwan. Britain and Spain also showed low levels of female participation, at 25 per cent each, while in Latin America, the picture was mixed. Women represented 42 and 40 per cent of journalists in Brazil and Chile respectively, while only 25 per cent were found in Ecuador and also in Mexico.

A survey conducted at the turn of the millennium by the International Federation of Journalists identified a rise in women journalists in the vast majority of countries studied (Peters, 2001). Female participation rates were again the highest for Europe and the Americas, where on average around 40 per cent of journalists were women, while in Africa that number fell to 25 per cent. It was even lower in the Asia-Pacific, where women made up only 12 per cent of journalists. Again, there were considerable differences globally, with Finland, Thailand and Mexico reaching figures around 50 per cent, while women made up only 6 per cent of journalists in Sri Lanka and Togo. The worldwide average percentage of female journalists was 38 per cent, considerably higher than the 27 per cent found in a similar survey 10 years earlier (Peters, 2001). Most striking, however, were the extremely low levels of women in decision-making positions. The average percentage of women editors, heads of departments or media owners was a mere 0.6 per cent around the world (Peters, 2001). Regional averages were highest for the Americas and Europe (5 and 3%, respectively). Even in the countries where the percentage of women in decision-making positions reached double figures (Cyprus, Costa Rica, Mexico and Sweden), it still varied only between 10 and 20 per cent. The findings prompted Peters to warn there was no room for complacency when it came to women's rights in journalism: 'Many issues remain unsolved and as long as women are still impeded by discrimination over the top jobs, or have less access to training, or continue to be forced into impossible choices between career and family, journalists' unions must keep women's rights at the top of their agenda' (Peters, 2001, pp. 16–17). She argued the three most important issues needing attention in order to improve the situation of women in journalism were: (a) negative stereotypes of women; (b) poor employment conditions such as the lack of equal pay, the glass ceiling effect as well as sexual harassment, age limits and job segregation; and (c) social and personal obstacles, such as conflicting family and career demands, lack of support facilities like day care centres, as well as lack of self-esteem (Peters, 2001, p. 17).

The latest available data from the Global Media Monitoring Project, which examines news coverage around the world on one day roughly every five years, also shows a noticeable increase in the number of stories written or produced by women. While during the first study, conducted in 1995, only 28 per cent of news items had been reported by women, in late 2009 this had increased to 37 per cent (Gallagher, 2010). It is worth noting, however, that this percentage did not change from the previous study, conducted almost five years earlier (Gallagher, 2005). Women were much more equally represented when it came to the number of news presenters on television and radio, where they constituted 49 per cent. Especially in television, where it is arguably more about appearances than journalistic skills, women have been in a slight majority since 2000 (Gallagher, 2010).

In terms of reporters, female newspaper journalists lagged behind their counterparts in electronic media in 2010, with 44 per cent of all television news reporters being female but only 33 per cent of print items written by women. While earlier studies found that women television presenters were predominantly young, the latest study shows that in the age group 50–64, women made up 51 per cent, as opposed to the situation in 2005 when that figure was only at 7 per cent (Gallagher, 2010, p. viii). However, Gallagher cautions that more research is required to examine whether this indeed points to some parity in terms of age. With reference to the various world regions, some significant differences are apparent. Female television presenters were most visible in the Caribbean (60%) and Asia (52%), with other world regions falling below parity (Africa, Europe and the Middle East each had 44%, Latin America 41%, North America 32%, and the Pacific 26%). In terms of the number of stories by female presenters and reporters, the world average was 42 per cent, with only the Middle East (46%) and Asia (44%) above the average. Women presenters and reporters were least represented in Africa (34%), the Caribbean (34%), North America and the Pacific (35% each). Latin America reported a figure of 38 per cent and Europe 41 per cent (Gallagher, 2010, p. 22).

A more recent survey of European journalists has confirmed the continuing trend towards higher representation of women in journalism, putting their average proportion at 47 per cent across the continent (Witt-Barthel, 2006). Countries with even representation of men and women in journalism included in particular Nordic and Eastern European countries, such as Finland, Latvia, Russia, Serbia and Slovakia. Yet, in Italy, Germany and the United Kingdom and Ireland, the percentage was still only slightly above one-third.

One of the latest comparative studies that examined gender as a variable is the *Worlds of Journalism* project, which was conducted in 18 diverse countries

around the world (Hanitzsch, 2011). The study, which surveyed 100 journalists in each of the countries, found the total proportion of women to be
42 per cent across the entire sample, a figure that is somewhat higher than
the roughly 30 per cent reported by Weaver's (1998a) collection of surveys
from around the globe. Yet, in the *Worlds of Journalism* study, the proportion
of women varied quite heavily, ranging from only 25 per cent in Germany and
30 per cent in Mexico, to a high of 65 per cent in Romania, 64 per cent in
Bulgaria and 61 per cent in Chile. It must be pointed out, however, that these
figures are not necessarily characteristic of the overall journalistic workforce
in the respective countries, as the sample size of 100 journalists per country
was quite small, and not intended to be representative. For example, Weaver
et al.'s (2007) study, which included a much larger, representative sample,
found a figure of 33 per cent for the United States, while Hanitzsch et al's
(2011) study put it at 42 per cent.

As we can see from the available baseline data from around the world,
there is valid evidence to suggest that the proportion of female journalists is
increasing almost everywhere, although it is also beginning to show signs of
stagnation in some countries. The extent of this increase varies considerably,
however, and while women are in the majority in some countries, they still
constitute only a small, though growing minority in others. However, when
we examine the positions in which women are employed, we can see they
remain highly disadvantaged at the middle and senior editorial and management levels, as well as in terms of media ownership. On these levels, men are
still in a strong majority in most countries, reinforcing continuing critiques of
journalism as a male-dominated profession.

Such baseline data as discussed here are useful in order to gain an understanding of the representation of women in journalism. However, in order
to better identify the ways in which journalism is still very much a gendered
profession, it is important to analyse the situation in more detail. As de Bruin
(2000, p. 225) points out, 'it is necessary to go beyond the "body count"
and to start looking at specific social practices, embodied in conventions and
rules, formally and informally, based on history and tradition, sustained by
people working in the media organizations'. This, she argues, is necessary
particularly as men have been the dominant influence on journalistic values
(de Bruin, 2000; see also de Bruin & Ross, 2004). Recent years have therefore
seen scholars move beyond such 'body count' approaches to examine gender
against the way in which it relates to journalistic culture (see, e.g., Steiner,
1998; van Zoonen, 1998; Carter et al., 1998a; Allan, 1999; de Bruin & Ross,
2004; Ross & Byerly, 2004; North, 2009a). In the following sections, we
examine some of these practices in more depth.

The role of gender in news production

The fact that many countries around the world, particularly developed countries, have experienced an increasing number of women in journalism in recent times has led to general claims about a 'feminization' of the profession, which, it is often claimed, has gone hand in hand with a softening of news values. In fact, the term tends to be used interchangeably for both the numerical representation of women and the presence of soft news. van Zoonen (1998, p. 34) notes that at the height of the movement for women's rights in journalism during the 1980s and 1990s, the predominant view was that if only more women worked as journalists, news reporting would change to reflect women's values and thus be more relevant to them. This aligns with Rush et al.'s (1982) argument that once women crossed the critical 33 per cent mark, they would become a significant minority that would be able to influence the direction within news organizations. North (2009a) has, however, pointed out that such approaches have increasingly fallen out of favour with researchers, who have realized that increasing the percentage of female journalists would not lead to the improvements that they had hoped for. She notes that scholars such as Gallagher, who had originally been a proponent of the 'critical mass' paradigm, later acknowledged that the problem lay much deeper than sheer numbers (in North, 2009a, p. 8). van Zoonen (1998) believes that the recent changes in journalism itself, such as its feminization in terms of an increase in soft news, have actually occurred despite women's minority position. Nevertheless, she sees these developments as encouraging, and believes that they can open up journalism to women (van Zoonen, 1998, p. 35). van Zoonen (1998, p. 36) is concerned with more significant aspects of what she calls 'the gendered nature of journalism'. These include

- the selection of topics (men report hard news while women focus on soft news);
- story angles (men focus on facts and sensation, while women approach them from backgrounds and effects, as well as compassion);
- the use of sources (men predominantly report about other men, women focus on women); and
- ethics (the masculine nature of journalism is detached, while the feminine nature is concerned with audience needs).

In terms of news writing, for example, van Zoonen (1998, p. 45) argues that women tend to favour 'a more human and involved approach that is seemingly at odds with professional values of objectivity and detachment', and as a result they have 'a much more fragmented and contradictory professional identity than men'. In short, women are able to provide a more 'intimate' journalism (van Zoonen, 1991). Recent trends in news reporting towards more 'soft' news have also often been seen as related to the increases in female journalists worldwide, and a resulting 'feminization' of news both in women's visibility and the presence of soft news. Yet, there is somewhat contradictory evidence in terms of whether gender has a significant influence on news, with some studies finding that gender has very little impact on journalists' decisions, despite the fact that women are often assigned topics that are significantly different from topics assigned to men. Chambers et al. (2004) note that, while men and women seem to approach news reporting quite differently, there is still no conclusive evidence to suggest that gender plays an overwhelming role. In fact, they point out that the 'evidence regarding the impact of gender on newsroom culture and news agendas is contradictory and ambiguous and may be related to whether the data has been generated through news content analysis or interviews with journalists' (2004, p. 122).

Many of the studies that have interviewed or observed journalists have found little evidence for the assumption that gender influences journalists' decisions or professional views. For example, Bleske (1991), in his replication of White's (1950) seminal work on gatekeeping, found that decisions made by the female writer editor he studied (as opposed to White's male wire editor) could rarely be attributed to gender. As a result, the question of whether and how gender influences the news product is only one of the factors that has been of interest to researchers of the gatekeeping process and the various levels of influence on news decisions. As we discussed in Chapter 3, there are varying levels of influence on journalists, which affect their decision-making. Gender operates on the individual level, and, as White (1950) argued in his study of 'Mr Gates', individual characteristics of a journalist can have an influence on their decisions. At the same time, however, newsroom influences, as well as wider professional ideologies, political, economic, social and cultural factors all play an important role in the gatekeeping process (Shoemaker & Reese, 1996). Assuming that professional and procedural influences are perceived as the most immediate influences on journalists (Hanitzsch et al., 2010), it could be assumed that women who have gone through a professionalization process in journalism schools, where traditional news values are taught, may internalize these to the same extent as their male counterparts. As a result, their reporting may not differ significantly from that of male journalists. Lavie and Lehman-Wilzig (2005, p. 67) point out that rather than gender, 'declarations of an existing professional model, of an obligation to objectivity, and of joint guiding principles have all characterized many interviews with news professionals'. However, as Steiner (1998) argues, this reluctance to identify gender as a factor may be due to the imposing limitations of a journalistic ideology that places supreme emphasis on objectivity and personal detachment, thus denying journalists the right to acknowledge their own biases. 'The celebration of objectivity as a standard for news writing forces reporters to erase themselves from their stories, distance themselves from their subjects, and proclaim their attempts to adopt a consistent stance of transparent neutrality' (Steiner, 1998, p. 146).

There is some degree of danger in assuming that women would automatically have different role perceptions or hold different news values merely because they are women. In her examination of British journalists' perceptions of their professional roles, Ross (2001) argues that gender and differences in values are not automatic.

> (G)ender alone will not make a difference in changing the culture of newsrooms or in the type of news produced, inasmuch as a journalist's sex is no guarantee that she or he will either embrace sentiments that privilege equality or hold specific values and beliefs that promote a more equitable and non-oppressive practice: some men may well be more sympathetic to the ideals (and realities) of inclusion than some women. (Ross, 2001, p. 542)

Similarly, in her edited collection of studies of the media in the Middle East, Sakr (2004) notes that gender roles are more complex than simply saying men always favour one approach and women another. Some men may actually hold more feminine values than typically masculine values, and vice versa. In fact, van Zoonen (1994, p. 4) points out that society 'is not constituted by orderly and dichotomous divisions of oppressor and oppressed'.

Studies of journalists' professional role perceptions have so far found little evidence to suggest that gender has a sizeable influence on the way journalists think about their jobs, giving support to the argument that professional ideology outweighs individual perceptions. For example, Weaver et al.'s (2007) survey of US journalists found that gender was not a significant predictor of perceptions of their professional roles. These results have been replicated internationally as well. A study of Indonesian journalists found that gender had little or no influence on journalists' role perceptions or their ethical views (Hanitzsch, 2005). Studies in Tanzania (Ramaprasad, 2001) and Israel (Lavie, 1997; cited in Lavie & Lehman-Wilzig, 2005) also did not find gender to be influential. Such similarities are perhaps not surprising if one considers that, according to survey results, women journalists almost everywhere are judged by male standards and performance criteria (Gallagher, 2008, p. 207). Thus, they may feel compelled to adhere to the journalistic values that were created by a dominant male proportion over centuries. Often, differences between the sexes are much more opaque. In her study in Canada, Robinson (2005, p. 92) notes that most women act 'as though they were equal partners in the heterosexual newsroom and use their gender *strategically* and merely under certain circumstances' (emphasis in original). Newsroom pressures also play an important role. In interviews with Australian journalists, North (2009b) noted that while some women held certain views about feminism, they rarely expressed them in their practice for fear of being labelled a feminist. North (2009b, p. 755) believes many women journalists hold feminist beliefs 'but rather than construct their identities around feminism or label their often private concerns as feminist – already alert to a fear or misunderstanding of feminism by the dominant newsroom culture – they merely attempt to fit in, rather than challenge dominant orthodoxies'. In general, North (2009a) identified strong elements of sexual harassment in the newsroom towards women, and a tendency by female journalists to adapt to the male-dominated processes in trying to become 'one of the boys' (North, 2009a, p. 208).

On the other hand, some academics argue that gender does matter when it comes to journalistic decision-making and general practice. Australian journalism academic Catherine Lumby (1994), for example, argues that there is a very clear distinction between men and women when it comes to reporting. 'There is no question that traditional news values split both format and content along traditional masculine and feminine lines. Facts, objectivity and the public sphere belong to the men' (Lumby, 1994, p. 50). Soderlund et al's (1989) analysis of Canadian television news noted that men were much more likely to report hard news stories, while women were relegated to reporting soft or feature news. Similarly, Liebler and Smith's (1997) analysis of policy stories on US television found that women reported only 14 per cent of foreign policy stories, while covering roughly half of the stories on social issues. In an analysis of Australian television news, Cann and Mohr (2001) also revealed that women reported the majority number of stories only in the topic areas of health, arts and the environment. For all other topics, such as politics, crime, economics and sport, the majority of stories were reported by men. Studies of female journalists in Korea have found they use more positive reporting styles, emphasize conflict values less, use fewer stereotypical references to women, report on a larger number of women's issues and perspectives and more generally aim to direct attention to women (Kim & Kim, 2005; Lim & Uhm, 2005; Kim & Yoon, 2009;). Taking a historical perspective, Chambers et al. (2004, p. 62) believe that 'while the 1960s marked a turning-point for women in journalism, as in many other professions, it was their ability to communicate as women rather than as professional journalists that was valued by the news media industry. None the less, the efforts of women in journalism in those days contributed to a change in news values still evident in the twenty-first century'.

The difference in topic assignment is not new and has been demonstrated in surveys and interviews of journalists as well as in the analyses of news contents around the world (see, e.g., Holman, 1992; Lont, 1995; McRobbie, 1996; Robinson, 2005; Gallagher, 2005, 2010; North, 2009a). However, De Swert and Hooghe (2010, p. 72) point out that 'while some studies see clear differences between female and male reporters with regard to the selection of news sources, other studies do not find any evidence for such a straightforward relation between gender and operating practices'. For example, a study of Brazilian journalists found that women did not tend to emphasize themes that relate to women or women's interests (in de M. Higgins et al., 2008, p. 242). A study of Israeli journalists was also unable to find any significant differences between men and women in terms of neither their reported news values nor their actual news selection (Lavie & Lehman-Wilzig, 2003). This finding led the authors to conclude that it does not appear to matter much whether more women join the industry, but rather that changes to news values are driven by audiences.

> Whether or not women journalists will produce the news in growing numbers, in the end the news belongs to – and is a reflection of – the common concerns and interests of both sexes among the readership. Thus, the growing empowerment of women may indeed change the news, but more from the bottom up (women as audience) than from the top down (women as editors). (Lavie & Lehman-Wilzig, 2003, p. 24)

Gender and news sources

Some evidence exists to suggest that women journalists across the world tend to be more likely to use female sources than their male counterparts. Gallagher's (2005, 2010) global studies of news content certainly point to such a difference. In the latest of these studies, women constituted 28 per cent of news subjects in stories reported by women globally, while they only made up 22 per cent in stories reported by men (Gallagher, 2010). De Swert and Hooghe (2010, p. 71) suggest there are three main reasons why women are selected as news sources: (a) the topic of the story may have an influence, in the sense that 'female topics' may be more likely to include female sources; (b) the gender of the reporter, assuming that women will be more likely to quote other women; and (c) with editorial policies that may be geared towards 'soft news' and therefore include more women as sources.

News reporting around the world generally shows a clear preference for reporting about men. Overall, only 24 per cent of news subjects are women. Considering news subjects central to a story, women's representation is even lower at merely 13 per cent of stories overall (Gallagher, 2010). There is some regional variation to be noticed here, however. Women in Latin America fare best, where they were news subjects in 29 per cent of stories. North America was closely behind, at 28 per cent, followed by Europe (26%), the Caribbean and the Pacific (25% each). Women fared worst in the Middle East (16%), as well as Africa (19%) and Asia (20%). Overall, women were the least likely to be central to the news in stories on the economy and politics and government (11 and 13%, respectively), while they were more visible in celebrity, arts and sports, crime and violence, as well as science and health stories (16% each) and social and legal stories (17%) (Gallagher, 2010, p. xii).

Yet, as our review of gatekeeping studies in Chapter 3 has shown, one needs to be careful when making assumptions about decision-making by analysing media content only. As Steiner (1998, p. 148) points out, 'the product delivered to the front door or newsstand reveals nothing about arguments over assignments, about stories not assigned or not published. Articles are critiqued and altered by many people before publication'. If women cover soft stories more than men, this may say much more about the respective newsroom politics and power relations than about any preference of women to cover soft news. Similarly, men remain more powerful in many countries around the world, and journalism tends to be oriented towards those in power, which may explain some of the discrepancies in terms of gender and news subjects. The fact that men still hold senior editorial positions in the vast majority of news organizations around the globe arguably has an effect on the types of news women get to report, thus influencing the types of stories that are traditionally associated with female news values. Women are assigned typical beats rather than choosing them for themselves, and therefore end up in stereotyped roles as reporters. For example, Gallagher's (2010) global study found that stories by male reporters exceeded those by female reporters in all topics. The strongest bias against women, however, appeared to be in politics and government, with 33 per cent, and crime and violence, with 35 per cent of all items reported by female journalists. Of science and health stories, on the other hand, stories written by women constituted 44 per cent, leading Gallagher (20010, p. ix) to note that 'the statistics strongly suggest that stories accorded high news value by newsroom decision makers are least likely to be assigned to female reporters, while those accorded lowest priority will most likely be assigned to female reporters'.

Gender in journalism: Non-western countries

Gender in journalism has mostly been approached from a Western stand-point, with comparatively few studies examining the situation elsewhere across the globe. In the following section, we take a closer look at the issues women journalists have to contend with in those countries, by way of a select number of case studies. One region where women have been disadvantaged quite considerably is the Middle East. Here, Sakr's (2004) edited collection has noted that while there have been some significant improvements in women's rights in general and the situation for female journalists in particular, numerous restrictions on women still persist in many countries in the region, particularly those who have a poor women's rights history. Pintak and Ginges' (2009) study of Arab journalists included 39 per cent women, while a 2008 study of women's representation on unions' governing bodies in the Middle East, North Africa and Iran showed that women made up only 12 per cent overall (International Federation of Journalists, 2009, p. 23). Women were best represented in North Africa, with five of nineteen board members in Morocco and three of nine in Tunisia identified as women. But even in countries such as Saudi Arabia, Sakr (2008) observed some positive developments that led to a heightened visibility of women in the media and thus a widening of the debate over women's status in society – despite the fact that women have very few rights in this patriarchal society. At the same time, Sakr notes, however, that this process is also related to commercial motives which, as apparent in our discussion of the history of women's involvement in journalism in the West, constitute a trend that has been occurring elsewhere around the globe. While recent developments in Saudi Arabia have not resulted in the promotion of women beyond the glass ceiling, Sakr (2008) notes that there is some reason to be optimistic for the future. 'Journalism training and senior editorial jobs, which were once off limits to Saudi women, were coming within their reach by 2006. But evidence also indicated that any reconstruction of media professions would be extremely uncertain and slow' (p. 403).

In Nigeria, men dominate the news landscape both as subjects and sources of news as well as among the journalism profession. Ugochukwu (in Harrison et al., 2008, p. 201) notes that few women in the country follow the news media which tends to focus strongly on political coverage. Such coverage, because of the local power structures, favours men: 'Serious issues affecting the ordinary Nigerian woman are mostly ignored and women's faces are obliterated in newsmagazines'. Anyanwu (2001, p. 71) reports that men also dominate the ranks of journalists in Nigeria, constituting 80 per cent of the profession. She notes that non-political journalism is generally regarded as trivial among Nigerian journalists and women tend to follow the male-dominated news agenda for fear of being branded as feminists. In Eastern Africa, the situation for women journalists remains dire, particularly when compared with some of the advances that have been made in many regions around the world in recent times. A 2008 report on the number of women journalists in the region found that only 20 per cent of all professional journalists were female (Okoko Tom, 2008). In addition, women make up only 3 per cent of those in senior editorial or management positions, glaring evidence of a very firm glass ceiling in force in Eastern Africa.

Yet, in countries such as India, women have made significant impacts in the first decade of the twenty-first century. Mishra et al. (2008) report that while there exists no comprehensive study of Indian journalists, let alone gender aspects, recent trends have indicated a large increase in the number of women practising journalism in metropolitan areas, in particular in broadcast media, aided by the introduction of satellite television in the 1990s. Once again, we can see the link between industry expansion and gender representation, which was also apparent in similar developments in Western countries decades earlier. Nevertheless, while women are making headway, significant obstacles still remain. Mishra et al. (2008, p. 217) report that negative attitudes among male journalists have been a major impediment, and 'many women journalists work in hostile environments'. Further, Joseph (2007) has pointed to important gender inequalities in the reporting of disasters and war on the subcontinent.

In a study of Nepalese journalists, Ramaprasad and Kelly (2003) found only 12 per cent to be female, although the authors noted that women were slowly making progress. Some of the more common concerns expressed by the respondents' parents were related to fears about late and uncertain hours of work. Other countries in Asia have seen a much higher participation rate of women, such as Taiwan. Here, recent statistics suggest that 43 per cent of journalists employed in the country were female, although there still exists a glass ceiling, with 64 per cent of those at the management level of news organizations being male (Mishra et al., 2008). Nevertheless, there have been noticeable improvements in recent years, leading Mishra et al. (2008, p. 229) to argue that 'women now share the power with men in the newsroom' and that many authoritative figures, particularly in television, are women.

In Latin America, female journalists have made the biggest achievements in countries such as Brazil and Chile, where women represent 45 and 40 per cent of the journalistic workforce, respectively, according to 2006 figures (de M. Higgins et al., 2008). Like elsewhere around the world, the highest proportion is in the fields of magazine and television journalism. In Brazil, only 18 per cent of radio journalists are female, pointing to a strong traditional male dominance in the sector (de M. Higgins et al., 2008, p. 242). In Chile, deeply entrenched cultural notions that women are primarily responsible for family life (Palacios & Martinez, 2006) have hindered women's participation in journalism, a profession where long and irregular hours are often the norm. In Chilean news stories, women have also rarely featured, although this appears to be changing with the ascendance of more women in the public sphere, most notably Michelle Bachelet, who was elected president in 2005. Nevertheless, as de M. Higgins et al. (2008, p. 247) point out, 'when a story covers these female leaders, it usually emphasizes the issue of how to cope with work and family duties'. A similar problem exists for journalists in Mexico, where a certain machismo is still highly pervasive, despite the fact that female journalists represent almost half of the workforce. And while good looks and certain beauty ideals are seen to play a role in the hiring of female television journalists the world over, Mexican television stations are apparently taking it a step further. de M. Higgins et al. (2008, p. 250) note that 'many females end up perpetuating a specific conception of beauty – European-blond, white skin, and blue/green eyes – characteristics which do not reflect the physical appearance of the majority of Mexican women who are mestizas with dark hair, dark eye, and brown skin'. Recent financial problems for the Mexican news industry have also resulted in women being given fewer stories to report. Such developments again highlight the close relationship between increases in female journalists and economic development – when times are good and news organizations are expanding, more women gain entry into the profession but when times are bad financially, they are also the first to be retrenched.

Conclusion

Gallagher (2008) acknowledges that journalism, at least in the Western world, has seen a number of important shifts. First, the numbers of women journalists have been increasing almost everywhere, and even in middle-level management positions. Second, publishers, faced with declines in circulation, have tried to attract new, particularly female audiences to their products. Third, the definition and presentation of news have changed, leading to a news agenda with broader public appeal and a more personalized style of reporting. Fourth, the increase in numbers may lead to women achieving a critical mass that would allow them to be 'less constrained by male-defined professional frameworks' (Gallagher, 2008, p. 202). van Zoonen (1998) has similarly argued that competitive pressure in the news media industry has seen a shift towards more human interest stories, which men in senior editorial positions believe women can cover better than male journalists. Yet, Gallagher (2008, p. 203) does not see these shifts as 'signalling a "happy ending" to the story of gender inequalities in journalism and the media'. Rather, she sees it as 'a temporary confluence of factors within a dynamic and fluid profession that, in terms of decision making and managerial power, is still largely dominated by men' (2008, p. 203). For example, she believes that shifts in journalistic cultures, brought about by the need to find new audiences, will not necessarily work to women's advantage, as men will adapt their practices to once more dominate in such fields, even if the original changes were pioneered by women. 'If audience behaviour causes a shift in the hierarchy of genres, or in professional beliefs about what constitutes "good" journalism, it is inconceivable that male journalists will ignore the new ground opened up by such a change' (2008, p. 210).

There appears to be a relationship between how societies value women more generally and the level of participation in journalism that is accorded to women, as well as their degree of success in the profession. It appears that those cultures that have been on the forefront of gender equality have higher rates of female participation in journalism, although this is not a universal trend. Yet, despite considerable progress in recent decades, numerous studies show that women are still disadvantaged in journalism around the world, particularly in terms of their attainment of senior editorial and management positions, as well as the ways in which they are marginalized as sources and topics of news. Journalism developed as a male-dominated practice and its underlying structures are still influenced by a number of factors, such as news values, that were developed by men. While the number of women journalists has undoubtedly been on the rise in many countries, the increase has also slowed somewhat in recent times, particularly in Western countries, where it appears that women may be reaching a certain threshold. More importantly, when it comes to professional roles, impact on the news, and power within news organizations, women have still not been able to make a considerable impact, leading some scholars to argue that some of the progress has been more of a smokescreen. In fact, Fröhlich (2007, p. 174) believes that 'the "feminization of journalism" is a myth: While making three steps forward in the 1980s, female journalists throughout the world have taken two steps backward since the mid 1990s'. It would seem there is still some way to go in creating a truly gender-equal journalism.

DISCUSSION QUESTIONS

1. What do you understand by the phrase – 'Ratio of Recurrent and Reinforced Residuum' – in relation to journalism (as discussed in this chapter)? Explain whether this ratio holds true for your home country.
2. What do you understand by the concept of 'feminisation of news', and what are its key features?
3. Discuss ways in which gender may or may not influence journalistic role perceptions.
4. Discuss some of the key barriers to active involvement of women in journalism and explain how they relate to the situation in your home country.
5. Discuss the representation of women as news sources and outline some of the ways in which it can be improved.

CHAPTER 6

Foreign news reporting in the digital age

Introduction

Foreign news reporting has never been a job for the faint-hearted. Reporting foreign cultures and people remains a major challenge to experienced and inexperienced journalists. The key challenge involves cultural sensitivity: how a reporter should explain another country and its culture to news audiences in their own country (*Media Studies Journal*, 1999). The challenge is seen as especially difficult because the way journalists report other countries is usually affected by the images they have of foreign places and cultures (*Media Studies Journal*, 1999, p. xiii). As d'Haenens (2003, p. 5) notes, the criticisms that are often lobbed at foreign correspondents tend to focus on their lack of contextual knowledge of the events and countries they report on, as well as their gender, social status and inadequate time allocated to the subject of news coverage.

There are a number of reasons why foreign news reporting should be considered quite important to people across the world. The way foreign news is reported affects not only how media audiences understand the world but also how they communicate and interact with people from different parts of the world. Thus, foreign news serves a number of functions for citizens across the globe (Wolter, 2006). Franks (2005, p. 1) has listed 'Globalisation, the interdependent nature of modern society and the precarious state of international relations post 9/11' as three reasons why everyone should be interested in foreign news coverage. In an increasingly interdependent world, the link between foreign and domestic events is clearly visible. Specifically, Franks (2005) emphasizes the relationship between national security and good foreign reporting, especially in a post-11 September 2001 world. 'Our security and well-being at home depends upon well-explained and informed foreign news. That is the best reason for monitoring and for ensuring that the standard of international coverage remains high' (Franks, 2005, p. 100). Apart from influencing cross-cultural perceptions and modes of communication, it has also been suggested that foreign news coverage influences the direction of foreign policy. This view is, however, contested in the literature on foreign news coverage. This debate will be addressed later in the chapter.

This chapter examines the changing landscape of foreign news reporting and the factors that influence foreign coverage, with particular emphasis on how technological changes have transformed foreign reporting. The chapter argues that new technologies have significantly transformed the way foreign news is reported, including the quantity, frequency, speed of coverage, global coverage of news events and the growing participation of news consumers – citizen journalists – in the collection, production and distribution of foreign news. The chapter draws on research conducted across the world to map how new technologies are transforming foreign coverage and some of the key factors that are driving foreign reporting in the digital age.

Declining attention to foreign news

There is a growing consensus among researchers that media attention to foreign news is declining in much of North America and Western Europe (e.g. Hoge, 1997; Utley, 1997; Hargreaves, 2000; Beaudoin & Thorson, 2001; Franks, 2005; Wolter, 2006; Altmeppen, 2010) despite the importance of foreign news. For instance, Altmeppen (2010, p. 567) argues that foreign coverage on German television is disappearing fast because of excessive focus on local news events, and emphasis on soft and entertainment-driven content such as sports, 'award ceremonies' and other forms of popular entertainment. He identifies the factors that account for this trend. 'Today, rules and resources for foreign news reporting are altered primarily by the process of economisation, whereby decisions made in news offices are increasingly based on economic factors rather than editorial standards of news reporting' (p. 568). In the United States, Fenton (2005, p. 4) makes a similar argument about how executives of television networks 'who decide what the nation wants to know, believe that tabloid news sells'. The commercialization of media and the impact of market forces on journalism are explored in greater detail in Chapter 8. Fenton also reports that, although there were a few flashes of interest in foreign news by American media following the events of 11 September 2001, the decline in foreign coverage did not stop as 'There was no mass reopening of foreign bureaus, no large scale hiring of skilled journalists' (2005, p. 17). Utley (1997) argues that the decline in attention to foreign news in American media may be informed by the perception – right or wrong – that audiences are not interested in foreign news. 'Producers and network executives believe the American mass audience's interest in daily events beyond their nation's borders is declining, so little such news is offered – which exacerbates the high cost/low return (or low visibility) nature of international coverage today' (Utley, 1997, p. 2).

In Canada, surveys of newspaper editors in 1988, 1995, 2000 and 2006 showed that editors continued to place international news last in relation to local, provincial and national news. When the editors were asked why they did not accord international news a higher priority, they 'consistently made the point that newspapers are essentially disseminators of local, not international, news' (Sutcliffe et al., 2009, p. 142). This suggests the high importance that Canadian newspaper editors attach to local news, and a consistent pattern of low priority accorded to international news in Western news media. In New Zealand, Tully (2005) reports that media coverage of Pacific news events has been undermined mostly by fewer resources allo- cated to foreign news, as well as journalists' lack of background knowledge of the Pacific region. He attributes the pattern of foreign reporting by New Zealand journalists to 'increased reliance on what has been variously called "hit and run" or "parachute" journalism' (Tully, 2005, p. 296). Research evidence also suggests that Western media coverage of Africa has declined. Knickmeyer, a former West Africa bureau chief for the Associated Press, noted that:

> the cold war days when Africa news would command headlines among the top stories for months and years at a time, as African proxies of the East and West did battle in Africa, seemed over. They probably had been since Zaire in the 1990s…Africa remains a compelling and internationally relevant story, but newspaper bosses are unlikely ever to return Africa staffing to what it was in the 1990s. (2005, pp. 113–14)

Despite growing evidence of declining coverage of foreign news by Western news media, a longitudinal study of foreign news coverage in the Flemish press (Belgium) between 1986 and 2006 reported that, although there were declines in foreign coverage in the decade of the 1990s, the general trend was that, over a 20-year period, Flemish newspapers did not follow the pattern of declining foreign news coverage observed in other Western media (Joye, 2010). This trend of foreign news coverage in the Flemish press would seem to be a radical departure from existing research evidence which shows that foreign news coverage is declining in North America and most countries in Western Europe. In his study, Joye (2010, p. 5) noted that 'The quality newspapers *De Morgen* and *De Standaard* devoted considerably more attention and space to international news as compared to the more popular *Het Laatste Nieuws*'.

Apart from increasing competition, entertainment and profit-driven agenda as factors that are influencing foreign coverage, there is also a growing audience interest in shorter news stories presented in digested formats (Cook et al., 1992, cited in Riffe et al., 1994). This changing reader habit has been attributed to readers being 'too busy, preoccupied, or uninterested in digesting long, detailed, newspaper articles. They want their news in short, pre-chewed morsels' (Cook et al., 1992: xv, cited in Riffe et al., 1994). There is a host of other reasons that account for declining attention to foreign news in the US media. For example, prior to 11 September 2001, Hoge (1997, p. 50) argues that 'A world less threatening to America is less newsy'. Utley (1997, pp. 5–6) supports this view. 'Without stories from abroad that could be presented as part of an overall threat to American security, newscasts suffered a severe loss in an increasingly competitive medium that thrives – perhaps depends – on drama and conflict to attract and hold an audience's attention.' Wolter (2006) and Bennett (2001) also adduced reasons for declining foreign coverage, namely rising cost associated with covering foreign news and lack of audience interest in foreign news. Another problem in foreign reporting is editors' obsession with foreign stories that have domestic link, appeal and relevance. This means that, in the case of the United States and Western European countries, editors are looking to find in their foreign reports stories that have some domestic relevance (Hess, 1996). Wolter (2006) and Parks (2002) contend that media attention to foreign news began to decline following the collapse of communism and the Cold War in 1989/1990. According to Parks (2002, p. 53), 'as the cold war ended and public interest faded, some organizations cut back'. This, it appears, marked the start of the decline in foreign coverage and the subsequent lack of audience interest. As mentioned elsewhere in this chapter, foreign news reporting has also been affected by a shifting news agenda (i.e. news organizations do not consider establishment of foreign posts as significant because they can fly journalists in and out of news locations – 'parachute' journalism – as events occur). Arguably, this practice contributes to low quality of foreign news (Wolter, 2006).

Prior to the emergence of digital technologies, the complicated costs of television coverage of foreign events posed a serious threat to foreign reporting. In those days, as Utley (1997) recounted, the job was much simpler for correspondents in the print media. For the broadcast media, however, the massive personnel and equipment required for television coverage of foreign news was overwhelming and challenging. Thus:

> A correspondent for a newspaper, magazine, press agency, or radio station or network is engaged in what is basically one-person journalism. He or she can travel to the scene of a story alone, cover it alone, write it up alone, and transmit it alone via telephone, fax, or E-mail... Television is of a different organizational magnitude. The basic working unit in international television news consists of a correspondent, a field producer, a cameraperson, and a sound engineer, plus some 600 pounds of camera and personal equipment. (Utley, 1997, p. 6)

In the new electronic environment, the high cost of television coverage of foreign news has compelled network executives to adopt cost-cutting measures. One such measure is the emergence of the 'lone person' foreign reporters equipped with digital technologies that allow them to cover overseas events. For example, American ABC television network is sending out one-person teams to foreign bureaus where they report with a range of portable digital technologies such as 'handheld digital video cameras, satellite dishes and laptops' (Dorroh, 2007/2008, p. 12). It is not very easy because the job obliges the reporters to perform multiple tasks which require them to: 'record, edit and transmit their own audio and video reports from Nairobi; Jakarta, Indonesia; Mumbai and New Delhi, India; Rio de Janeiro, Brazil; Seoul, South Korea; and Dubai, United Arab Emirates, as well as from neighboring countries' (Dorroh, 2007/2008, p. 12).

Other reasons given for the decline in foreign news include: public perceptions of foreign news as confusing and a difficult subject to understand; the rise of television as a news medium and its emphasis on coverage of dramatic events presented in 'short narratives' without contextual background – all of which confound rather than assist audiences to understand international events (Hoge, 1997, p. 50).

Why is media attention to foreign news declining? Wu and Hamilton (2004, p. 518) argue that, in the case of the United States, market forces and editors' assumption that readers are not interested in foreign news account for the decline. In the United Kingdom, Hargreaves (2000, p. 57) states that newspaper editors and readers lost interest in foreign news because there are no wars that threaten the lives of the citizens and this has redirected media attention to health-related issues. It is important to clarify that Hargreaves' article was published in 2000, before the British government joined the United States and other coalition forces in the wars in Iraq and Afghanistan. Since the British involvement in the Afghan war started in late 2001 and British participation in the Iraq war started in 2003, London streets and train stations have experienced at least one major bomb explosion on 7 July 2005 which resulted in large casualties. So, it is not quite correct, as Hargreaves stated, that Britain is not threatened by any war. More fundamentally, as international events demonstrate, what happens in distant locations overseas can have repercussions for local audiences at home. Contrary to popular argument, Kohut (2002) insists that the positive response by the United States' public to media coverage of the 11 September 2001 attacks on the country and the ensuing war on terrorism underline the relationship between the press and the public. 'First and foremost, it shows that the public's need to know trumps everything else. It not only drives public attentiveness to the news, it also shapes evaluations of media performance' (Kohut, 2002, p. 54).

Declining media attention to foreign news has enormous implications not only for cross-cultural understanding but also for foreign policy direction of many governments. As Wu and Hamilton (2004, p. 529) argued:

> If media conglomerates continue to scale down foreign news operations and reduce the time and space given to foreign affairs, then we have strong reason to be concerned. Policy-making depends heavily on public opinion. Episodic coverage of foreign affairs will not alert Americans to the growing reality that foreign affairs are, in truth, local affairs.

Hoge (1997, p. 52) points out that when editors, journalists and news organizations show little or no interest in foreign news, it is the public that pays the price as they may be left unaware of developments that may affect their lives. Franks (2005, p. 92) also believes that having a permanent correspondent in a location may lead to an obligation to cover stories to justify the investment, while when stringers or casuals report foreign news, fewer stories will be covered.

'Parachute' journalism

Scholars have identified the phenomenon known as 'parachute journalism' as one factor that has undercut the quality of foreign reporting. Franks' (2005) reference to 'stringer', for example, raises the question about the extent to which media organizations are closing foreign bureaus (as a financially prudent measure) and opting to send journalists to cover foreign events as and when events occur. This is the practice widely referred to as 'parachute journalism'. Wolter (2006, p. 59) believes 'parachute' journalism leads inevitably to poor quality of foreign coverage and to a decrease in public interest in foreign news. The practice of 'parachute' journalism has drawn severe criticisms from journalism academics and professional journalists because it is deemed to privilege the reporting of foreign news by inexperienced journalists who lack basic skills and who have no background knowledge of the countries and events they are reporting on. Despite growing criticisms of the practice, Erickson and Hamilton (2007, p. 132) argue that parachute journalism is not new and is not necessarily a bad thing: 'Long before they could parachute by plane, reporters overseas jumped off ships, trains, horses, or whatever other transport was available to hop from story to story.' Some of the redeeming features of 'parachute journalism' include: use of parachute journalism to complement foreign coverage, not to cut down on it; the desire to add more expertise to the pool of foreign correspondents maintained by news organizations (e.g. US news media that sent experts on religion to Rome to cover the death and funeral of Pope John Paul II); and the notion that parachute journalism is 'better than nothing' – it also provides an opportunity to retain former foreign correspondents who might be intent on joining other news organizations that could post them overseas again (Erickson & Hamilton, 2007, pp. 141–4).

Although the Internet may encourage the emergence of the independent, freelance foreign correspondents 'who are free to go wherever they wish' (Wu & Hamilton, 2004, p. 529), there are risks associated with hiring such breed of reporters. For example, the new type of foreign correspondents may lack specialized training and news editing skills, and they may refuse to be bound by the professional code of ethics that conventional journalists subscribe to (Wu & Hamilton, p. 529). There is no doubt that parachute journalism has its consequences, one of which is the likelihood that it could engender low quality foreign news (Wolter, 2006). Although parachute journalism or what Franks (2005, p. 94) describes as 'fireman-style reporting' might save money for news organizations, some scholars insist the practice degrades foreign news (Hess, 1996; Franks, 2005; Wolter, 2006). In foreign news coverage, there is no substitute for quality and 'intelligent reporting'. Franks (2005, pp. 94–5) contends that nothing beats foreign reports that are properly contextualized, well explained and interpreted in a meaningful way. One of the problems in television coverage of foreign news is the lack of context, the failure to explain why a conflict has erupted or has continued unabated. The challenge of foreign news reporting, as argued at the beginning of this chapter, lies in the ability of journalists to reflect cultural understanding and sensitivities in reporting other people and places.

In order for journalists to do a good job of covering and explaining events in distant locations, it is imperative that foreign correspondents be attuned to the culture, the people, the language and history of the countries and regions from which they are reporting. A very good foreign correspondent must be experienced, must have an in-depth knowledge of the history of the country or region from which they are reporting and must be competent. Above all, a very good foreign correspondent must demonstrate cultural sensitivity in their reports, including expertise in the language of the country or region (i.e. language skills). These are the essential qualities that shape well-rounded foreign correspondents. Hess (1996, p. 76) highlights how parachute journalism undermines the quality of foreign news. 'Crises are covered by "parachutists", who know a great deal about covering crises but who do not necessarily know much about the crisis they are covering.'

It has been argued that the difference between coverage and non-coverage of foreign events depends inexorably on the presence or absence of journalists (Franks, 2005, p. 91). Thus, if an event occurs and there are no journalists to report the event, it will not make the news. Whether news depends on the presence of journalists or whether journalists' postings are based on where news unfolds, there are circumstances that uphold and at the same time challenge these assumptions.

'Citizen journalists' as foreign correspondents

The assumption that journalists' presence or location determines the coverage of foreign news events may no longer hold true in the digital era because new technologies have empowered ordinary citizens to gather and report news as professional journalists do (e.g. citizen or participatory journalism). 'Armed with lightweight camcorders and computers and able to post images and words on websites with the click of a button, anyone overseas can now become a foreign correspondent, whether carrying press credentials or not' (Hamilton & Jenner, 2003, p. 134). Livingston (2007) notes that the explosion in camera phones and digital cameras (and other portable devices) has spawned a generation of 'pocket paparazzi'. He illustrated how this phenomenon occurred in 2005 during the funeral of Pope John Paul II.

> In an attempt to maintain the dignity of the event, Vatican officials issued rules prohibiting the use of 'cameras' by the million plus persons who viewed the body of Pope John Paul II as he lay in state at the Vatican. What Vatican officials didn't realize is that the definition of camera is not what it used to be. Thousands of people took camera phone photographs. (Livingston, 2007, p. 52)

Whether citizen journalists should be taken seriously or not, the trend is growing rather than waning. Associated with citizen journalism is the phenomenon of blogging. New technologies have indeed spawned the phenomenon of blogging in which ordinary citizens participate in news generation and reporting. As Yemma (2007, p. 121) explained it, 'blogging has in effect made everyone a potential news gatherer'.

> ...technology enables talented journalists, amateurs, and ordinary citizens to become ad hoc foreign correspondents, to fact-check foreign news or to join in the global discussion about international issues. (Yemma, 2007, p. 122)

Trammel and Perlmutter (2007, p. 72) contend that 'Foreign blogs complement traditional foreign affairs coverage' but they also point out that, while bloggers may not displace foreign correspondents, they will complement the range of information that media audiences receive about events and people from around the world. Of course, blogs, no doubt, serve their purposes. 'Blogs enable all of us – if we have access to them despite economic or political obstacles – to engage in such "conversations" for our own edification and,...to the enrichment of both democracy and foreign affairs coverage' (Trammel & Perlmutter, 2007, p. 83). Although blogs might be a growing practice particularly in developed Western countries, it is important to not forget that 'peasants don't blog' (Perlmutter, cited in Trammel & Perlmutter, 2007, p. 72). This is particularly true because most of the people who engage in blogging 'are middle-class people or intellectuals who have computer skills: students, academics, businesspeople, professionals ...' Despite the fact that blogging is becoming a popular preoccupation in economically developed Western countries, a majority of people especially in the developing world still lack access to the Internet owing to poverty, illiteracy and the dearth of communication infrastructure such as reliable telephone lines and regular supply of electricity. Owing to underlying problems of access to, and cost of, new technologies in non-western societies, Berger (2009, p. 361) has cautioned against optimism about the widespread use of the Internet. If blogging is practised on a massive scale in the West, it does not imply that a similar experience is occurring in non-western countries. That a lot of people are engaged in blogging should not imply that it is a worldwide practice. As Tuinstra (2004, p. 102) noted, 'There are still many countries, of course, where most people are not connected to the Internet, and so this makes its use as a mass communication tool still problematic there'. With specific reference to Internet presence and use in Africa, Wall (2009, p. 399) notes that 'most African countries are far from wired, and use of the Internet, much less a video site such as YouTube, is limited'.

Although new technologies have empowered ordinary citizens to participate in news gathering and reporting, opinions are divided as to whether citizen journalism should be taken as seriously as traditional forms of journalism. Livingston (2007, p. 61) contends that it should not be regarded as professional journalism practice:

> The raw immediacy of some information delivery systems (including live television) lacks the qualities that define news: a thoughtful, vetted, edited presentation of information that has benefited from the experience of news professionals. In this view, amateurs telling stories or posting pictures on the Internet is not journalism.

Hamilton and Jenner (2003, pp. 136–7) subscribe to this view, warning that 'Internet international news provided by untrained and unsupervised journalists, however, can flood public discussion with error, rumor, and disinformation that is often difficult to sort out from the authentic and factual'. These are valid concerns but it is worthwhile recognizing that the definition of journalism has changed significantly in the age of new technologies. As Paulussen and Ugille (2008, p. 26) argue, 'the question of whether blogging and other forms of citizen journalism are threatening professional journalism is losing relevance, as both forms of news production' are essentially complementary. They contend that 'professional journalists will increasingly have to share their control over the news production process with their users, who are becoming more and more actively involved in the creation of content. This could not only result in an increased use of user generated content by journalists, but it could also stimulate collaboration between professional and amateur journalists' (Paulussen & Ugille, 2008, pp. 24–5). Bucy et al. (2007, p. 144) cite a number of examples to illustrate how news organizations are promoting interaction between journalists and news audiences, one of which is the establishment of 'blogging sections for reporters to post their reflections about issues in the news and for visitors to interact with editorial staff ...'

One consequence of ordinary citizens' involvement in foreign news reporting is that traditional foreign correspondents have lost their monopoly of knowledge of foreign cultures and places, including the ability to provide exclusive news reports (Hamilton & Jenner, 2003, p. 137). For example, the first reports of the Asian tsunami of 26 December 2004 were provided by bloggers, just as they did soon after the July 2005 terrorist bombings in London (Livingston, 2007). One of the widely cited impacts of new technologies on foreign news reporting is the loss of autonomy previously enjoyed by foreign correspondents (see Yemma, 2007). Prior to the emergence of new technologies, foreign correspondents enjoyed autonomy. They were self-directed. They operated in foreign capitals with no one directing them what to do or how they should report foreign news. They enjoyed the authority of providing accounts of events in foreign countries. However, the emergence of new technologies has diluted the authority, independence and autonomy previously enjoyed by foreign correspondents (Yemma, 2007). Even as foreign correspondents enjoyed autonomy prior to the emergence of new technologies, there were certain snags associated with journalistic independence and authority. They included: foreign correspondents often provided more colourful or dramatic reports of events; they also plagiarized quotes from other media without attribution; and they often manufactured events or quotations (Yemma, 2007). These fraudulent practices were possible before now because: news sources lacked access to their statements in print owing to distance; and, editors and other reporters lacked good knowledge and understanding of events in distant places. Without this knowledge, editors could not challenge the 'authoritative' reports written by foreign correspondents (Yemma, 2007).

Not only have new technologies generated multiple sources of foreign news such as the participation of private citizens as content generators and consumers, some organizations are also taking on the role formerly reserved for foreign correspondents such as governments (e.g. Saudi Arabia) that are 'building their own news distribution systems to go directly to the American public' (Perlmutter & Hamilton, 2007, p. 10). In essence, foreign news reporting is no longer the exclusive reserve of professional journalists, thanks to the Internet and the phenomenon of 'do-it-yourself-journalism'.

New developments in communication technology have made foreign news reporting to become a more collaborative and open enterprise whereby reporters, editors and news consumers are constantly in touch by means of portable technologies. Specifically, mobile phone and electronic (e-mail) technologies have made it easier for the foreign correspondent to remain in constant touch with their editor at the head office. News consumers are now able to contact journalists directly through their e-mail addresses and telephone numbers which are published alongside their stories. These facilities give news audiences the opportunity to provide direct feedback to journalists, to suggest story angles, to rate news articles and to comment on news stories. Similarly, the provision of e-mail addresses of newspaper reporters in news stories has encouraged readers to respond quickly to news reports, thus 'inviting dialogue with the public over journalistic conduct and encouraging the public to voice their grievances against the news media' (Hendrickson, 2006, p. 52). Gasher and Gabriele (2004, p. 311) believe the growth of numerous news sites on the World Wide Web and the ability of news consumers to access the websites imply that the Internet is well positioned 'to globalize media content'. On their part, Ahlers (2006) and Deuze (2003) believe the Internet represents the most practical platform to assist humanity to achieve some parity in global information flow. Similarly, Wu (2007, p. 540) argues that, on the Internet, 'the working environment and the approaches of storytelling for journalists have been changed dramatically'. He suggests that the subsequent change emanating from the Internet environment and the ensuing journalistic practices 'might result in a different presentation of news – particularly international news' (2007, p. 540).

Owing to the increasing use of the Internet for domestic and international news reporting, technological determinists have argued that the Internet has rendered foreign correspondents irrelevant in the digital age. That argument can be challenged on the basis that foreign correspondents are still important because they are on the ground, talking to their sources and contacts on the spot. The foreign correspondent is well equipped to provide us with information on what is happening on the ground and what is likely to occur in the forthcoming weeks and months. Foreign correspondents have an advantage over the Internet and other new technologies because they have news sources on the ground. These news sources have in-depth knowledge and expertise in regard to news events and geographical regions. Foreign correspondents can draw on the expertise of these contacts when news breaks. These constitute valid reasons why media organizations should establish and maintain their staff of foreign correspondents. Media organizations need foreign correspondents to make a difference, to add value to their outputs. Foreign correspondents provide invaluable and worthwhile service which media organizations cannot get from the Internet or from wire services.

New technologies and quality of foreign reports

To understand how well journalists are reporting the world in the age of new technologies, we must ask, as Franks (2005, p. 93) alluded in her essay, not just how well informed media audiences are of events in other countries and cultures but also whether there has been a significant shift in foreign news reporting in terms of volume and quality of coverage, as well as global reach, that is, coverage of hitherto unknown regions and countries. In terms of news quality, evidence suggests that nothing has changed. Franks (2005, p. 99) argues that 'news from developing countries is the same diet of war, disaster and poverty. This breeds a clichéd view of these countries and leads to image fatigue amongst audiences'. Similarly, Joye (2010) found evidence of Eurocentrism and predominance of hard and negative news in his study of Flemish newspapers. This suggests that foreign news is still dominated by news of Western Europe and North America, offering evidence that nothing much has changed in the way traditional mainstream newspapers report world news. Worried by the shortcomings that are evident in foreign news reporting, Franks (2005, p. 99) and Hargreaves (2000, p. 60) recommend a drastic change in editorial policy of the media to ensure a more representative and global coverage of the world. This implies that foreign news which is diverse, well packaged, properly explained and interpreted would restore honour to a field fast losing its appeal and audience.

In examining foreign news coverage, the direction, flow and pattern of coverage have been studied. Among the numerous news flow studies, two worldwide studies were initiated under the auspices of the International Association for Mass Communication Research (IAMCR) and United Nations Educational, Scientific and Cultural Organization (UNESCO). In the first study, undertaken in 1979, foreign news coverage in 29 countries was examined, with the researchers finding that, primarily, foreign news coverage had concentrated on events in a country's immediate geographic region (Sreberny-Mohammadi et al., 1984). In news about developing countries, the emphasis was on hotspots, such as political crises. There also existed an imbalance of news flow, with the Third World receiving far more news about the First World than vice-versa. In addition, there had been a shortage of developing regions covering one another (Sreberny-Mohammadi, 1982, p. 88).

In a second major international study in 1995, researchers found that the dominance of Western news agencies had receded (Stevenson, 1997). However, news in Central and Eastern Europe was more directed towards the West and the United States enjoyed unique prominence as a news superpower. Geographic proximity to the newspaper's country and national linkages remained the dominant news values in media worlds mostly defined by politics and economics (Stevenson, 1997). Koponen (2003) argued that these two major global news flow studies showed that the two most dominant factors influencing international news coverage were regionalism and politics. In the studies, African countries were most concerned with African affairs, South American countries with Latin American news, and so on. 'And it was exclusively geographical regionalism, unable to transcend itself into a common "Third World Perspective"' (Koponen, 2003, p. 148).

Specifically, a study of foreign news coverage in Nigerian and Ghanaian newspapers (Obijiofor & Hanusch, 2003) found that more than half of the foreign news stories (52%) reported in the five newspapers were African news. In essence, Nigerian and Ghanaian newspapers gave more prominence to news about Africa than they did to news stories from any other part of the world. This suggests that geographical proximity continues to influence the coverage of foreign news even in the digital era. As further evidence of the importance of geography, Kariel and Rosenvall (1995) found in their study of 21 Canadian newspapers that 49.8 per cent of the foreign news stories published in the Canadian newspapers were from the United States. The findings reported by Obijiofor and Hanusch (2003) and Kariel and Rosenvall (1995) support the argument in the literature which shows that geographical proximity is a major determinant of foreign news coverage. In fact, Mosco (2000) insists that the advent of new technologies has not invalidated the importance of geographical proximity as a news value. He argues that, 'it may take less time to move a person or a message from one place to another. But this does not eliminate or even diminish the importance of place itself because places contain characteristics that matter irrespective of distance' (2000, p. 40). Obijiofor and Hanusch (2003) also found that more than two-thirds of the foreign news stories published in the African newspapers were negative.

One salutary feature of the findings reported by Obijiofor and Hanusch (2003) was that African newspapers' preoccupation with negative news was not reserved for African and developing countries only. Of all the foreign news stories published in the five African newspapers, more than 70 per cent were negative. This implies that, irrespective of the region or country of origin, a large majority of foreign news stories reported in the five African newspapers were decidedly negative. Emphasis on negative news seems to be a common trend in international news reporting (e.g. Franks, 2005; Joye, 2010).

Impact of new technologies on the broadcast industry

New technologies have created new challenges for foreign correspondents who report in all media platforms. In the electronic age, a successful foreign correspondent must not only demonstrate informed knowledge of international events but must also serve as an all-rounder, an expert in specific fields, regions, countries and events (Utley, 1997). More fundamentally, the foreign correspondent who aims to succeed in the digital era must show that they have the capacity to report across all three media platforms, namely print, broadcast and online (i.e. convergence). Parks (2002, p. 57) believes the introduction of smaller and cheaper technologies such as cameras and video phones would impact foreign news coverage by US television networks in two principal ways. First, cheaper and small technologies would lower the cost of foreign news coverage by US television networks. Second, lower cost of news production would lead to an increase in the amount of foreign coverage. However, there is no guarantee that cheaper technology would necessarily lead to greater amount of foreign news coverage. It is possible that television networks might channel the cheaper cameras and video phones to those units that produce more revenue for them. If the British television experience is anything to go by, it could be argued that this is the more likely prospect (Franks, 2005).

Taylor (2000, p. 35) states that although new technologies have generated real-time (live) reporting of events, there are double consequences both for news organizations and media audiences. For example, the global competition in a deregulated news market which has also promoted real-time reporting of events (the urge to be 'first with the news') can undermine professional requirements that journalists should ensure accurate reporting by checking and cross-checking their sources and facts before reporting. Unfortunately, with real-time television reporting, there is hardly sufficient time for journalists to reflect on their stories or to cross-check their sources. According to Taylor (2000, p. 35), real-time reporting puts 'extra pressure on policy makers to make decisions at a speed that might not be in the best interests of the watching audience'. This is the dilemma that confronts broadcast and online news channels that are driven by growing competition to engage in real-time reporting. However, as Seib (2007) points out, if the technologies for real-time reporting are available, journalists should not hesitate to use them. In essence, it is the journalist, not the technology, who should be responsible for ensuring accuracy in news reports.

Seib (2007, p. 151) suggests two reasons why real-time news coverage is the new fad. First, the technologies that facilitate live coverage are available, less expensive and easier to operate. However, the question must be asked: does better technology produce better journalism? The second reason why real-time news coverage has persisted is because 'the global audience for international news is increasingly accustomed to finding real-time coverage available through various media' (Seib, 2007, p. 156). Despite the growing practice, there are two serious consequences of real-time television coverage of events. Live coverage of news can lead to production of hasty, inaccurate and incomplete reports designed to satisfy media consumers' appetite for dramatic live coverage. Additionally, real-time coverage tends to privilege speed of news coverage over background material which is critical to public understanding of the nature and context of foreign news (Seib, 2007, p. 152).

One of the canons of journalism practice requires journalists to verify and authenticate their reports before publication or broadcast. Real-time coverage of news undermines this professional obligation. The opportunities that new technologies offer for in-depth coverage, greater interaction between foreign news producers and consumers and the choices available to news audiences to access the kind of news they want when they want it are regarded as major attractions of technological changes in journalism (Tait, 2000, p. 51). Feist (2001) believes that converging technology has lifted the number of news consumers who can access foreign broadcasts through the Internet or television channels. 'Around the world, the shrinking costs of small satellite receiving dishes and the rapid expansion of cable television have allowed hundreds of millions of people to see the broadcasts of CNN, the British Broadcasting Company (sic) (BBC), and other Western television news organizations' (Feist, 2001, p. 710). It could also be argued that the involvement of the United States in two global conflicts in Iraq and Afghanistan suggests that media interest in, and public attention to, foreign news – at least in the United States – should be on the rise rather than on the decline, owing to diverse online sources of foreign news. For example, Best et al. (2005, p. 65) report in their study of online foreign news usage that 'approximately a quarter of all U.S. Internet users gather information about news and current events via an online foreign source'. However, they underline one of the strengths of online sources of foreign news, as different tools for alternative sources of foreign news, such as the opportunity to access alternative news sources and news framed in ideologies that are different from those of the United States (2005, p. 65). This implies that foreign news consumers can use foreign news sources to evaluate news stories that are consistent with their opinions. They can also use foreign news sources to gratify their appetite for political news. For traditional news media such as newspapers, radio and television, such opportunities are severely limited.

Contrary evidence

Just as evidence exists to show how new technologies are transforming foreign news reporting, there is also research suggesting that new technologies are not affecting foreign reporting in a significant way. For example, Wu (2007) examined and compared foreign news published in the hard-copy editions of *The New York Times* and its online counterpart nytimes.com, as well as international news broadcast on CNN and its online version – cnn.com. He found that the web (new technology) has not changed the way foreign news is reported (Wu, 2007, p. 549) and that the traditional determinants of foreign news are still dominant even in the age of new technologies. Joye (2010) made a similar finding in his study of Flemish newspapers. For example, foreign coverage in the newspapers was still predominantly negative and concentrated on hard news.

In another study, Wu and Hamilton (2004, p. 517) noted that while the Internet may be having 'a profound impact on the way foreign correspondents go about their work', nothing in their study 'suggested that the general neglect of traditional foreign newsgathering will be reversed in the near future'. However, of the 354 respondents, 34 per cent said that, owing to the Internet, they were compelled to file stories more frequently while 37 per cent reported more frequent updating of their news stories. What was remarkable in the study was that foreign correspondents expressed disappointment with the quality and quantity of foreign news reported in the US news media. According to Wu and Hamilton (2004, p. 527):

> About one in three expressed disappointment over the current quality and quantity of international news content in the US media. They attributed these problems to lack of resources, inadequate editorial support and attention, insufficient reader interest and the trend toward sensationalised treatment. 'General tendency', said one typical respondent, 'is to look for topics that appear exotic, cute and entertaining for a Westernised audience.'

When the foreign correspondents were asked to list regions or foreign news topics that required more attention, Africa popped up, as did 'environmental issues, poverty and development, social and religious tensions and culture' (Wu & Hamilton, 2004, p. 527). While the Internet may have led to an increase in independent freelance reporters who report freely around the globe, the Internet has also compelled reporters to rely more on their computers than on their established news sources (Wu & Hamilton, 2004, p. 527). One of the respondents in the study said 'the increasing dependence on the Internet for information will cause journalists to spend more of their time behind a computer screen instead of getting out of the office to properly report stories' (cited in Wu & Hamilton, 2004, p. 529).

Further evidence that new technologies have not affected the quality of foreign news or the way foreign news is reported has been observed by other researchers. For example, Chia (2007) studied foreign news in four online newspapers and found that, 'Although developing countries received greater foreign news coverage as a whole, North America and Western Europe consistently emerged as the top three most covered regions in all four online newspapers'. She also found, as Gasher and Gabriele (2004) did, that the four online newspapers she studied were dependent on the leading international (Western) news agencies for their foreign news. Chia (2007, p. 89) reported that quantitative inequities in foreign coverage between developing and developed countries were prevalent in the four online newspapers, namely the *Gulf News* (United Arab Emirates), *The Daily Mirror Online* (Zimbabwe), *Globe and Mail* (Canada) and *Guardian Unlimited* (UK).

Chia's (2007) arguments echo concerns that new technologies may not have changed the quality of foreign news, including journalistic culture and practices that influence foreign news coverage. Could it be that foreign news reporting is still entrenched in the traditional news reporting genre: that is, emphasis on negativism and conflict, as well as the dominance of news from the United States and Western Europe? Research results reported by Gasher and Gabriele (2004) and Chia (2007) echo the age-old trend in foreign news reporting. News events from the United States and Western Europe tend to dominate the foreign news pages of leading newspapers across the world. This fits with Galtung and Ruge's (1970) hypothesis, proposed more than four decades ago, that events involving 'elite nations' are more likely to be reported than events concerning developing (non-elite) nations. The only time developing countries receive prominence in Western news media, Bonney and Wilson (1983) have argued, is when there are issues that tie developing countries to the interests of the First World ('elite') countries, or, more commonly, when extraordinary events such as natural disasters and political instability occur in non-elite countries (i.e. Second or Third World countries). 'News about other Second World or Third World countries is reported chiefly when First World interests are involved' (Bonney & Wilson, 1983, p. 301). For example, since 2003 when the war in Iraq began, Iraq has featured consistently in the foreign news menu of the media across the world, even though Iraq is not a 'First World' country.

The 'CNN Effect' and the 'YouTube Factor'

Amanpour (1996) draws on endless media coverage of the conflict in Bosnia in the late 1990s to illustrate the power of foreign correspondents to influence foreign policy. She argued that the US government ignored the conflict in Bosnia until three-and-a-half years later when the 'genocidal ethnic cleansing, concentration camps, mass murder, cities under siege, shell-fire and sniping' forced the United States to take the lead to intervene in the Bosnian conflict, in concert with NATO member states.

> Governments simply hated seeing the constant stream of blood from Bosnia spilling onto the front pages and TV news broadcasts, increasing the pressure

on them to do something. It's a phenomenon that has become known as the CNN Factor. (Amanpour, 1996, p. 16)

The 'CNN Factor' or 'CNN Effect' is an allusion to the power of the American Cable News Network (CNN) to influence domestic and international politics. Utley (1997), like Amanpour (1996), notes how television coverage of foreign events influences domestic policy in the United States. 'Television had an impact on public opinion, which in turn affected the government's formulation of foreign policy, during and after the Tet Offensive in Vietnam in 1968, the seizure of the American embassy in Tehran in 1979, the terrorist attack on the Marine Corps barracks in Beirut in 1982, and the killing of American troops in Somalia in 1994' (Utley, 1997, p. 4). Former US secretary of state James Baker endorsed this notion in his book (1995) when he wrote: 'In Iraq, Bosnia, Somalia, Rwanda, and Chechnya, among others, the real-time coverage of conflict by the electronic media has served to create a powerful new imperative for prompt action that was not present in less frenetic [times]' (Baker, 1995, p. 103, cited in Gilboa, 2005, p. 28). Wu and Hamilton (2004, p. 519) concur that foreign news reporters influence the public's and the government's knowledge of foreign events. 'Foreign correspondents have a dominant role in informing the public and, at times, the government about foreign events'. While all this may be the case, other scholars such as Hallin (1986) have argued that in the case of Vietnam there was a shift in the US government policy prior to the decision to end American involvement in the war, which then led the media to follow the policy rather than the media serving as a catalyst for foreign policy development.

Beside what has been referred to as the 'CNN Factor' or 'CNN Effect', some researchers have noted how the video-sharing website known as *YouTube* influences political decisions and election campaigns across cultures (e.g. Naím, 2007). Gilboa (2005, p. 28) draws on comments by US government officials which suggested that live television coverage often influenced policy decisions. The CNN effect has been described in various ways by various authors. Feist (2001, p. 713) describes it as an assumption 'that compelling television images, such as images of a humanitarian crisis, cause U.S. policy-makers to intervene in a situation when such an intervention might otherwise not be in the U.S. national interest'. Robinson (2002, p. 3) has argued that the CNN effect, on one hand, looks at the 'direct impact of media coverage on policy-makers and the broader group of politicians, experts and commentators who make up the foreign policy elite'. Schorr (1998, p. 11) explains the CNN effect as 'the way breaking news affects foreign policy decisions'. Naím (2007, p. 103) sees the impact of the CNN effect from a global perspective:

'Since the early 1990s, electoral frauds that might have remained hidden were exposed, democratic uprisings energized, famines contained, and wars started or stopped, thanks to the CNN effect.'

Apart from recognizing how 24-hour cable television has transformed international politics, Naím (2007) believes *YouTube* would have a more profound effect on foreign news reporting and greater participation by ordinary citizens in foreign news reporting, essentially through recording, posting or sharing news videos. He describes the two-stage process in *YouTube* through which new technologies are transforming world events. Although *YouTube* may have empowered ordinary citizens to record and post videos online, surely there are drawbacks. For example,

> How do we know that what we see in a video clip posted by a "citizen journalist" is not a montage? How do we know, for example, that the YouTube video of terrorized American soldiers crying and praying for their lives while under fire was filmed in Iraq and not staged somewhere else to manipulate public opinion? (Naím, 2007, p. 103)

For more on the impact of *YouTube* on national and international politics, see Grove (2008) and May (2008).

Conclusion

The factors that affect foreign news reporting in the digital age, including the differences and similarities in foreign coverage in mainstream and online media constitute the main focus of this chapter. The chapter also explored the major challenges that confront foreign reporting in the age of new technologies. The significance of foreign news in a globalized world was examined in-depth, in particular how foreign news coverage influences public perceptions, cross-cultural understandings of people and government policy direction.

The overarching observation is that new technologies have significantly transformed the way foreign news is reported, including the quantity and diversity of foreign news, frequency and speed of coverage and the greater participation of news consumers (citizen journalists) in the production and distribution of foreign news. Although new technologies and cost-cutting measures may have resulted in a reduction in the number of foreign posts and the number of foreign correspondents, concerns persist about whether the phenomenon of parachute journalism has encouraged in-depth or low quality foreign coverage.

One of the radical transformations in foreign news reporting spawned by new technologies is the participation of ordinary citizens in foreign news gathering, production and reporting. However, citizen journalism has its drawbacks some of which are unethical practices and the notion that untrained citizen reporters could dilute professional journalism practice and inundate traditional media and online news sites with inaccurate reports and rumours. The chapter noted that, although the Internet has promoted global coverage of foreign news even in hitherto obscure locations, it should equally be acknowledged that the Internet has also generated complacency among journalists, compelling some reporters to rely more on their computers rather than on their established news sources. Other ways through which technological advances have affected foreign reporting include generation of multiple sources of foreign news, enhancement of interactions between media organizations and news consumers, as well as the availability of multiple sources of foreign news that present news consumers with opportunities to access foreign news when they want it. However, the prevalence of factors such as geographical and cultural proximity, emphases on conflict and negativism and the dominance of Western news reports over reports from non-western countries suggest that, in news selection decisions, foreign news editors and reporters are still influenced more significantly by cultural practices and professional news values rather than by the new technologies.

If new technologies have not had significant impact on the quality of foreign news, the chapter suggests that it may be necessary to examine professional journalistic conventions (e.g. news values such as conflict and negativism), as well as cultural practices that inform how journalists perceive, select, interpret and write news in various parts of the world. Further research is required to investigate these issues. The chapter argued that greater research on foreign news coverage on the Internet, for example, would enhance research-based knowledge of the cultural and professional dynamics that influence the coverage of foreign news on the web, including how foreign news published in traditional mainstream media differ in terms of volume, source and slant from their online counterparts. Why, for example, have journalists not used new technologies to reflect balance and diversity of news in their reports of foreign events? Why, for example, are online newspapers still reliant on international news agencies as the main sources of foreign news, even with diverse online news sources? Why is negative news still the dominant form of foreign news reported in traditional and online media? How can the web transform foreign news reporting (in traditional and online media) in such a way as to address the issues that have dominated foreign news reporting for the past 50 years? These questions constitute an agenda for future research on foreign news reporting.

DISCUSSION QUESTIONS

1. Outline and discuss the drawbacks of journalistic independence and authority enjoyed by foreign correspondents prior to the emergence of new technologies.
2. Discuss the three reasons why the broadcast media are practising real-time coverage of news events. What are the implications of real-time news reporting for journalism practice in your country? Should new technologies be blamed for professional errors in real-time news coverage? Does better technology produce better journalism?
3. What do you understand by the phrase 'CNN Effect' or 'CNN Factor' in foreign news reporting? Identify and discuss arguments for and against the 'CNN Effect'. Can you identify an example in your country where media reporting helped to influence the development of government policy?
4. Analyse the arguments for and against 'parachute journalism'. In the digital age, do you believe that media organizations should practise parachute journalism?
5. Outline and discuss the underlying reasons why media attention to foreign news is declining in much of North America and Western Europe. How could the trend be reversed?

CHAPTER 7

Approaches to reporting peace and conflict

Introduction

The role that news media play in wartime has been an important topic in the scholarship of journalism around the world. This is perhaps not surprising, given that it is during times of national and international crises that journalists play a crucial role in informing audiences about what their governments are doing in their name or in the national interest. Wars have constituted a central part of news reporting ever since the accounts distributed to the Roman people in the *Acta Diurna Populi Romani*, a publication some scholars deem to be the forerunner of the newspaper (Giffard, 1975, p. 107). Similarly, the early newssheets of the sixteenth and seventeenth centuries were full of accounts of the various wars being fought in Europe, though most of these were not written by reporters in the field. Modern war correspondence traces its beginnings back to the Crimean War (1853–56), when reporters sent dispatches from the field and new technologies such as the telegraph and the railway allowed them to be distributed quickly (Tumber, 2009, p. 386). The Crimean War is also regarded as the first war to be photographed for newspapers, with Roger Fenton gaining the title of 'first war photographer', although the American Civil War (1861–65) is nowadays regarded as the first widely photographed conflict, allowing readers at home to follow events at the frontline in increasing detail (Griffin, 1999). From this time onwards, 'modern warfare was to be marked not only by mass armies and machines of mass destruction, but also by mass witnesses' (Paschalidis, 1999, p. 122). The apparent realism first relayed by early war photographers was later extended by the emergence of radio and particularly television news reporting, which allowed audiences to follow wars in real time, following the arrival of 24-hour news channels.

In these contexts, war therefore has played a crucial role in the history of the news media, leading to a number of publications about the news media's role in conflict reporting (e.g. Allen & Seaton, 1999; Allen & Zelizer, 2004; Löffelholz, 2004; Wolfsfeld, 2004; Spencer, 2005; Cottle, 2006). In particular, attention has been given to the performance of journalists, including the relationship between the media and governments during war, as well as the potential for the news media to make a difference through 'peace journalism alternative' (Lynch & McGoldrick, 2005). This chapter explores these strands of perspectives with respect to their application globally. First, we examine the way in which journalism has played a role in the reporting of wars and conflict against a variety of cultural backgrounds. This includes conflicts across regions but also within nations, as the concept of war has taken on ethnic dimensions, such as the wars in the Balkans, in Rwanda, Sri Lanka and Indonesia. Furthermore, we explore the relationship between the media and governments in terms of influence, as the debate over the so-called CNN effect shows. Although heavily contested, the 'CNN effect' suggests that journalism has a profound influence on government policy in times of war and conflict (see also Chapter 6). Finally, a large part of this chapter explores the idea of peace journalism, which has become a popular concept in the study of the media's role during war in the early twenty-first century. Here, we critically examine the theory of peace and conflict reporting and speculate about its potential for success. This discussion is set against a background of numerous examples from across the globe.

Examples of war reporting around the world

News media have been used to support war efforts for quite some time, mostly for nationalist purposes but also at times merely because proprietors had a vested interest in creating tensions. William Randolph Hearst, one of the founders of 'yellow journalism' in the late nineteenth century, was involved in a fierce battle over newspaper sales with Joseph Pulitzer at a time when tensions were running high between the United States and Spain. Hearst and Pulitzer are often held responsible for having exacerbated the conflict with their sensationalized news coverage (West, 2001, pp. 44–5). Hearst in particular is said to have fanned the flames, filling his pages with accounts, often untrue, of Spanish atrocities in Cuba. An exchange with his illustrator Frederic Remington is frequently held up as evidence that Hearst wanted a war at all costs. In the famous telegrams, Remington, who had been despatched to Cuba to illustrate the atrocities there, was said to have told his boss: 'Everything is quiet. There is no trouble here. There will be no war. I wish to return.' Hearst, however, reputedly wanted none of this, telling his illustrator to stay put with the instruction: 'Please remain. You furnish the pictures, and I'll furnish the war' (Campbell, 2000, p. 405). While the fact that this particular exchange actually occurred has since been challenged (see Campbell, 2000), there is ample evidence of Hearst and Pulitzer's newspapers creating an environment in which the public increasingly demanded a war with Spain – one which they eventually got (West, 2001, p. 45).

A further example of the disastrous impact of the media on war propaganda stems from the time before and during the Second World War. Following the rise to power of the National Socialist Workers' Party in Germany in 1933, the country's media was subjected to the steady process of *Gleichschaltung*, which meant that all media outlets eventually came under the control of the Nazis. Subsequently, most mass media were used for propaganda purposes in order to maintain the support of the German people for Nazi policies, and specifically to propagate hatred of Jews. One extreme, but significant example was *Der Stürmer*, a weekly newspaper that had been edited by Julius Streicher since 1923. The paper was widely available, particularly in public places, and reached a weekly circulation of 500,000 copies in 1937 (Ryszka, 2002, p. 302). Using real stories and highly dramatized accounts, the *Stürmer* consistently portrayed Jews as stealing and thieving criminals. And while Ryszka (2002, p. 303) points out that the newspaper was actually not much approved of by the elite of the Reich, its 'activity can be considered effective as far as anti-Jewish discrimination and "*Rassenschande*" are concerned'. In this way, the *Stürmer* contributed to a climate of hatred towards Jews in the 1930s and 1940s Germany, leading to Streicher's conviction for crimes against humanity and his subsequent hanging after the war.

This climate of fear was propagated again more recently, in the lead-up to and during the 1994 genocide in Rwanda, when 800,000 people were killed in roughly 100 days (Thompson, 2007). The role played by radio in the incitement of the genocide has been documented in popular films such as *Hotel Rwanda*. But it was not just the extremist Hutu radio station, Radio Télévision Libre des Mille Collines (RTLM), which spread a constant stream of anti-Tutsi propaganda immediately before and during the genocide. The newspaper *Kangura* also did its part to contribute to the situation. Tutsi were constantly referred to by Hutu media as 'inyenzi' (cockroaches), who needed to be exterminated. During the massacres, RTLM would broadcast the names of Tutsi and their hideouts, allowing Hutus to hunt them down and murder them. As Hamelink (2008, p. 80) pointed out, 'ordinary people turned into crazed killing machines – because they were made to believe that a dangerous and hideous enemy lived next door'. The role played by Rwandan hate media in the genocide has been well-documented in considerable detail in Thompson's (2007) edited collection. Reminiscent of the case of the *Stürmer*, two founders of RTLM and the editor-in-chief of *Kangura* were later convicted for genocide, conspiracy to commit genocide, direct and public incitement to commit genocide, as well as crimes against humanity (see the judgment as reported in Thompson, 2007, pp. 277–307). The role of the media in inciting conflicts in central African countries more generally has also recently been examined in some detail by Frère (2007).

Further, during the conflict in Bosnia and Herzegovina in the early 1990s, Serbian-controlled television was reported to be transmitting hate-filled anti-Croat and anti-Muslim messages. Benesch (2004, p. 63) quoted a British journalist as saying: 'It was a message of urgency, a threat to your people, to your nation, a call to arms, and yes, a sort of instruction to go to war for your people…It pushed and pushed. It was rather like a sort of hammer bashing on people's heads.'

In Asia, which in recent years has experienced its share of ethnic conflicts in countries such as the Philippines, Indonesia and Sri Lanka, the news media have also played an important role. Hanitzsch (2004) reports that when conflict broke out in Indonesia's Moluccan Islands in early 1999, there was only one daily newspaper in the capital Ambon. The *Suara Maluku* (Voice of the Moluccas) quickly found itself caught in the escalating conflict between Christians and Muslims. The situation was made even more difficult for the newspaper, as it employed a number of Christian and Muslim journalists.

> During the first weeks of fighting, ethnic cleansing was occurring throughout Ambon. The town was divided into several territories controlled by either Christian or Muslim groups. Coincidence or not, the location of the *Suara Maluku* office was within Christian territory which meant that Muslim journalists working for the paper could not access the editorial office without risking being killed as soon as they enter Christian territory. Consequently, Christian journalists reported from Christian sectors and Muslim journalists reported from Muslim territories. Since the Muslims could not enter the editorial office, the *Suara Maluku* was entirely controlled by Christian editors, who eventually shifted their editorial policy from independent to pro-Christian. (Hanitzsch, 2004, p. 483)

Hanitzsch reports that eventually the newspaper's owners decided to split the enterprise into two, creating a Muslim paper, the *Ambon Ekspres*, in order to service the Muslim minority population.

> As a result, the Christian population was reading reports on the destruction of Christian villages by "evil Muslims", provided by *Suara Maluku*; while the Muslim population was reading news about bloody attacks on Muslim civilians and a "conspiracy" of Christian clerics, provided by *Ambon Ekspres*. Journalists became combatants; their media became inflammatory pamphlets. (Hanitzsch, 2004, p. 483)

The potential effect that journalism can have on war has also been a reason for some governments to censor the media in times of conflict. During the Second World War, the US government put in place stringent censorship restrictions on photographs of fallen US soldiers, for fear that they had the potential to demoralize the public at home. Only when President Roosevelt decided in 1943 that the American people should see the ugly side of the war did such images appear in newspapers and magazines back home (Rainey, 2005). The Vietnam War proved a watershed for the perceived power of the news media as, for the first time, audiences in Europe and the United States were able to follow the war through television. They could witness the horrors in the jungles of Indochina for themselves, and saw images that many will never forget. There was the image of AP photographer Nick Ut, which showed a group of distressed Vietnamese villagers running towards the camera, including a naked nine-year-old girl with burns to her back from a napalm attack. Similarly, the photograph of Saigon police chief General Loan executing a Vietcong prisoner during the Tet Offensive, right in front of Eddie Adams' camera, stirred emotions. The view that the news coverage was responsible for turning the public against the war is still 'accepted so widely across the American political spectrum that it probably comes as close as anything to being conventional wisdom about a war that still splits the American public' (Hallin, 1986, pp. 105–6).

Wars led by Western powers have been much more tightly controlled since, with the shadows of the Vietnam experience hanging over every war the United States or Britain has been engaged in since. One of the more or less direct results was the establishment of the 'pool' system of reporting during the Gulf War, which saw journalists placed into so-called Media Reporting Teams attached to US and British military units, which were closely supervised by military censors (Taylor, 1992, pp. 51–2). During the Iraq War which started in 2003, journalists were individually embedded with the troops, and although they were given more freedom in reporting, they arguably witnessed only small slices of the action at the frontline. Feelings of gratitude to and attachment to the soldiers they accompanied also led to somewhat biased reporting (for a discussion of how journalists were embedded with troops in the Iraq War, see Katovsky & Carlson, 2003; Tumber & Palmer, 2004). Both the Gulf War and the Iraq War have been the subject of insightful and in-depth comparative analyses that examined the coverage of the wars around the globe, noting broad similarities in their reporting and framing, but also important local differences. See Mowlana et al. (1992) for analysis of the Gulf War and Nohrstedt and Ottosen (2005) for examination of the Iraq War.

The influence that news reporting can have on policy decisions has been a topic of debate in journalism and communication studies for some time. Hallin (1986) examined comprehensively the role played by the news media during the Vietnam War and found little evidence that the media coverage alone led to a change in public opinion against the war. In fact, he argued that the news coverage only became anti-war once politicians at the elite level had already turned against the conflict, and when many members of the public were also beginning to doubt the need for the war effort. Previously, the media had been extremely supportive of the war effort, a fact demonstrated by empirical studies which found that news programmes showed very little details of actual fighting and when they did, took great care not to show American casualties in graphic detail (Hammond, 1989; Cook, 2001). Hallin (1986, p. 130) also noted that television networks had explicit guidelines 'not to show film of identifiable American casualties, unless their relatives had been notified by the Defense Department'.

The discussion of the role of the media during times of war shows that news media can at times have an impact on the events they report on. A number of studies have argued that war reporting is profitable for media organizations, especially television news, because of the drama and the pictures, and so it is no surprise that war reporting tends to be stereotypical and focused on strongly negative issues. The belief that what the media do actually matters in terms of affecting audience attitudes towards a conflict therefore has influenced members of the public with a desire for the news media to engage in peace-oriented reporting.

The philosophy behind peace journalism

The idea of journalism as a tool for the cultivation of peace – or at least to help foster a more peaceful climate – can be traced back to the work of the Norwegian peace researcher Johan Galtung (1969, 2002; Galtung & Höivik, 1971). Galtung (2002) was instrumental in the development of the theoretical perspectives called 'peace/conflict journalism' on the one hand, and 'war/violence journalism' on the other. According to this terminology, peace and war journalism can be distinguished along four major dimensions: an orientation towards peace and conflict, truth, people and solutions. War journalism, on the other hand, is oriented towards war and violence, propaganda, elites and victory. Peace journalism attempts to explore the formation of a conflict, sees a multitude of parties involved and aims for 'win-win' situations. It makes conflicts transparent, is proactive in that it aims to help prevent violence before it occurs and exposes untruths on all sides. The focus of reporting is on the suffering among all participants, including non-combatants, as well as grassroots efforts of conflict resolutions. Peace initiatives are regularly highlighted (Galtung, 2002).

War journalism is the polar opposite of this approach. In this perspective, journalists focus on the conflict arena rather than its formation; only two parties are seen as being opposed to each other, and there can only be one winner, akin to a sports report. This type of journalism is reactive in that it waits for violence before it is reported, and focuses mainly on the visible effects of violence. Galtung sees war journalism as oriented towards propaganda because it attempts to expose the opponent's untruths and helps to cover up government's lies. The sources of such stories are often elites rather than ordinary people, thus reflecting elitist discourses as opposed to grassroots movements. Whereas peace journalism equates peace with non-violence and creativity, war journalism sees peace as the result of a victory and ceasefire. Galtung believes that peace journalism is quite a serious undertaking.

> Peace journalism is a "journalism of attachment" to all actual and potential victims; war journalism only attaches to "our" side. The task is to report truthfully both war and peace, shaming the adage that "peace must be working, there is nothing in the media". The task of peace journalism is serious, professional reporting, making these processes more transparent. The task of peace advocacy is better left to peace workers. (Galtung, 2002, p. 262)

The idea of peace journalism as a useful tool for de-escalation of wars and violence had been around for some time but over the past two decades it has found increasing attention from a number of academics and peace activists. Three main reasons have been identified for this: (a) public disenchantment with the way journalists report on conflicts; (b) the increasing number of global conflicts in the early 1990s; and (c) increasing media focus on conflicts and negative events, including natural disasters (cited in Obijiofor, 2009). In fact, particularly during the first decade of the twenty-first century,

journalism's role in times of war has been an increasingly popular topic in
academic research, with numerous articles on peace journalism published in
established journals. The establishment during this time of scholarly journals,
such as *Conflict & Communication Online* and *Media, War & Conflict*, is further evidence of the significance the field has achieved in the academic and
research communities.

The most commonly used definitions of peace journalism are firmly
grounded in Galtung's framework. Lynch and McGoldrick, who have published extensively on peace journalism and who draw heavily on Galtung's
approach, have defined it as journalism that occurs

> when editors and reporters make choices – of what stories to report and about
> how to report them – that create opportunities for society at large to consider
> and value non-violent responses to conflict. Peace Journalism:
>
> - uses the insights of conflict analysis and transformation to update the con-
>   cepts of balance, fairness and accuracy in reporting
> - provides a new route map tracing the connections between journalists, their
>   sources, the stories they cover and the consequences of their journalism – the
>   ethics of journalistic intervention
> - builds an awareness of non-violence and creativity into the practical job of
>   everyday editing and reporting. (Lynch & McGoldrick, 2005, p. 5)

Applying this definition and expanding on Galtung's ideas, Lynch and
McGoldrick (2005) provide an in-depth overview of the potential for peace
journalism, replete with numerous ideas and tips on how to practise it. A
further influential approach to peace journalism has been formulated by
German social psychologist Wilhelm Kempf (2002, 2003), who expands on
Galtung's work but sees the goal of peace journalism as a two-step process.
He differentiates between de-escalation-oriented coverage in the first place
and solution-oriented coverage. Kempf (2002) believes that peace journalism
in Galtung's sense can only be supported by a majority once a peace treaty
or armistice has been reached. When a conflict is still ongoing, however, de-
escalation-oriented coverage is what is needed. This type of reporting, according to Kempf, is closely connected with what is generally referred to as quality
journalism.

> It is characterised by neutrality and critical distance from all parties to a conflict
> and goes beyond the professional norms of journalism only to the extent that
> journalists' competence in conflict theory bears fruit and conflict remains open
> to peaceful settlement (win-win orientation as an option, questioning violence

as an appropriate means of resolving conflict, questioning military values, and examination of conflict formation processes). (Kempf, 2006, p. 3)

Only once a peace treaty has been reached can a more proactive, people-oriented peace journalism gain the support of the majority. However, there are other constraints which can impact on how audiences receive peace journalism, such as the degree to which the audience is entangled in the conflict, societal beliefs, journalists' assumptions about audience preferences, the text genre, the format of the media and the audience itself (Kempf, 2002).

Melone et al. (2002, p. 3) argue that 'the media have a large potential for creating a common basis and thus cultivating conditions for conflict transformation through a variety of activities'. They believe that the media can do so in three primary ways: (a) It can inform and educate about the roots of conflict and point out common misperceptions; (b) it can build confidence and mediate between the parties involved in a conflict; and (c) it can act as a watchdog on those in power in order to make certain there is long-term accountability. As a result of the peace journalism initiatives, there have been a number of handbooks and manuals published around the world, highlighting the potential for the approach (see, e.g., Maslog, 2000; Howard, 2003).

Ideally, according to the philosophy and definition behind the concept, peace journalism would contribute to peaceful alternatives to conflicts, and help to act as a bulwark against a culture of violence. Yet, while this is certainly a worthy undertaking, peace journalism has been subjected to intense scrutiny over how realistic a prospect it really is.

Critique of peace journalism

One of the most prominent critics of the peace journalism concept has been German scholar Thomas Hanitzsch, who defines peace journalism as 'a programme or frame of journalistic news coverage which contributes to the process of making and keeping peace respectively to the peaceful settlement of conflicts' (2004, p. 484). He admits that peace journalism has noble intentions, but argues that peace journalism unintentionally overburdens journalists with responsibilities that ought to be reserved for politicians and policy makers. Hanitzsch notes that much of the discussion on peace journalism has been normative, with proponents rarely grounding their arguments in mass communication theory. He argues that peace journalism as advocated by its opponents runs the risk of being merely a subjective enterprise, which contravenes long-held journalistic norms of 'objectivity, neutrality and impartiality' (Hanitzsch, 2004, p. 487). This point has also been made by Cottle (2006, p. 103) who identifies a problem in the 'epistemological assumption embedded in peace journalism' that allows those who practise it to be able to decide between truths and untruths.

> This contradicts everything that we know about the way that different his-
> tories and identities fuel each other, and how claims to the facts, much less
> the "truth", are frequently destined to remain in dispute, notwithstanding (or
> maybe because of) appeals to "history", "evidence", "reason" and "expert tes-
> timony". (Cottle, 2006, p. 103)

Cottle believes that peace journalists are no more able to have a monopoly on what constitutes the truth than anyone else. This has also been acknowl-edged by peace journalism advocate Kempf (2007, p. 7), who believes that a turn away from objectivity would endanger 'the acceptance of the peace jour-nalistic project in the journalistic community' and twist 'peace journalism into a form of advocacy journalism, which leads directly to PR and propaganda and can squander the trust bonus which its recipients grant to peace journal-ism'. Nevertheless, McGoldrick (2006) sees the whole notion of objectivity as the cause of the problem. She argues that the conventions of objectivity in journalism actually privilege official sources, examine events rather than proc-esses and favour a dualism when reporting conflicts. Thus, she says, this type of objectivity is much more likely to lead to war journalism.

Hanitzsch also criticizes what he sees as peace journalism's overestimation of media effects. He argues that the current state of media effects research shows that media effects are selective rather than all-encompassing. Indeed, media effects research has undergone a number of phases since its initial stages in the early twentieth century, with McQuail (2005) identifying four broad historical phases, beginning with a view of the media as all-powerful up until the 1930s, to more limited effects between the 1930s and early 1960s. With the arrival of television in most Western countries in the late 1950s and the early 1960s, the belief in the powerful mass media returned, though not in terms of direct effects, but rather long-term cultivation of audience attitudes. From the late 1970s, a social constructivist view emerged, which sees the news media as constructing images of reality in predictable and pat-terned ways, while audiences interact with the media content and construct their own social reality from it (McQuail, 2005, p. 461). Nowadays, some scholars believe that certain messages can have certain effects for some people under certain circumstances (Hanitzsch, 2004, p. 489). Yet, McQuail (2005) believes that during times of crisis and war, perhaps mass media actually are more influential as audiences are more reliant on them than normally for information, and as such governments, business and other elites try to use them even more so to influence public opinion. Later in this chapter we will return to the issue of media effects when we look at the emerging body of evidence that has examined the effect of peace journalism.

Another point of Hanitzsch's (2004) critique of the peace journalism concept relates to the way in which it is often targeted at individual journalists. Arguing from a systems theoretical perspective, Hanitzsch believes that it is impossible for individuals to have a long-lasting effect on the nature of news coverage. Rather, change is needed at a much higher level. He sees potential for the success of the peace journalism approach only when it is also targeted at the media structure.

> Peace journalism ... cannot be induced from the "outside", but can only evolve within a "culture of peace". Thus, the question of how the mass media construct reality gains a socio-critical dimension. We should rather ask: what kind of society is it that creates the sort of journalism that has no sense of peace? (Hanitzsch, 2004, p. 491)

This point is also borne out in research on newspaper coverage of the conflict in Northern Ireland. Here, Fawcett (2002) argues that journalists who work for a media organization that aligns itself with one side in a conflict cannot serve as detached or objective peacemakers owing to the way news is packaged and framed. According to her, 'the rhetorical and narrative forms used by the news media facilitate certain frames or discourses, while closing off the development of alternative ways of viewing a set of events' (Fawcett, 2002, pp. 220–1). Wolfsfeld (1997, p. 68) explains why journalists would prefer to report war rather than peace: 'War provides drama and conflict and an abundance of visuals. It is also easier to deal with a war as a series of events, and journalists can normally report on a specific beginning and end.' Hanitzsch similarly notes that many news values are adhered to by journalists because they are in line with what audiences desire. 'Those who are critical of news values-oriented news coverage need to realize that the media would have to pay for any insufficient consideration of news factors with a loss of readers, listeners, viewers or users' (Hanitzsch, 2004, p. 490). Change, according to Hanitzsch, could therefore not be induced on journalism from the outside. What is needed is a much broader change of the entire journalistic system.

The argument that many journalists are simply hungry for conflict has also been reflected in research conducted by Richter (1999) who, in interviews with German foreign correspondents, found they aimed to focus mainly on reporting the situation and civilian suffering, rather than focussing on the military. Ozgunes and Terzis (2000) found that Turkish and Greek journalists expressed a desire for more balanced reporting of conflict between the two countries, proposing a variety of measures that would enhance training and structures of journalism. At the same time, Bläsi (2004) notes that theoretical models need to be operationalized so they can be employed in the reality of news reporting. Based on qualitative interviews with 30 German journalists engaged in conflict reporting, Bläsi (2004, p. 2) believes there are 'six main factors that influence conflict coverage production: structural aspects of the media, the situation on site, the personal characteristics of individual journalists, the political climate, lobbies, and the media audience'. He argues that all these would need to be addressed in specific ways if peace journalism is to be a successful prospect. Nevertheless, as past reporting of conflicts such as the Persian Gulf War and the Iraq War has shown, military operations have often tended to be at the forefront of reporting, perhaps in large part due to government restrictions on journalists. In both these wars, the United States and its allies implemented strict conditions on journalists who travelled into the war zone either in pre-arranged media pools, or were 'embedded' with allied troops.

Hanitzsch's (2004) critique has stirred much debate around the issue of peace journalism, eventually leading to the publication of a special issue of the journal – *Conflict & Communication Online* – in which two critics (Hanitzsch, 2007b; Loyn, 2007) and two prominent peace journalism advocates (Lynch, 2007; Peleg, 2007) put forward their arguments, followed by rejoinders written once they had read each others' contributions. Despite the attempt at dialogue, some arguments were more polemic than academic, and reading the often heated debates one could easily forget that at the heart of the issue was the topic of peace. As a result, some of the criticisms put forward by Hanitzsch still remain unresolved.

The editor, Wilhelm Kempf (2007), subsequently provided a synthesis of the main arguments in the debate. He believed that peace journalism certainly does have a chance, even if it would occupy a minority position in the field for some time to come. He called for more basic research and clarification of paradigms. In attempting to reconcile one of the major discussion points, the need for objectivity, Kempf believes that while there needs to be a change in the way that objectivity is currently understood and applied by journalists, it is also dangerous to call for a radical turn away from it. This, he fears, 'endangers the acceptance of the peace journalistic project in the journalistic community .... (and) twists peace journalism into a form of advocacy journalism, which leads directly to PR and propaganda and can squander the trust bonus which its recipients grant to peace journalism' (Kempf, 2007, p. 7).

Peace journalism initiatives

Despite various criticisms of peace journalism as a realistic undertaking, a number of initiatives have emerged around the world in recent years to encourage news media to help in the search for peaceful solutions to conflict. Bratic (2008), for example, documents a total of 40 media projects in 18 countries. Additionally, efforts exist or have existed at one time or another in all continents.

In Colombia, the best-known group to advocate media peace initiatives is the journalist-run not-for-profit organization *Medios para la Paz* (Media for Peace). Colombia is well known for its decades-old civil war and narco-terrorism, which has seen tens of thousands killed and more than 1.5 million people displaced (Caballero, 2000). Despite the hostile environment, Colombian journalists have tried to contribute to peaceful solutions to the conflict for some time. In 1997, a group of journalists founded *Medios para la Paz*, and the organization has since delivered countless workshops, round tables and publications across the country (Adam & Holguin, 2003). In 1999, it published the dictionary *Desarmar la Palabra* (Disarming Words), which has aimed to instil the use of conflict-sensitive language. *Medios para la Paz's* goal is to understand the challenges that reporting the conflict poses for the news media, and 'help journalists face them by providing support for their work, and by offering tools and training with an aim to improve analysis and coverage of the country's state of affairs' (Adam & Holguin, 2003).

In Africa, a number of peace-oriented initiatives by media have also taken hold. One example is the project Radio for Peacebuilding, Africa, which was put in place by the conflict resolution non-governmental organization, Search for Common Ground (SFCG), a leading organization in the production of peace-oriented media content. The African project aims to increase the knowledge and skills of radio broadcasters in covering issues from multiple perspectives, to encourage effective communication by government officials with their constituents, as well as to improve the flow of communication between policy makers, civil society members and radio broadcasters (Search for Common Ground, 2010a). To this end, the project has assessed media environments in a number of African countries, such as Angola, Burundi, Côte d'Ivoire, Democratic Republic of Congo, Sierra Leone and Guinea, and developed guidebooks for radio broadcasters. The project has also produced and broadcast programmes reflecting the main themes in the guidebook. A number of the guidelines are aimed at developing so-called peace techniques for use in talk shows and news journalism.

One such example is *Studio Ijambo* (meaning 'wise words' in Kirundi), which was launched by SFCG in Burundi in 1995, shortly after the genocide in neighbouring Rwanda and at a time during which there was much ethnic and political violence in Burundi. The station is 'a radio-production studio that employs an ethnically balanced team of journalists to produce high-quality radio programs that promote reconciliation, dialogue and collaboration' (Search for Common Ground, 2010b). *Studio Ijambo* tries to achieve its objectives through news programmes, special features, round-tables, as well as a very popular soap-opera series. The soap opera, called *Umubanyi Niwe Muryango* ('Our neighbours, ourselves'), features the complex relationships of a Hutu and Tutsi family in a rural area and attracts listenership of around 80 to 90 per cent of the population regularly (Bratic, 2008, p. 497). A further example is the documentary series *Heroes*, which traced the stories of people who had put their own lives in danger to save members of the other ethnic group from being killed. It appears that these series have had an effect, with many listeners citing *Umubanyi Niwe Muryango* as having helped them to change their attitude or behaviour towards the other ethnic group (Bratic, 2008, p. 497). According to Bratic (2008, p. 494), *Studio Ijambo* has become 'a model for production of peace-oriented media content not only for the conflicts in Rwanda and Burundi but throughout the African continent'. In addition, Frère (2007) has noted how some media in the central African region at large are contributing to peace processes.

Following his in-depth examination of case studies of peace initiatives undertaken by media in Rwanda and Bosnia, Bratic (2008, p. 500) argues that such projects do have the potential to make a lasting impact on peace processes, even if they can never 'single-handedly end a conflict'. Nevertheless, he believes there are three approaches from which such projects could benefit. First, he sees a need to integrate several media channels and practices, rather than the haphazard organization and lack of coordination among projects that currently exists. 'In essence, what is needed is a peace relations agenda closely resembling a commercial public relations campaign. A joint and integrated set of measures involving more than a single media channel or technique is vital to the success of the practice' (2008, pp. 500–1). Second, Bratic recognizes that media are only one portion of a conflict society and therefore must be integrated into legal, political, economic and other institutions. 'In order to be productive, media need to accompany the other social and political institutions in their pursuit of peacebuilding' (p. 501). Finally, he believes that there needs to be a regulation of propaganda, to avoid the re-emergence of hate media. 'Reducing the level and amount of hate messages inciting violence during the conflict would significantly minimise the negative impact of the media on the audience' (p. 501).

Peace-building projects employing local media can have powerful effects in transforming local audiences, particularly when violent conflict has abated and there exists a climate of reconciliation. Many of these projects, however, have focussed on small-scale, grassroots levels of using media technologies to advance peace. The mainstream media play equally if not more important role in that they shape debates on a national level. There is certainly a perception in the majority of peace journalism literature that mainstream media heavily favour war journalism. Until relatively recently this assessment was not based on much empirical evidence. In recent years, however, a number of studies have attempted to investigate more closely the content of news media output in order to understand the extent to which journalism may be peace-oriented. In the remainder of this chapter, we examine the existing empirical evidence. First, we take a look at various content analyses which have been conducted around the world. Later, we review the emerging literature that is concerned with the effects of peace journalism on audiences.

Empirical studies of peace journalism

The best-known empirical studies of peace journalism have been conducted mostly in an Asian setting by communication scholars Seow Ting Lee, Maslog C. Crispin and Kim Hun Shik, who examined Asian newspapers' coverage of conflict (Lee & Maslog, 2005; Lee et al., 2006; Maslog et al., 2006; Kim et al., 2008). In order to examine whether newspapers displayed predominantly peace- or war-oriented journalism, Lee and Maslog (2005) operationalized Galtung's classifications of the terms. They based their analysis on framing theory, which Entman (1993, p. 52) defined thus: 'To frame is to select some aspects of a perceived reality and make them more salient in a communicating text, in such a way as to promote a particular problem definition, causal interpretation, moral evaluation, and/or treatment recommendation for the item described.' The concept of framing has been widely employed by communication researchers interested in the way journalists shape certain texts in a variety of contexts.

Lee and Maslog (2005) believed that the majority of scholarly efforts on peace journalism had been normative or prescriptive and argued for a more evidence-based approach in order to better inform the debate. On the basis of Galtung's (1998) peace/war journalism classifications, they devised 13 coding categories for both a war journalism and a peace journalism frame, structured along the themes of approach and language (Lee & Maslog, 2005). In terms of approach, there were 10 categories, which included:

(a) reactivity, i.e. whether the approach was proactive and anticipated war before it began, or reactive and only reported war once it was just about to break out;
(b) visibility of effects of war, i.e. whether the story focused only on the visible effects of war such as casualties or property damage, or whether it reported the invisible effects of war such as the emotional trauma of those involved and the damage war was doing to their society;
(c) elite orientation, i.e. if stories focused only on leaders and elites as actors and sources of information, or whether they focused on common people;
(d) differences, i.e. the extent to which a story focused on differences or agreements between the parties in the conflict;
(e) focus on here and now, i.e. if stories focused only on the here and now or actually reported causes and consequences of the conflict;
(f) good and bad dichotomy, i.e. whether stories dichotomised only between good and bad, victims or villains, or whether such labels were avoided;
(g) party involvement, i.e. whether stories had a 'one party wins, one party loses' approach, or if they gave voice to many parties in the conflict;
(h) partisanship, i.e. the extent to which stories were biased for one side or whether they took a neutral stance;
(i) winning orientation, i.e. a zero-sum orientation or a win-win orientation;
(j) continuity of reports, i.e. whether the approach stopped reporting once a peace treaty was signed or if journalists stayed to report the aftermath of war. (Lee & Maslog, 2005, pp. 325–6)

The three categories in terms of language included:

(a) victimising language using words such as destitute, devastated or defence-less, or language that avoided such terms and reports on what has been done and could be done by people;
(b) language that was demonising (e.g. vicious, cruel, brutal, terrorist, fanatic, etc.) or language which used more precise and less demonising terms; and
(c) emotive language, which includes terms such as genocide, assassination, massacre, as opposed to language that is more objective and moderate, avoiding such emotive terms. (Lee & Maslog, 2005, pp. 325–6)

Lee and Maslog then used this framework to examine the news coverage of four Asian conflicts (Kashmir, the Philippine Mindanao conflict, Sri Lanka's war with the Tamil Tigers, as well as Indonesia's Maluku and Aceh civil wars) in 10 English-language newspapers from five Asian countries: India, Pakistan, Philippines, Indonesia and Sri Lanka. They found that a majority of stories in all papers were framed as war journalism (56%), while only roughly one-third were framed as peace journalism (35.7%), with 8.3 per cent of stories neutral. In terms of regional differences, Lee and Maslog (2005) found that Pakistani and Indian newspapers displayed the strongest war journalism frames, with 74.2 per cent of Pakistani stories classified as such, as well as 63.7 per cent of Indian stories. In Indonesia, war journalism stories (48.1%) also outweighed peace journalism content (41.8%). In the Philippines, however, peace journalism stories were in the majority, with 52.5 per cent of stories classified thus. In Sri Lanka, that percentage was even higher, at 58 per cent. Lee and Maslog were at pains to point out, however, that the classification of peace journalism is highly dependent on criteria that are of a non-interventionist nature, such as the avoidance of demonizing language or good-bad labels, a non-partisan approach and multiparty orientations. They note that these criteria are merely extensions of the objectivity credo and 'do not truly exemplify a strong contributory, proactive role by journalists to seek and offer creative solutions and to pave a way for peace and conflict resolution' (Lee & Maslog, 2005, p. 324). Further, the fact that Sri Lankan newspapers displayed a strong peace journalism orientation may have been affected by the peace negotiation between the government and the Tamil Tigers during the research timeframe (Lee, 2009, p. 268).

Lee and Maslog's (2005) study was followed by further examinations of war and peace journalism frames in the Iraq War. Here, Maslog et al. (2006) examined the reporting of the Iraq War in eight newspapers from India, Pakistan, Sri Lanka, Indonesia and the Philippines. This time, the coverage suggested a minor tendency towards peace journalism framing overall. And while non-Muslim countries India and Sri Lanka had a stronger war journalism framing, they were more supportive of the United States and its allies while newspapers from Muslim Pakistan and Indonesia displayed stronger support for Iraq. As in their previous study, Maslog et al. (2006) found that the international news wire services displayed a stronger tendency towards war journalism and were more supportive of the war and the United States and its allies.

Most recently, Kim et al. (2008) examined the dominance of war or peace journalism frames in Asian vernacular-language newspapers. They did so because the vernacular press is seen as playing a significant role in influencing public opinion and 'are more likely to be swayed by communal feelings to the extent of inciting violence with irresponsible reporting' (Kim et al., 2008, p. 254). Kim et al. (2009) examined the coverage of the Kashmir, Tamil Tiger and Maluku/Aceh conflicts in eight vernacular newspapers in India, Pakistan, Sri Lanka and Indonesia and, once again, found evidence that was in line with the previous studies which had been conducted on English-language newspapers. War journalism frames dominated in similar ways to the previous study of Asian conflicts; the most salient indicators of peace journalism were similar, and feature stories were more likely to be framed as peace journalism.

> While there is some demonstration of journalists' appreciation of the conflict by the inclusion of ordinary people and taking a non-partisan approach, the peace journalism frame did not receive adequate support in terms of journalists focusing on a conflict's causes and consequences, commonalities between warring groups, and the invisible effects of war. (Kim et al., 2009, p. 265)

In a review of their studies, Lee (2009) highlights this shortcoming in much of the conflict reporting the team investigated and argues that more needs to be done on the part of journalists to change their reporting practices.

> But until journalists covering war and conflict are willing to acknowledge and overcome their internal biases and external influences, rethink their over-reliance on objectivity and detachment, and break free of the professional shackles that detract from universal proto-norms of nonviolence and respect for human dignity, peace journalism will always remain a child of its time. (Lee, 2009, p. 270)

Recently, there have been other attempts at investigating empirically the salience of peace and war journalism frames around the world. In Central America, Gutiérrez (2005) has examined the coverage of the San Juan River conflict. The river runs along much of the border between Costa Rica and Nicaragua and was the site of a long-running dispute between the two countries. In 2002, however, the governments of Costa Rica and Nicaragua decided to resolve the conflict and worked towards cooperation. In order to examine how the press covered the conflict, Gutiérrez (2005) analysed two Costa Rican newspapers' reporting of the dispute in 1998, when conflict momentarily reignited, and in 2002, when the decision to cooperate had been made. She developed six variables to indicate pro-conflict coverage, and six variables for pro-cooperation coverage, which in their themes are somewhat similar to the 13 variables developed by Lee and Maslog (2005). Not surprisingly, Gutiérrez found that during 1998, when the dispute had reignited, pro-conflict coverage dominated the reporting. When the governments began cooperating, the frame also changed to include more pro-cooperation stories, but only so much as to achieve a balance with pro-conflict coverage. So, while the policy framework had changed to cooperation, the media coverage was not as quick to fully embrace this frame, leading Gutiérrez (2005, p. 1) to argue that 'the two newspapers (...) lag behind in favouring the policy that supports co-operation and peace. Thus, the two newspapers endorse media culture's preference for conflict, confrontation and drama'. Further, despite recognition of the area as a river basin, 64 per cent of which is on Nicaraguan territory and 36 per cent belonging to Costa Rica, Gutiérrez found the news media continued to see the area only through the narrow prism of a border river.

The Niger Delta in West Africa has also been the site of a long-running dispute, which has been ongoing since the formation of the modern Nigerian state in 1914. Originally grounded in various ethnic groups' displeasure at being amalgamated into the new Nigeria, in recent decades much of the conflict has centred on the subject of oil exploration and environmental damage in the region, with many now demanding compensation for the damage that countless oil spills had caused to the area. Over the past four decades, the Nigerian authorities have used force to resolve the conflict in the Niger Delta, but so far their efforts have proved unsuccessful. Obijiofor (2009) conducted a content analysis of four online newspapers and examined the presence of three frames in the reporting, which were based on Fawcett's (2002) earlier work in Northern Ireland. These included the 'law and order', 'injustice and defiance' and 'win-lose' frames. According to Fawcett (2002, p. 214), 'the law and order frame is used to portray one side of a conflict as a threat to "law and order", while the injustice and defiance frame focuses on constructing one party as being the victim of injustice and determined to stand up for its rights'. Fawcett's (2002, p. 215) definition of the win-lose frame refers to 'the underlying assumption (...) that one side would lose while the other would win'. Examining the newspaper coverage between January and May 2008, Obijiofor found that the Nigerian press constructed the conflict in the Niger Delta predominantly in a law and order frame, 'suggesting that the journalists were concerned about how the conflict might threaten law and order. This pattern also suggests that Nigerian journalists were more peace journalism oriented rather than war journalism focused' (Obijiofor, 2009, p. 199).

The above examples show that there are still formidable challenges for peace journalism in its quest to gain a foothold in mainstream media reporting, let alone for it to become the norm. Yet, the analyses conducted around the world have also identified some encouraging signs. Only longitudinal analyses will show whether peace journalism is actually making inroads into the mainstream media. Having examined the content of peace and conflict reporting, we will now turn to the question of whether peace journalism can actually make a difference in terms of audience perceptions. As we discussed previously, one criticism levelled at peace journalism proponents has been that they overestimate audience effects. We have already seen from the example in relation to *Studio Ijambo* in Burundi that there are some measurable effects which can come from peace-oriented media. In the following, we will look at further empirical support for this argument.

Effects of peace-oriented coverage

While there have been few empirical examinations of the effects of peace journalism, a team around German peace journalism advocate and social psychologist Wilhelm Kempf has built a research agenda around the issue in recent years. Kempf has been highly influential in the advocacy of peace journalism as the editor of one of the most important journals in the field, *Conflict & Communication Online*. We have already seen that Kempf has put forward his own two-stage process for de-escalation-oriented journalism to be successful.

In order to study how de-escalation oriented coverage – the first step in his strategy towards peace journalism – can impact on audiences, Kempf (2006) conducted a number of experimental studies to measure both the acceptance and impact of news, editorial and background in both war and post-war scenarios. He and his team designed a number of different versions of the same articles in order to account for a variety of escalation- and de-escalation-oriented coverage. This framework was applied in a number of experimental settings, ranging from assessments of regular newspaper readers in Germany and Austria to students at the University of Konstanz in Germany. Reader reactions to the various versions of articles were then measured using a variety of specifically-designed questionnaires. Perhaps somewhat surprisingly, and contrary to the opinions of some peace journalism opponents, Kempf found that 'de-escalation-oriented coverage is *no less* acceptable to audiences than traditional reporting. *Nor* is escalation-oriented coverage more suitable for the purpose of arousing interest, and (at least in the quality press) de-escalation-oriented coverage has the same potential to do so' (2006, p. 14;

italics in original). Kempf argues specifically that articles which offer more complexity, balanced reporting and cover structural issues have the potential to lessen the impact of escalation-prone factors like simplification, negativism and personalization.

Thus, reporting that follows many of the tenets of de-escalation-oriented, or even peace journalism appears to have a considerable chance of attracting readers. As one of the experiments reported in the study showed, 'the avoidance of simplification in favour of presenting sufficiently detailed and balanced information about a conflict context is a powerful method to counteract mental models which divide the world into "good" and "evil" and to immunise audiences against moral disengagement – even when the presentation of information is not completely unbiased' (Kempf, 2006, p. 15).

However, Kempf also points to some limitations of constructive conflict coverage. He is wary of the potential that such coverage may not be seen as a real alternative if it is perceived as too radical an undertaking.

> Explicit arguments rejecting the escalation-oriented bias of mainstream coverage may produce a boomerang effect, making articles seem partial, and de-escalation-oriented coverage has a better chance of evoking a positive response if it does not interpret the situation within a too radically reversed framework. (2006, p. 14)

This caution would also point to Hanitzsch's (2004) argument which related to the need for the journalistic structures to change along with individual journalists in order for peace journalism to be successful. This recognizes that if systemic structures accept alternative models which in turn are accepted by audiences, peace journalism has a chance to take hold.

Conclusion

The role the media play during conflict has received considerable attention from journalism and communication researchers. And with numerous conflicts around the world still flaring, this interest is unlikely to wane any time soon. In fact, the amount of research appears to be increasing rapidly. The discussion of the inflammatory effect that irresponsible news reporting can have has shown that it is desirable to try to develop a peace-oriented journalistic format, and as a result, the peace journalism option was born. It tries to instil better quality in journalism, and works against long-held beliefs and practices in order to achieve a better balance in reporting. Mostly, however, peace journalism is predicated on many of the assumptions about conventional journalism practices, which, for a variety of reasons – many of them related to the fact that news has to be sold to audiences – have apparently declined in quality in recent times.

At its most basic level, peace journalism aims to provide a forum for all participants in a conflict, tries to achieve win-win outcomes rather than win-lose situations, and focuses on common people and the consequences of a conflict. Kempf (2002) has introduced a necessary step for peace journalism to be possible, in that he developed a concept of de-escalation-oriented coverage, but the aims of both follow along similar lines. The evidence on the content and effectiveness of peace journalism as well as de-escalation coverage has shown that there is potential for such content to make a difference. Audiences do not appear to spurn peace-oriented coverage, and such coverage can have a positive influence on their attitudes. This is important at a time when ethnic conflicts in particular are ongoing all around the world and societies desire more peaceful solutions.

At the same time, however, peace journalism has its critics, who believe the idea is normative and not based on sufficient evidence. There certainly is a desperate need for more research in the field in order to present a stronger case for peace journalism to succeed. Critics have taken aim at peace journalism proponents' calls to do away with the notion of objectivity and their perceived lack of understanding of the journalistic system. In fact, even peace journalism advocates have acknowledged some of these critiques and called for renewed efforts to establish a better foundation. In particular, it appears crucial that peace journalism, if it wants to be successful, should target and engage with the structures of journalism. Research documented here has shown that many journalists favour peace-oriented coverage. However, they are aware that they cannot change, on the basis of their individual efforts, the structures in which they work. As Hanitzsch (2004, p. 491) has said, peace journalism 'cannot be induced from the "outside", but can only evolve within a "culture of peace". The need to target more systemic factors also emerges from other research that examined peace journalism (e.g. Bläsi, 2004; Ross, 2006) and will certainly need more attention in the future.

The value of peace journalism, or at least de-escalation-oriented coverage, needs to be made palatable for news organizations as a whole, and be formulated in ways that do not break from traditional journalism practices too radically so as not to drive away audiences. And, in keeping with the theme of much of this book, such attempts at change must be made from an approach that reflects local cultural values in order for peace journalism to make sense to audiences. There is no point attempting to induce a form of reporting that does not receive support from the population or the journalists. So, while peace journalism certainly appears to be making inroads and has the potential for a positive impact, much remains to be done in order for it to become an accepted approach in news reporting.

DISCUSSION QUESTIONS

1. Summarize the ways in which journalism has, over the past century, contributed to inflaming conflict.
2. Outline the philosophy behind peace journalism and, reviewing existing definitions, propose your own definition of the approach.
3. Discuss the main criticisms directed at peace journalism and highlight how they could be overcome by peace journalism advocates.
4. Summarize Lee and Maslog's (2005) categories for war and peace journalism frames, and apply those frames by examining local news coverage of a recent international conflict.
5. Discuss the potential for de-escalation oriented news coverage to lead to journalism that contributes to conflict resolution.

CHAPTER 8

Commercialization of journalism

Introduction

The rapid transformations engendered by new technologies and the hyper-mobility of capital create new forms of power imbalances in the global landscape. A number of scholars in the critical mass media tradition (e.g. Garnham, 1990) have examined processes of commercialization and inter-nationalization of media, and their consequences for journalistic practices. These authors explore the processes of commodification of the media and focus on, for example, how historically the commercial, popular press undermined the ability of citizens to act as rational actors engaged in public debate. Dahlgren and Sparks (1991), among others, assert that the commercial media fail to provide for informed citizenship. Despite claims and promises proffered by the private, commercially-oriented media that they do serve the information needs of consumers, research evidence suggests that commercial media provide an inadequate space for public debate (e.g. Calabrese & Ruth-Burke, 1992).

Growing commercialization of media is a sensitive topic within the media industry. Journalists know what it is but cannot do much about it. Editors detest it but are compelled to accommodate the trend. Media owners and managers do not see any problem with it because they believe the media is like any other business. Commercialization of media has raised concerns among professional journalists, editors and media audiences not because it is something new but because the practice is on the rise.

This chapter looks at how contemporary journalism across the world faces similar pressures in regard to technological and commercial changes that threaten to disrupt more traditional journalism practices. For example, in Eastern Europe, after the fall of communism, new democratic elites are becoming uncomfortable with investigative journalism since they see the media as serving commercial or state interests but not the interests of the public. As in most Western European countries, Slovenia, for example, has deregulated the print media and regulated broadcasting. Splichal (1995) argues this has serious implications for journalists, since they are discouraged from political reporting. The ways in which newsrooms are managed and the respect that journalists have for directors and editors suggest that journalists generally fail to serve as models of democratic beliefs and values. In Russia, as Becker (2004) writes, journalists are under enormous pressure from the government and commercial companies, which create distrust among Russian journalists and the public.

Against this background, this chapter maps some of the debates on commercialization of journalism and communication. The chapter also discusses the contests over journalism as one of the elements of the public sphere. Further, it conceptualizes the notions of the public sphere and citizenship and focuses on the role that the mass media play. The concept of the public sphere has been one of the most important aspects of contemporary discourse on democracy and journalism. There exists a view of the media as reinforcing a public sphere and public discourse as being reinvented as media discourse. The public sphere is important for journalism because it is within this sphere that citizens receive the necessary enlightenment concerning public issues (Habermas, 1989).

Public sphere debate

Jürgen Habermas's theory of the public sphere has been widely cited in studies that examine the contributions of media (old and new) to participatory communication and the sustenance of the public sphere in the electronic age. Habermas (1989) attributed the development of the public sphere to the growth of capitalism in Europe in the seventeenth and eighteenth centuries. In its simplest form, the public sphere refers to an informal gathering of members of the public for purposes of debating, exchanging and sharing information and ideas. An important element of the public sphere is that it can function without being influenced by the agency of government and other powerful institutions in society such as the church, political parties, educational institutions and market forces. According to Calhoun (1992, p. 3), 'The early bourgeois public spheres were composed of narrow segments of the European population, mainly educated, propertied men, and they conducted a discourse not only exclusive of others but prejudicial to the interests of those excluded.' However, in contemporary society, a public sphere which is acceptable for democratic development should reflect the 'quality of discourse and the quantity of participation' (Calhoun, 1992, p. 2).

Calhoun notes how the transformation of the public sphere was influenced by the open involvement of more participants. It was this openness, the inclusion of all classes of 'men', that ultimately led to the decline in the quality of discourse in the public sphere. Another factor that contributed to the decline of valuable discourse was the commercialization of media. In fact, Habermas (1989) explained that the same forces of capitalism that led to the development of the public sphere were also responsible for undermining it. In analysing the role of the public sphere in modern democracies, Dahlberg (2004, p. 2) states that 'a public sphere of informal citizen deliberation is central to strong democracy'. Chambers and Costain (2000, p. xi) concur. In their view, 'Healthy democracies need a healthy public sphere where citizens (and the elite) can exchange ideas, acquire knowledge and information, confront public problems, exercise public accountability, discuss policy options, challenge the powerful without fear of reprisals, and defend principles'. In the European Union, for example, the argument has been made that a link exists between public service broadcasting and effective operation of a public sphere. Specifically, public service broadcasting 'is seen to have a specific role in educating the masses, providing impartial information which will enlighten the viewer and encourage public debate, perhaps ultimately helping to foster a European public sphere' (Harrison & Woods, 2001, p. 480).

Thus, the mass media today remain the central ideological battlefield and they certainly perform an important role in providing a range of news and entertainment that fit with the imperatives of the existing socio-economic structure. Current trends characteristic of online journalism and blogging prove that the debates on the public sphere are still crucial to the idea of journalism (Pavlik, 1997; Jankowski & Van Selm, 2000). In rethinking the public sphere, this chapter argues that the media need to promote greater democratic participation at all levels of society (Calabrese & Ruth-Burke, 1992). As Splichal (1995) argues, the issue of democracy is still an open question for journalism. These issues are explored in depth in this chapter.

Commercialization of news: What is it?

To understand how commercialization has affected journalism, we must understand what it is. McManus (2009, p. 219) defines commercialization of news as 'any action intended to boost profit that interferes with a journalist's or news organization's best effort to maximize public understanding of those issues and events that shape the community they claim to serve'. When media organizations place greater emphasis on their business interests rather than on the public interests, quality journalism suffers (Picard, 2004, p. 55). The key reference term in these conceptualizations which should help us to engage critically with the analysis of commercialization of journalism is media's preference for profit over public service or good. So, when media abandon their traditional role of providing information that serves the public good in preference for profits, the quality of journalism is undermined. Basically, profit motives and public service goals of media are at odds. Yet the tensions between public service objectives of the media and the goal of making profit set out by media owners and managers have existed for more than a century. The source of the current public discontent is the rising trend of media commercialization. The emergence of new channels of communication spawned by technological transformations has led to growing competition in the media industry, as media organizations explore new ways of reaching larger audiences, in order to increase their share of advertising revenues and therefore maximize profits. In the search for new business models to survive the tough competitive environment, media organizations are leaning more towards production and presentation of cheap, low quality light entertainment to attract and sustain readers, viewers and listeners (McManus, 1995, 2009; Overholser, 1998; Getlin, 1999; Bogart, 2000, 2004; Hamilton, 2004).

Hamilton (2004) illustrates in his widely cited book how consumer demands underpin news content and news reporting practices. He argues that market forces which have encouraged the commodification of news and commercialization of media have made it possible and easier for audiences to determine what the quality and content of news can be. News, he contends, should be seen as a commodity rather than a reflection of social reality. Adopting a framework which defines news as an economic good, Hamilton states that:

> News content is clearly a product. Its creation and distribution depends on the market value attached to the attention and tastes of different individuals, the technologies affecting the cost of information generation and transmission, and the values pursued by journalists and media owners. (2004, pp. 7–8)

Thus, profit maximization achieved through advertising revenue is seen as the ultimate aim of business-oriented media. McManus (1992) explores this theme by examining the interlocking relationship between media audiences and advertisers, as well as the relationship between media organizations and advertisers. With reference to the latter, he notes that advertisers contribute to the bulk of the cost of news production in newspapers and in television. 'Advertisers contribute 70% to 90% of the gross revenues of newspapers and almost all the income that networks or stations derive from news programming' (McManus, 1992, p. 788).

To understand news as a commodity, we need to understand the relationship between media, audiences and advertisers. 'News consumers trade their attention, and perhaps per-copy fees, to news providers for information. The news providers then sell that attention to advertisers for rates based on the size and commercial value...of the audience whose attention is delivered. Although intangible, consumer attention is extremely valuable' (McManus, 1992, p. 788). In terms of economic value, media are attracted to advertisers who pay more in order to reach their target audience than consumers who pay virtually nothing to access news and current affairs contents, including entertainment. As McManus explained it, 'National advertisers are paying, not for news quality, but for audience "quality" and quantity. All else held equal, advertisers can be expected to support the program generating the largest audience likely to purchase the products offered, at the lowest cost per thousand viewers' (McManus, 1992, p. 789). Therefore, in the marketplace of news, media organizations compete also 'in a *public attention market*' (McManus, 1992, p. 790).

Commercialization of newspapers

McManus (2009, p. 220) states that commercialization of journalism is likely to have deleterious impacts on the industry owing to 'a temporary decline of journalism's expensive but vital watchdog function...' These practices are already occurring. Picard, for example, points out that:

> The primary content of newspapers today is commercialized news and features designed to appeal to broad audiences, to entertain, to be cost effective and to maintain readers whose attention can be sold to advertisers. The result is that stories that may offend are ignored in favour of those more acceptable and entertaining to larger numbers of readers, that stories that are costly to cover are downplayed or ignored and that stories creating financial risks are ignored. This leads to homogenization of newspaper content, to coverage of 'safe' issues and to a diminution of the range of opinion and ideas expressed. (2004, p. 61)

One criticism of media commercialization is that the conglomerates that own and manage the media are more interested in making profits rather than enhancing the quality of journalism. That is, media owners make demands on editors and journalists for profit maximization while quality is overlooked (Ureneck, 1999, p. 3). To maximize profits, media organizations are adopting cost-saving strategies that significantly hurt their news reporting business. The measures include reducing budgets for news coverage, reducing circulation and distribution costs, closing down overseas bureaus and cutting back on the number of journalists (Ureneck, 1999). The new business models that are being embraced by media organizations to achieve profit goals have significantly overturned the philosophical assumptions that underpinned the way print media organizations, for example, conducted business in the first half of the twentieth century. During that time, print media organizations upheld the principle that 'newspapers had to construct their business strategies around stronger and more credible journalism which, in turn, would drive demand, sales and profits' (Ureneck, 1999, p. 5). That is no longer the case, as success and performance are now measured by profit margins.

A worrying trend in the commercialized media environment is that, rather than increase news budgets, media organizations are increasing marketing budgets aimed at hiring and training more staff in the advertising and marketing departments, and in acquisition of new technologies to boost production and marketing strategies. Essentially, emphasis has shifted from strengthening the quality of staff in news departments to investing in advertising strategies that would increase sales, as well as higher profits and dividends for shareholders (Overholser, 1998; Ureneck, 1999). In the United States in the 1980s, the newspaper industry flourished as a result of two main factors, namely technological transformations that introduced more efficient production processes, and steady growth in revenue earned through advertising (Ureneck, 1999, p. 6). Although new technologies assisted newspapers to introduce more cost-effective means of production, introduction of technologies also resulted in layoffs of staff especially those employed in the production department (Ureneck, 1999, p. 6). However, the era of economic boom experienced by the American newspaper industry began to weaken in the 1990s as the newspapers faced stiffer competition from television and other news channels such as the Internet, as well as a weakened American economy (Overholser, 1998; Ureneck, 1999, p. 7). The end of the good times and the desire to maintain profits compelled the newspaper industry to halt staff recruitment, to reduce editorial budgets, to reduce news staff and to adopt other strategic measures that would ensure survival in the hostile business environment. One consequence of these measures was the shift towards production of less expensive but more entertainment-oriented contents. The changes in the business model of the American newspaper industry had a tremendous impact on the way newspapers re-positioned themselves in order to meet the challenges of the new environment.

Bogart (2000) describes how entertainment-driven media have lowered quality journalism and deprived citizens the information they require to make informed judgments about their society and welfare. According to Bogart (2000, p. 4), 'Entertainment increasingly overshadows information, blurring the difference between what is real and what is not, and thus weakening the public's will and capacity to confront the world and its problems.' Part of the public concern over commercialization of media is the adverse influence of entertainment on media content. Entertainment draws larger audiences which the media sell to advertisers in order to earn advertising revenue. In essence, media entertainment is produced with an eye on its impact on the audience; audience attention translates to high ratings and high audience ratings attract advertising revenue. McManus (2009, p. 227) notes that 'Since entertainment has historically generated a larger audience than information, and consumers are poor at evaluating news quality, there is economic pressure to generate newspapers, newscasts and Web sites that look newsy, but entertain as much or more than they inform.'

Media managers believe that entertainment offers audiences what they want. However, entertainment, particularly superficial forms of entertainment, often make little contribution to participatory democracy. When citizens are deprived of useful information about events in their society, they are unable to contribute to civic deliberations or to participate in the political process. Essentially, poor quality information is not seen to contribute to the political process. Bogart (1995, p. 4) argues against entertainment-oriented media on the basis that entertainment often distorts social reality. However, other scholars believe that media entertainment has its value. Hartley (2000), for example, argues that media entertainment which focuses on lifestyle and other softer contents has salutary impacts on media audiences in terms of helping them to ease the boredom that ensues from overexposure to hard news diets served by traditional media. Hartley believes that such media contents are 'the ones who extend the reach of media, who teach audiences the pleasures of staying tuned, who popularize knowledge' (2000, p. 40).

Focusing editors' attention on revenue-generating strategies seriously undermines the public service mission of newspapers. The transition from public service orientation of media to market-driven contents shows that newspapers have shifted from providing a service to local communities and exposing corruption and injustice in government to become a new vehicle for making money. Making money and surviving in the new competitive environment have therefore become the key concerns of commercial media. Even with the new business model in place, newspapers have not experienced an easy time. Thus, the:

> proliferation of alternative sources for news and information on such outlets as the Internet, the convenience and immediacy of television and radio, the expansion of what constitutes a broadening definition of "journalism" to include infotainment – from Oprah to Rush Limbaugh to "Hard Copy" to Matt Drudge – battered the newspaper industry. (Ureneck, 1999, p. 13)

Overholser (1998) notes that, in the new business climate in which American newspapers operate, 'Declining readership compels editors to be marketers. Corporatization compels them to be entrepreneurs' (1998, p. 50). As evidence of the growing corporatization of the American newspaper industry, Overholser observes that of the 1500 daily newspapers as at 1998, approximately 300 were independently owned. This compares to the figure of 1300 as at 1940. These figures are already dated as they relate to the situation 12 years ago and beyond. However, ownership of more newspapers by fewer companies implies growing demands for profits on investment. As profits become the primary objective of news organizations, the quality of journalism suffers. The new business model requires media organizations to create products that would generate profits. Editors sit at the receiving end of the new challenges. They wonder how they could improve the quality of news and achieve more profits for their organizations with fewer resources at their disposal. As a former editor who experienced the consequences of market-driven media, Overholser (1998) argues that over-commercialization of news undervalues journalism.

Commercial pressures on the media

Zurawik and Stoehr (1993, p. 27) identify two kinds of pressures that are facing television news. One source of pressure comes in the form of cost-cutting which is imposed on editors through reduction in staff, hiring of inexperienced and inexpensive staff, closure of news bureaus and business takeovers. Cost-saving affects the television industry negatively. It compels television networks to sack experienced journalists and producers (who cost a lot of money to retain), and to hire rookie reporters and producers who cost little. The second source of pressure is competition between news and entertainment programmes that are broadcast during prime time. This conceals the line between news and entertainment. When hard news competes with light entertainment, the victim is 'depth and quality' of news which is forfeited in preference for longer hours of light entertainment programmes (Kovach, 1999, p. 2). The shrinking of television news audience and the trend towards entertainment-driven programming have occurred because the television industry chose to make news more entertaining in order to contain stiff competition from other forms of media such as cable television and the Internet. Bogart (2000, p. 175) notes how the pursuit of commercial imperatives has compelled television directors and producers to 'conform to the rules of show business. It gives us a vivid first-hand view of great events, but that view is often fragmentary and distorted'. Getlin (1999, p. 68) draws on Neal Gabler's work (*Life, The Movie: How Entertainment Conquered Reality*) to argue that entertainment-driven journalism has become popular because of our appetite for 'amusement'. He notes that 'the very structure of all-news cable channels like Fox, MSNBC, and CNN requires a steady diet of talk, gossip and punditry – news as entertainment – to fill a 24-hour news hole' (Getlin, 1999, p. 68). This raises the question: should we blame new technologies or journalists who use the technologies to entertain audiences?

The influence that advertising is having on the media's obligation to serve society is a key concern over media commercialization. More than five decades ago, Peterson (1956, p. 79) noted the pervasive influence of advertising on the American media: 'As advertising became increasingly important to newspapers, it was viewed as a sinister force which tainted the news columns and caused editors to suppress material unfavourable to big business.' In his book entitled *Commercial Culture: The Media System and the Public Interest*, Bogart (1995) identifies the subliminal ways through which advertising influences the choices we make, the life we live and the products we consume.

> Advertisements tell us to consume, and to consume now, right away. They represent an enormous affirmation of the importance and value of the material comforts that are available in a wealthy industrial society. They teach us to take pride in our outer appearance, in the way we present ourselves to others. They reinforce traditional conventions and values, in contrast with the moral anarchy that suffuses the surrounding news and entertainment. They represent a continuing advocacy for hedonism, for making our lives easier, more enjoyable. They urge us on to accumulate more goods and new experiences, and reassure us that these are well within our reach. They tantalize us with visions of pleasures beyond our capacities to taste and often beyond our ability to afford. (1995, p. 74)

More competition, higher costs of producing news, current affairs and entertainment programmes and decline in ratings have all added to the pressure on the television industry to perform, to attract more advertising revenue and to maximize profits through production of low-cost entertainment programmes that appeal to a mass audience. In the new media environment, particularly in the competitive ethos of the television industry, there is a trend towards the production of news and entertainment programmes that appeal to a mass audience. Audience appeal translates to higher ratings which invariably attract advertising revenue. Gunther (1999, p. 21) outlines three factors that influenced the development of the market-driven model of television programming. The first was the requirement to produce more entertainment programmes directed at a mass audience. This implied a lowering of emphasis on hard news. The second was the requirement to produce more hours of programming. Logically, more programmes would ultimately yield greater returns on investment. That is, more programmes attract more audiences who attract advertising revenue and therefore profits. The third factor was the requirement to reduce costs through closure of local and overseas news posts, sacking of staff and overall control over spending.

There are of course dangers associated with cost-saving measures adopted by the television industry. Staff layoffs, shutting down of overseas and national bureaus and pooling resources to share news are definitely designed to cut costs but they have adverse consequences on the media industry. They result in poor quality of news such as reporting that lacks depth, contextual background and analytic rigour. Gunther concludes that in the ruthless business environment in which the media now operate, it is valid to ask 'whether the core requirements necessary to provide solid journalism – time to pursue stories and develop sources, a recognition that not all coverage is going to produce immediate profit, an ability to focus on important topics that won't bring high ratings but can build viewer trust – can be sustained' (1999, p. 32). Hickey (1998, p. 29) has documented the serious problems that confront American journalism in the era of commercialization and how the problems have compromised journalists' commitment to professionalism. These include increasing competition, decline in public confidence in news media, the trend towards tabloidization such as emphasis by media on "lifestyle" stories such as celebrity gossips and scandals, emphasis on profit maximization, collaboration between editors and advertisers and other forces in the market, as well as declining numbers of newspaper and television news audiences. Lehrer (1999) echoes these worries, arguing that commercialization of journalism has undermined the quality of news and therefore the credibility of journalists and media organizations. In his view, the problems confronting journalism in the era of increasing competition and greater demands for profit have generated confusion over the differences and similarities between straight news reporting style and reporters who position themselves as expert commentators, including the confusion over reporters who place more emphasis on their personal opinions and those who report across multiple media platforms.

Commercialization has engendered the conflict between the pursuit of shareholder interests and the public interest goal of media. In the highly competitive environment in which media operate, it is the shareholder interests that tend to dictate editorial content and direction. Commercialization of media has therefore transformed the model on which media business was based for many decades. This has seen the shift in emphasis from a media business that targeted small audiences that constitute active members of the community (with an eye on earning modest revenues) to the current model which seeks to reach large audiences as a strategy to bolster large circulation (sales) and large advertising revenue (Picard, 2004). Beyond market forces, McChesney (2004, cited in McManus, 2009, p. 224) believes that government policies have contributed significantly to the emergence of media that take advantage of audience emotions and weaknesses. However, he recommends the development of new policies that would lead to growth of media that support deliberative democracy.

Concerns about commercialization of media

Traditionally, public concerns about media commercialization had their origins in the history of the development of the press in the United States and the United Kingdom. Hallin (2000, p. 218), for example, points out that American media operations were defined by commercial objectives right from the era of the penny press, with the exception of the 'small institution of public broadcasting created in 1967'. Specifically, the dangers inherent in media commercialization informed the development of the social responsibility theory of the press (Peterson, 1956, pp. 73–103). The social responsibility theory thus served as a natural response to growing criticisms of the American media, not least of which were the growing concentration of media ownership and the 'unholy' alliance between media owners and business organizations. Bogart canvasses four reasons why commercialization of media should be reversed: media are preoccupied with commercialism; media contents are designed to serve the interests of advertisers rather than the needs of media consumers; media organizations focus on scandals, sensational and vulgar news in order to capture a larger share of the audience; and media sensation tends as much to falsify social reality as it distracts public attention from problems that deserve public attention (Bogart, 1995, p. 9).

Public concerns about commercialization of media have reinforced the debate over the role of the media in modern society. Are the media set up to serve public interests (public service orientation) or to serve the interests of the owners (profit-driven, market motive)? Croteau and Hoynes (2006) have wondered which of these two underlying media objectives – public service and profit maximization – should serve as a more accurate yardstick for measuring media performance. These two conflicting objectives dominate discussion about the role of the media in democratic societies. Questions about the role of the media in society underline the significant functions the media perform in democratic societies. The media are regarded as an important institution in democratic societies not only because they furnish the citizens with information necessary for achieving their goals in life (e.g. information, education and entertainment) but also because they help to promote and support active participation of citizens in the democratic process (Schultz, 1994a, p. 16).

Historically, making money was not the original intent of the founding fathers of the media (Schultz, 1994a, p. 16). Some scholars agree. For example, McManus (1995, p. 308) believes that, while television developed as an entertainment-driven medium and therefore fits the market model of media, newspapers were, right from their origins, regarded as purveyors of news. This explains why early newspapers were regarded as a channel of public information – a medium designed to inform and educate the public (Williams, 1969). However, the extent to which newspapers still adhere to their original mission in the era of commercialization remains contested. Schultz (1994a) notes that the Australian public has grown increasingly sceptical about the media's ability to meet their public service obligations. This is because, in the past couple of decades, 'the media in Australia, as in much of the world, have undergone fundamental changes and become more enmeshed in business' (Schultz, 1994a, p. 18). Mwangi (2007) found a similar trend of commercialization even in community newspapers in South Africa. Her study found that 'the content in the conglomerate-owned community newspapers has a market-driven orientation. The newspapers have allocated huge percentages of their space to advertising and in the remaining newshole, the volume of consequential news was relatively low' (2007, p. 75). This is not particularly surprising because the community newspapers are distributed free and are therefore dependent on advertising to generate revenues. In this context, Mwangi concluded that:

> the proliferation of community newspapers does not necessarily mean that the media is fulfilling its role of keeping the readers informed, or being a public platform where the citizens can deliberate on issues affecting their community and

be empowered to make critical civic decisions or understand their environment. (2007, p. 78)

Still in Africa, Oso (1991) notes that the commercialization of the Nigerian press preceded the country's independence in 1960. 'The capitalization of the Nigerian press and its subsequent commercialization started with the arrival of the *Daily Times* in 1926. The paper was established by European financial interests... in alliance with some wealthy Nigerians' (Oso, 1991, p. 43).

Market and public service models of media

The conflict between market-driven journalism and public service obligations of the media has dominated academic debate and research investigations for many decades. A number of authors have identified the core issues (see McManus, 1992, 2009; Schultz, 1994a,b; Hallin, 2000; Hamilton, 2004; Croteau & Hoynes, 2006). The tension between business-oriented media and public service media was clearly articulated by McManus (1992, p. 800) thus: 'The central purpose of journalism is to maximize public understanding. There is potential for conflict between such a norm and the business goal of maximizing benefit for investors ...' Croteau and Hoynes (2006) identify the elements that distinguish the market model of media from the public service form of media. In the market model of media, the emphasis is on capturing audiences to be sold to advertisers. 'The market model of media is based on the ability of a network to deliver audiences to... advertisers. The more people watching a programme, the higher the price the networks can charge for ad time. Lost audiences mean lost profits' (Croteau & Hoynes, 2006, p. 8). In this media model, journalists are perceived as a part of business enterprises whose primary objective is to make money. McManus (1995) notes four related models of market-driven journalism that underpin commercialization of news.

> ... at the heart of commercial news production lie four markets: In the first and most familiar, readers and viewers trade their attention, and perhaps a subscription or per copy fee, to media firms in exchange for information. In the second, sources trade their information – the raw material of news – to reporters for the attention inclusion in the news may bring them, their ideas, or both. In the third, advertisers pay money in return for attention of potential customers. Finally, owners-investors contribute capital and expect to share in profits and growth in the value of stock. (1995, p. 305)

Merits of market-driven media

The market model of media offers a useful framework for analysis of media because it enables us to understand not only the roles that commercial media play in democratic societies but it also expands our knowledge of the business rationales (or marketing objectives) that inform the operations of media in the marketplace (Croteau & Hoynes, 2006, p. 16). Despite its drawbacks, some scholars believe there are some redeeming features of the market-driven media (Meyer, 1987; McManus, 1995). According to Meyer (1987), the market model of media is desirable because it lessens the potential for unnecessary government censorship of the media as well as official use of the media for government propaganda. Another important element of the market model of media is that it leans on advertisers as a primary source of revenue and also as a means to reduce the cost of news that could have been passed on to consumers. This model of media is also regarded as useful because it can respond to consumer needs or it can lose its relevance and energy and disappear (Meyer, 1987). Beyond these advantages, the market model of media is also valuable because: it facilitates our understanding of the market forces that underpin the way news is reported and produced (e.g. news values, professional conventions/norms that guide news selection decisions, etc.); the model challenges age-old assumptions that 'the news content that best serves the market also serves the public best' (McManus, 1995, p. 332); the model challenges neo-Marxist theories of the media which claim that media represent the ideological state apparatuses that serve the interests of the elite and the bourgeoisie; and the model questions the fundamental principles that guide journalism education and training and suggests that journalism educators should pay significant attention to educating the public about how to identify and select quality news rather than concentrate on the training of journalism students on how to improve professional news selection and reporting practices (McManus, 1995, p. 332).

Croteau and Hoynes (2006, p. 18) highlight other merits of the market model of media such as profit motives driving commercial media to seek ways of lowering their operating costs by engaging in more efficient ways of doing business in the market. Market-driven media also operate on the basis that they are in business to provide their audiences with what they want. Thus, media are seen as being 'responsive to what people want' (Croteau & Hoynes, 2006, p. 18). Other merits of the market model of business include promotion of flexibility and the development of new products, services and ideas (Croteau & Hoynes, 2006, p. 18). Hallin (2000) also argues that the market model of media is not all that bad because it serves the interests of a mass audience rather than the good of a narrow audience. He points out that the culture of 'hard news' which dominated media contents for a long time privileged the interests of the political and economic elite because they focused on political events in Washington, the official seat of the government of the United States (2000, p. 230). Journalists who emphasized 'hard news' were seen to be biased because the news they projected mirrored the profile of the journalists themselves – their race, socio-economic class and gender (Hallin, 2000, p. 230). Despite his qualified support for commercialized media, Hallin believes there are serious drawbacks of media commercialization. Nevertheless, Hanusch (2010b) believes that entertainment-driven genres, such as travel journalism, can provide benefits to audiences that news may not be able to.

Drawbacks of the market model of media

Despite the enduring features of the market model of media which account for its survival and its attraction to media owners, managers, shareholders and audiences, the philosophical foundation of this model of media is seriously flawed. Hallin (2000) believes that diversification of media contents spawned by commercialization has also led to tabloidization of news and current affairs programmes, as well as other forms of entertainment. Trivialization of media contents has also affected the news agenda, such as the allocation of fewer resources to international news reporting, closure of overseas bureaus and the practice of flying journalists in and out of foreign locations ('parachute' journalism) to report on overseas events. Additionally, profit cannot serve as the only barometer for assessing the usefulness of media. Media are expected to serve certain essential functions in society. They are required to contribute to the development of society, to encourage and support civic deliberations and active citizen participation in society and to strengthen the democratic process. Emphasis on profits diverts attention from the public service obligations of the media. When media owners and managers argue that the media is no different from any other business, they overlook the civic responsibilities of media that are not measured in terms of profits and dividends distributed to shareholders. So, commercial media that record huge profits or returns on investments are not necessarily the media that contribute most to a healthy democracy.

Croteau and Hoynes also argue that markets are undemocratic because they operate on the basis that people who are endowed with more financial resources should enjoy more power and recognition, hence the rich get richer and the poor become poorer (2006, p. 23). Furthermore, markets do not make moral judgments about what is good and what is bad in the buying and selling of goods and services. As Croteau and Hoynes (2006) argue, markets are not designed to meet the democratic needs of society essentially because the forces that drive markets are at odds with the core principles of democracy. Market forces seek to satisfy consumer needs, regardless of whether the products (e.g. shocking scandals and sensational news reports) undermine the moral health of society. For example, if there is a market for indecent and pornographic material, market forces will aim to provide those services as long as they are permitted within the laws of society (Croteau & Hoynes, 2006, p. 25). Market forces may encourage the production of goods targeted at a small group of consumers owing to their financial status. This practice may lead to denial of access to a greater number of people. Markets tend to target consumers who have the resources to buy products that will facilitate profit maximization. Thus, markets do not seek to correct existing social and economic inequalities (Croteau & Hoynes, 2006, pp. 25–6).

The public service model of media

The philosophical objectives of public service-oriented media differ markedly from the central motives that drive the market model of media. Public service media are assumed to engage in the production and delivery of quality material that helps to build informed citizens. Public service media provide information which helps to develop healthy dialogue among citizens. In the public service model of media, news coverage is seen as a part of the educational and public service obligations of the media. In this type of media:

> Journalists, commentators, and analysts speak to you as a citizen. They invite you to learn about the public issues that face society and perhaps improve your community by acting on this knowledge – in the voting booth, in your community, and beyond. This model of media is based not on ratings and profits but on the ability to serve the impossible-to-quantify 'public interest'. (Croteau & Hoynes, 2006, p. 8)

The core public service obligations of the media underline the argument that media business cannot be regarded as just another business. In many democratic societies, the media enjoy certain legal protections and privileges which are not accorded to other businesses. In the United States, for example, the First Amendment is widely cited as evidence of the protection the media enjoys. The First Amendment to the Constitution of the United States says: 'Congress shall make no law...abridging the freedom of speech, or of the press' (cited in Croteau & Hoynes, 2006, p. 31). In a poignant critique of the book – *Four Theories of the Press* – Nerone identified the key contradictions that undermine commercial press in capitalist societies:

> The press cannot logically be free from capital because it is capital in form and use...the press driven by capital cannot be expected to provide a thorough critique of the economic system or to offer alternatives because it is not 'free from control or domination' by capital. Naturally, from its very beginning, the capital-driven press did not have as its aim to be a watchdog over the system of which it is a part. Watchdogs don't bite their owners. (1995, p. 26)

This raises the moral question whether, for example, it is possible for an editor of a commercial newspaper to openly criticize the business interests of their publisher or employer. Realistically, editors are not appointed by media owners and managers to serve as critical watchdogs over the business interests of their employers. The conflicting roles of media – providing a service to the public and focusing on profit goals – constitute a serious threat to professional and ethical journalism practice. Professional journalists and editors are worried about the dual roles which they are expected to play – whether they should concentrate on the editorial side of their job or on the commercial interests of their organization. In Australia, Schultz (1994a, p. 29) reports how a survey of business journalists revealed such a dilemma. She said the study showed that 'although the majority were strongly committed to a separation between editorial and commercial interests, one-third said they "would not pursue a story that was potentially damaging to my employer's commercial interests as actively as a story about an unrelated company"'. Essentially, it is very difficult for journalists to satisfy two masters who are pursuing conflicting objectives. One way through which journalists have tried to resolve this tension is through reference to their professional values as an organizing framework for professional practice. For example, whenever journalists refer to professionalism in journalism, they allude to the canons of the industry such as truthfulness, fairness, objectivity, accuracy and balance in reporting. The extent to which these values are reflected in news reported by journalists is highly contested. Unfortunately, professional values which journalists regularly refer to as defensive shields also have their origins in commercialism (Schultz, 1994b, p. 43).

Hallin (2000, p. 220) provides evidence which suggests that professionalization of journalism has not eliminated the tensions between the quest for truth and the pressure to aim for profit in the interests of media owners and shareholders. One such conflict concerns the foggy line between the business interests of media owners and journalists' autonomy. As Hallin (2000, p. 221) stated: 'the increasingly blurred line between news and entertainment, and the journalists' growing uncertainty about their voice and standpoint ... clearly fit the description of postmodern culture.' Two factors have accounted for this. The transformation in the economics of the media which has tilted the balance between journalists' obligation to professional values and the pursuit of the business mission of their news organizations has been identified as one factor (Hallin, 2000, p. 221). The second factor has to do with political and cultural modifications which have weakened the circumstances that previously promoted professional journalism practice. In recognition of the danger that trivialization and commercialization of media content might have on the industry and on the larger society, Hallin (2000) states that:

> If we are to avoid the collapse of news media with some sense of public service, two things will probably have to happen. First, journalism will have to change. The 'high modernist' conception of professionalism is clearly no longer viable and needs to be rethought in important ways. For one thing, ... journalists will probably have to shift from conceiving of themselves as, in effect, a representative or stand-in for a unitary but inactive public, to a role of facilitating and publicizing public dialogue. Second, we will need a new public debate over the question asked more than 50 years ago by the Commission on the Freedom of the Press: what can be done, through public policy or the structuring of media institutions, to 'free the press from the influences which now prevent it from supplying the communication of news and ideas needed by the kind of society we have and the kind of society we desire'. (pp. 234–5)

Theories of market-driven journalism

Two 'theories' have been proposed to explain market-oriented journalism. They are the 'readership theory' and the 'stockholder theory' (Hallin, 2000, p. 222). The readership theory argues that newspaper organizations are experiencing serious declines in readership. It is in response to this development that newspaper organizations have adopted new strategies not only to retain the loyalty of their existing readers but also to attract the attention of more readers and to provide them with what they want. The stockholder theory states that public listing of newspapers in the stock market has whittled down their public service obligation. Although former newspaper proprietors in the United States were interested in the profit margins of their business, they were generally satisfied with the low returns on investment. More fundamentally, they were also interested in the public rating of their newspapers (Hallin, 2000, p. 222). The stockholder theory blames the decline in readership and circulation on newspaper organizations because of their obsession with profit which invariably has undermined quality. In some situations, newspapers opted to respond to the demands of a lesser but more prosperous audience members because the newspapers could afford to charge higher advertising rates (Hallin, 2000, p. 223). All these meant that the interests of the larger audience were ignored. This had a double impact on newspapers: circulation and readership declined significantly. Hallin also explained that concentrated ownership which had adverse impact on diverse media channels favoured newspaper owners. They enjoyed high profits generated through their monopoly position in the market. High profits, however, came at a cost – decline in circulation (2000, p. 223).

Newspaper readership and circulation: Declining or rising

Within the media industry and academic community, there is a serious debate about whether newspaper readership is declining or increasing. For example, while statistics on declining newspaper readership abound, there is equally compelling evidence to show that newspaper readership is rising, especially in developing societies in Africa (e.g. South Africa and Nigeria), Asia (India) and some parts of Latin America and Europe. First, we examine the evidence that suggests newspaper readership is declining. It will be followed by proof that newspaper readership is in fact rising in many parts of the world. Drawing on a study conducted by the Newspaper Association of America and the American Society of Newspaper Editors, *The Economist* (1999) reports that, as at 1977, 67 per cent of the American audience read daily newspapers frequently, compared to the 51 per cent that did so 20 years later in 1997. Another study confirms the decline in newspaper readership in the United States. The percentage of adult newspaper readers in the United States declined from 73 per cent in 1967 to 51 per cent in 1991 (Hallin, 2000, p. 222). The decline in newspaper readership has been attributed to technological changes and increasing competition among media for people's time. According to *The Economist* (1999), 'technology and economics have produced more and more ways of occupying people's leisure hours: more television channels, more magazines, more theme parks, and now video games, chatrooms and all the other delights of the digital age'.

Decline in newspaper readership is particularly pronounced in the United States. A useful insight into this trend has come from the demographics of newspaper readers in the United States and some parts of Western Europe: the younger generation is abandoning traditional media and using newer media such as the Internet to satisfy their news needs (see Flanagin & Metzger, 2001; Lauf, 2001; Coleman & McCombs, 2007). Specifically, in his study of newspaper readership in nine European countries, Lauf (2001) examined the trend over a period of 18 years (between 1980 and 1998) and concluded that newspaper readership is on the decline among younger readers across Europe (especially France, Denmark, Luxembourg and the UK), with below average declines recorded in the Netherlands and Italy. It was only in Germany that readership rose marginally during the 18-year period. However, rather than technology driving that change, age was found to be the strongest determinant of daily newspaper reading. In fact, Lauf (2001, p. 241) argued that, 'it does not matter what the newspaper market provides them with primarily – tabloids, prestige press or regional newspapers – young people do not read daily about politics anyway'. The results should be qualified because the study was concerned with newspaper readership for political news, not for general news. Other problems include: the data were collected about 12 years ago; the data predate the mass spread of the Internet, in that by 1998 Internet usage was not really as widespread as it is now; and the study only examined the trend in Europe. A more recent study of individual and national differences in newspaper readers in Europe (Elvestad & Blekesaune, 2008, p. 442) reported that 'gender, age, education and household income' accounted for differences in newspaper reading although the effect differed across countries. Nevertheless, based on evidence reviewed in this section, the trend of newspaper readership is obviously downward in Europe and North America, although the decline is slower in Europe but much more pronounced in the United States. Against this background, more global evidence is warranted to facilitate a compelling conclusion.

Data by the World Association of Newspapers (WAN) show a different picture, identifying an upward trend in newspaper circulation and readership in other continents (except Oceania). For example, according to WAN (2009):

- Global newspaper circulation increased +1.3 percent in 2008, to almost 540 million daily sales, and was up +8.8 percent over five years. When free dailies are added, circulation rose +1.62 percent in 2008 and +13 percent over five years. Europe is the hotbed for free newspaper development −23 percent of daily newspapers in Europe were free in 2008.
- Newspaper circulation increased +6.9 percent in Africa last year, +1.8 percent in South America, and +2.9 percent in Asia. It decreased −3.7 percent

in North America, −2.5 percent in Australia and Oceania, and −1.8 percent in Europe. But in many mature markets where circulation is declining, newspaper reach remains high – many European countries continue to reach over 70 percent of the adult population with paid newspapers alone. In Japan, it's 91 percent. In North America, it's 62 percent.

- Circulation gains are not only occurring in the emerging markets of China and India; 38 percent of countries reported gains in 2008, and 58 percent saw circulation increase over five years. (http://www.wan-press.org/article18148.html)

Franklin (2008) offers equally strong evidence to counter arguments suggesting the imminent death of newspapers. Although figures show differences in different regions, his verdict is that 'the global newspaper business is booming' (Franklin, 2008, p. 632). Similarly, Friedlander (2009) argues that in India, 'Hindi newspaper sales and readership have grown immensely since 1991. Readership had increased from 29 per thousand in 1991 to 69 per thousand in 2001 and has continued to grow up to the present day'. So, while there is research evidence suggesting a decline in newspaper readership (Lauf, 2001; Flanagin & Metzger, 2001; Coleman & McCombs, 2007), data produced by WAN (2009), Franklin (2008) and Friedlander (2009) show quite clearly an upward trend in readership in many parts of the world. More significantly, data by WAN show that the reported decline in readership is not uniform. For example, where declines have been recorded at all, they have occurred principally in the United States, Europe and Oceania.

Conclusion

Across the world, public discontent is rising over the increasing trend towards commercialization of journalism. Growing concerns about commercialization of journalism reflect public unease over declining quality of journalism. This has reinforced the debate over the role of the media in modern society. Are the media set up to serve public interests (public service orientation) or to serve the interests of the owners (profit-driven, market motive)? Commercial interests are conceived of as fundamentally at odds with the democratic, public interest model of journalism. Questions about the role of the media in society underline the significant roles the media perform in democratic societies. The media are regarded as an important institution in democratic societies not only because they furnish the citizens with information necessary for achieving their goals in life but also because they help to promote and support citizen deliberation (Schultz, 1994a, p. 16). One consequence of commercialization of journalism is increasing scepticism among media consumers about the public service role of media. In the larger society, there is a prevailing view that the quest for high ratings and high circulation figures by the media is fuelling commercialization of journalism in modern democratic societies.

A major criticism of commercialization of media is the pervasive influence of market forces on media contents. These influences are reflected in profit maximization; the production of low quality entertainment material; less emphasis on expensive public journalism projects and investigative report- ing that tend to antagonize advertisers and other sources of revenue; editors being compelled to serve as marketing managers, to cut editorial budgets and to freeze hiring of news staff, to close foreign bureaus and to hire less experienced journalists who cost less – all in the attempt to cut costs and to increase profits. Croteau and Hoynes (2006, p. 9) describe the phenomenon thus: 'Bottom-line pressure usually steers media content away from serious substance that challenges people, to light entertainment that is familiar and comforting. Although such programming may be profitable, it usually makes little contribution to a more vibrant civic culture.' This represents a key con- cern about growing commercialism in journalism.

The emergence of new channels of communication spawned by technologi- cal changes has led to increasing competition in the media industry, as media organizations explore new ways of reaching larger audiences in order to increase their share of advertising revenues and to boost profits. New business models introduced by media organizations to survive the tough competitive environ- ment have also forced media companies to lean towards production and pres- entation of poor quality light entertainment intended to attract and sustain readers, viewers and listeners. Media commercialization is also influenced by the close and symbiotic relationship between advertisers and media organizations. Advertisers provide commercial media with the revenue they require while the media sell audiences to advertisers who need to reach their target audience so they can market their products. It is this relationship between the media, adver- tisers and the audience that defines public conception of news as a commodity. There is therefore the concern that commercialization of news undermines quality journalism. Despite criticisms directed at commercialization of media, one view holds that there is value in market-driven media. Essentially, this view argues that market model of media facilitates an understanding of why and how commercial media do business in democratic societies.

One effect of growing commercialization of media is the media's loss of their watchdog function in democratic societies. As Picard (2004, p. 61) points out in regard to newspapers, 'The result is that stories that may offend are ignored in favour of those more acceptable and entertaining to larger numbers of readers, that stories that are costly to cover are downplayed or ignored and that stories creating financial risks are ignored.' Additionally, the pursuit of market goals has had negative consequences for media in various ways, including the adoption of cost-saving strategies that significantly hurt quality news reporting objectives. As Ureneck (1999) described it, rather than strengthen the quality of journalists in news departments, media organizations are placing greater emphasis on investment in advertising strategies that boost sales and higher profits for owners and shareholders.

To overcome the dangers that commercialization of journalism poses to the industry, it is perhaps fitting that we draw on Hallin (2000) to conclude as follows: journalists and media owners need to rethink notions of professionalism and public service goals of media which have proved inadequate to address the pervasive and diluting influence of market forces on quality journalism. Additionally, public debate needs to be reinvigorated to address how to overcome those factors that undermine the role of the media as channels of information and citizen deliberation, keeping in mind, as Dahlberg (2004, p. 2) states, that 'a public sphere of informal citizen deliberation is central to strong democracy'.

DISCUSSION QUESTIONS

1. Outline and discuss three reasons why the public sphere is deemed to be important for journalism.
2. Discuss the market and public service models of media and analyse the strengths and weaknesses of each model.
3. Analyse the major arguments for and against growing commercialization of media. Identify instances of commercialization of the media in your country.
4. How does the relationship between the media, audiences and advertisers influence public perceptions of news?
5. Researchers are divided over whether newspaper readership and circulation is rising or declining. Drawing on evidence, identify the key trends across the world and compare them to the situation in your own country.

CHAPTER 9

Impact of new technologies

Introduction

This chapter examines systematically the impact that new technologies are having on journalistic practices across cultures. It explores how technological convergence has affected journalism, including the development of multiple platforms of news delivery and consumption, the emergence of alternative forms of journalism such as participatory journalism (i.e. the increasing involvement of ordinary citizens in news reporting and production processes), multiple tasks performed by journalists, the growing interaction between journalists and news consumers, as well as ethical issues spawned by technological changes. The chapter also looks at how new technologies have transformed journalism practices around the world.

The introduction of new technologies in many newsrooms has not been without well-founded fears and some form of resistance. Henningham (1995, p. 226) reports that the introduction of new technologies in Australian newsrooms generated concerns about how the technologies would affect the health of journalists as a result of sustained use of video display terminals (VDTs). Consequently, 'As a result of industrial lobbying by the journalists' union, free eye checks for journalists were introduced, as well as ergonomically designed furniture and agreed rest breaks'. Historically, journalists have never been known to embrace new technologies without some form of objection or resistance (Henningham, 1995; Deuze, 2008). In fact, Deuze (2008, p. 8) notes that 'journalists tend to be cautious and sceptical towards changes in the institutional and organizational arrangements of their work, as lessons learnt in the past suggest that such changes tend to go hand in hand with downsizing, lay-offs, and having to do more with less staff, budget, and resources'. However, both Henningham (1995) and Deuze (2008) acknowledge that journalists normally accept new technologies that are introduced into their work practices if they perceive the technologies to improve efficiency in their work routines, if the technologies help to ease their workload and if the technologies minimize errors in their work.

The impact of new technologies on journalism practices has received extensive attention from researchers across the world (e.g. Atton, 2002; Williams & Delli Carpini, 2004; Singer, 2005; Allan, 2006; Kim & Hamilton, 2006; Atton & Hamilton, 2008; Paulussen & Ugille, 2008; Deuze, 2008, 2009; Conboy, 2009; Reese, 2009). Deuze (2007) argues, for example, that there has been a fundamental shift in mainstream news media practices in recent years, partly due to the phenomenon that is participatory journalism. Similarly, Bruns (2005) contends that increased audience participation in the news process (e.g. citizen journalism, blogging, etc.) is generating a new form of journalism, one of collaborative online news production.

Have technological changes that transformed journalism generated better ways of practising journalism? Scholars are divided on this question. While predicting the demise of traditional journalism as it is known and practised, Deuze (2008) summarizes some of the ways that technological changes have transformed journalistic practices, including the relationship between news producers and consumers:

> The boundaries between journalism and other forms of public communication – ranging from public relations or advertorials to weblogs and podcasts – are vanishing, the internet makes all other types of newsmedia rather obsolete (especially for young adults and teenagers), commercialization and cross-media mergers have gradually eroded the distinct professional identities of newsrooms and their publications (whether in print or broadcast), and by insisting on a traditional orientation toward the nation, journalists are losing touch with a society that is global as well as local, yet anything but national. (Deuze, 2008, p. 4)

Singer (2006) argues that the free, participatory and democratic appeal of online media invites all genres of news, including all manner of news reporters and differing quality of news content. Thus, in the new media environment, 'Journalists' hegemony as gatekeepers is threatened by an audience able to actively participate in creating and disseminating news' (Singer, 2006, p. 268). See Chapter 3 for more on the role of journalists as gatekeepers. Similarly, Williams and Delli Carpini (2004) identify diverse ways through which new technologies have transformed journalistic practices such as the increased volume of news, empowerment of news consumers who now serve also as content producers, greater interaction between journalists and news consumers, as well as an increase in the speed with which journalists collect and report news (Williams & Delli Carpini, 2004, p. 1212).

New technologies are also seen as enhancing economic efficiency in the management of newsrooms. In terms of democratization of information, new technologies are said to have introduced a new form of the Habermasian public sphere through the promotion and sustenance of various online discussion forums. Habermas' (1989) public sphere refers to an informal assembly of members of the public for debating, exchanging and sharing of information and ideas. In the digital era, Hurwitz (1999, p. 655) explains that the Internet is particularly suited to promote the public sphere because the 'libertarian and communitarian visions built on the Internet's technology, particularly its non-hierarchical structure, low transaction costs, global reach, scalability, rapid response time, and disruption-overcoming (hence censorship-foiling) alternative routing' make the technology suitable for communication in the public sphere. These elements promote greater democratization of information on the web, allowing civil society groups and activists to meet online, to make their voices heard, to report news events, to challenge established authorities in democratic and non-democratic societies, and to spread their ideology worldwide. See Chapter 8 for more on Habermas' public sphere.

In its online publication, the World Association of Newspapers (WAN), an umbrella organization that represents the newspaper industry world-wide, outlined in 2006 six trends that are affecting newsroom practices across the world, not least of which new technologies have a dominant impact. They are:

- The explosion of participative journalism, or community-generated content;
- The rise of audience research by media companies to learn new patterns of media usage;
- The proliferation of personalised news delivered online and on mobile devices;
- The reorganisation of newsrooms optimised for audience focus;
- The development of new forms of storytelling geared toward new audiences and new channels;
- The growth of audience-focused news judgment and multimedia news judgment. (WAN, 2006)

Pavlik (1999, p. 54) reinforces the influence that technology has had on journalistic practices, arguing that journalists' routines and practices have always been affected by technology. Similarly, Ursell (2001, p. 178) makes an important point about how technological changes have affected news reporting and production routines, although the changes have not been identical across multiple platforms. With specific reference to online news, Fenton (2010a,b) identifies three main characteristics of the Internet that distinguish online journalism from traditional forms of journalism. These are speed and space, multiplicity and polycentrality, and interactivity and participation. While traditional print and broadcast media suffer from space and time constraints, online journalism enjoys unlimited news space. Unlimited online space opens up huge opportunities for news, information and data storage and retrieval on the Internet. The Internet therefore assists journalists to cross-check and verify facts quickly, and to access contextual and background information. This implies that journalists who expect to survive in the electronic environment would have to upgrade their skills in order to be able to report and research at the same time (i.e. multi-tasking or multi-skilling). Although the Internet may have enhanced the speed of information retrieval and storage, as well as the pace of news production, certainly there are drawbacks. Ethical issues that confront journalists in the digital era are examined later in this chapter.

Real-time news reporting

One consequence of faster news reporting facilitated by technological changes and growing competition is that journalists are increasingly pressured to be 'first with the news', with all the negative consequences that that culture entails. Immediacy of news reporting has implications for ethical journalism practice. Coming out first with the news does not necessarily mean that the news is accurate or complete. Therefore, placing greater value on speed of reporting rather than on accuracy and verification of facts diminishes rather than enhances ethical journalism practice. One of the canons of journalism enjoins professional journalists to be truthful, fair, accurate and balanced in their reporting. However, debate persists on the ability of journalists to uphold these professional values in the new media environment in which emphasis is placed on real-time reporting. While new technologies may be having tremendous impact on journalism practice, there are aspects of the new journalism that pose serious challenges to the integrity and credibility of journalists and their news organizations. Fenton (2010b, p. 8) draws on Gunter (2003) to identify one of the drawbacks of multi-skilling. Multi-skilling involving the journalist serving as reporter, research librarian and newspaper page designer can 'lead to a reduction in levels of professionalism associated with standards as individuals are expected to do everything from acquiring the pictures, to writing the copy and designing the page' (2010b, p. 8). This echoes similar sentiments expressed by Bromley (1997) about the drawbacks of multi-skilling in journalism.

In regard to multiplicity and polycentrality of the Internet, Fenton (2010b, p. 8) contends that it has the potential to provide a level playing field between major multinational news providers and their small counterparts. This means that smaller news providers have the space to accommodate and disseminate alternative news and viewpoints that do not receive attention from major news providers. Significantly, multiple news platforms imply that journalists no longer enjoy the monopoly and control over news and information as they did prior to the emergence of the Internet. Online journalism is open to all players, who constantly contest, challenge or modify professional journalism conventions of 'objectivity', accuracy and fairness. Fenton (2010b, p. 9) notes that multiplicity of views on the Internet is not necessarily evidence of diversity of views and news content. For instance, she argues that online news research has shown that newspapers that have online presence often publish in their online edition a little bit of the news stories carried in the print version; or the newspapers use the same news reports based on comparable news decisions. However, if multiplicity does not equate to diversity of print and online news contents, it can at least add to greater quantity (Fenton, 2010b, p. 9) because of the diversity of news platforms that are available to a global audience.

Increasing interaction between content producers and consumers

Across the world, new technologies have changed the relationship between journalists (news providers) and news consumers. Through e-mail addresses and telephone numbers provided as part of the by-lines of reporters, news consumers are able to contact reporters directly. These facilities give news audiences the opportunity to provide direct feedback to reporters, to suggest story angles, to rate news reports, to comment on news stories and to make judgments about perceived levels of bias or balance in news reports. Interaction between news providers and news consumers is seen as part of the 'demystification' of journalism which is also believed to have broken down 'the barriers between audience and producer facilitating a greater deconstruction of the normative values embedded in the news genre and a re-imagining of what journalism could and/or should be' (Fenton, 2010b, p. 10). Hendrickson (2006, p. 52) notes that in the digital era, the provision of e-mail addresses of newspaper reporters in news stories has encouraged readers to respond quickly to news reports, thus 'inviting dialogue with the public over journalistic conduct and encouraging the public to voice their grievances against the news media'. According to him: 'If reporters are perceived as accessible, that carries positive implications about how much the newspaper cares about its readers' perceptions and opinions and of how much its reporters are in touch with community needs' (Hendrickson, 2006, p. 56). A number of examples have been cited to illustrate how news organizations are promoting interaction between journalists and news audiences. For example: 'Most major newspaper and magazine sites have also established blogging sections for reporters to post their reflections about issues in the news and for visitors to interact with editorial staff...' (Bucy et al., 2007, p. 144). The increasing avenues provided to ordinary citizens to report, comment on and rate contents of online newspapers underline the growing consciousness on the part of editors and journalists to improve their relationship with their audiences. As Hendrickson (2006, p. 65) observed:

> Journalists and their news organizations must consider that their personal successes depend on being accepted – viewed as truthful or credible – by those they serve, the audiences for news and opinion. It just makes common sense to include these most important people – their readers – in their day-to-day conversations via the new channel of the Internet.

Increasing interaction between journalists and ordinary citizens reflects recognition of the phenomenon known as citizen journalism. When editors and journalists encourage citizen involvement in journalism, they promote civic deliberation by the citizens.

Alternative journalism and civic deliberation

The growing involvement of ordinary citizens in news reporting and production at local, national and international levels is one of the effects of technological changes in journalism. See Chapter 6 for detailed discussion of this. Citizen journalism (also referred to as participatory journalism) extends the world of journalism beyond the roles attributed to, or monopolized by, professional journalists. A number of scholars (e.g. Atton, 2002; Atton & Hamilton, 2008) have explored unconventional forms of journalism (otherwise known as alternative journalism and media), including community media (e.g. Meadows et al., 2007), models of alternative journalism, the factors that are driving the practice, the profile of alternative journalists, challenges that confront citizens who engage in non-standard journalistic practices and theories that inform alternative forms of journalism (Atton & Hamilton, 2008).

To the question – 'What is alternative journalism?' – Atton and Hamilton (2008, p. 1) point out that concepts such as 'citizen journalism, citizen's media, community media, democratic media, emancipatory media, radical media, and social movement media' are all driven in practice 'by the desire to provide news, information, comment and analysis to specific, identified communities defined in geographic or socio-cultural terms (such as ethnic minority journalism, gay/lesbian journalism, or community media)'. As the name suggests, alternative journalism represents unconventional journalism practices that differ from mainstream journalistic cultures. Alternative journalism is therefore fundamentally at odds with conventional news writing, news reporting and news production practices, including other key characteristics of traditional journalism such as objectivity, an inactive media audience, the 'professional, elite basis of journalism as a practice' and the role of news sources in the news production chain (Atton & Hamilton, 2008, p. 1). In its conceptualization, alternative journalism represents public disappointment with entrenched journalistic practices that have failed to satisfy audience needs. Thus, alternative journalism is most often

> produced not by professionals, but by amateurs who typically have little or no training or professional qualifications as journalists: they write and report from their position as citizens, as members of communities, as activists or as fans... Much of the work of alternative journalism is concerned with representing the interests, views and needs of under-represented groups in society. (Atton & Hamilton, 2008, pp. 1–2)

Silverstone (1999, p. 103) argues that alternative media provide alternative spaces and voices that facilitate the projection of community interests as well as 'contrary' and 'subversive' opinions. Local community members are attracted to alternative journalism because of the opportunities it provides to ordinary citizens to express their views and to participate in the democratic process. For example, a study of the Australian community broadcasting sector (Meadows et al., 2007) identified a number of reasons why a significant section of the Australian population tune in or listen to community radio. Among the reasons were: community radio is 'accessible' and 'approachable'; and listeners use community radio to satisfy their need for local news and information (Meadows et al., 2007).

Citizen journalists have made significant contributions to journalism in different parts of the world, such as reporting major world events like the

Asian tsunami of 26 December 2004 and the terrorist bombings in London in July 2005. Other instances include 'bloggers...helping to organize and co-ordinate protests over the Iraq war; boosting the presidential hopes of Howard Dean and Barack Obama by gaining them followers and cash contributions' (Fenton, 2010b, p. 10), and helping to convey to the world the deep social divisions and unrests that followed the contested outcomes of the 2009 presidential election in Iran. Thus, new media have equipped ordinary citizens with the tools to contribute to online and traditional media contents, and to set the agenda of public and media debate. However, citizen journalism is not without its blemishes. Livingston (2007) has argued that, free from strict editorial control and routine news reporting and production checks, citizen journalism cannot be regarded as professional journalism practice. Similarly, Stephenson and Mory (1990, p. 25) argue that 'Technological change, and the associated changes in working practices, are serving to blur...distinctions between journalists and non-journalists'. However, the question ought not to be whether ordinary citizens have the capacity and skills to report news as professional journalists do but whether they are contributing to and complementing news reports provided by established media organizations.

There is no doubt that citizen journalists have contributed in some significant ways to reporting major news events across the world. In the new media environment, professional journalists and ordinary citizens recognize that the definition of journalism has changed significantly. News is no longer restricted to what professional journalists define it to be. In this context, we cannot deny the useful contributions that citizen journalists make to various forms of journalism practice (see Paulussen & Ugille, 2008).

Drawbacks of technological changes

Even as news organizations and some journalists celebrate the positive impacts of new technologies on newsroom practices, some researchers are not so enthusiastic. For example, although new technologies have expanded the terrain of journalism and the global audience for news has also increased, these have not eliminated certain flaws associated with online commentary and news reporting. For example, online report published in the form of commentary, analysis or news is deemed to conceal the distinction between straight news and commentary. Rather than enhance journalism, this practice is seen to promote rumour and therefore undermines journalism because of the anonymity of contributors to online content, the difficulty of verifying the accuracy of online reports in some circumstances and the lack of accountability by online contributors (Fenton, 2010b, p. 10). Technological changes have also empowered non-professional journalists who are involved in the production of online content in ways that were not previously regarded as serious threats to editorial independence. For example,

> advertising and marketing personnel influence what gets covered via topic selection and budget allocation to a greater extent than in traditional media as online news sites strive to be profitable. Technical and design personnel also have a greater contribution to play in how news gets reported from the use of multimedia and interactive tools to the visual interface. (Fenton, 2010b, p. 12)

All these issues transform traditional journalistic practices, including the conventions, ethical codes, the changing business models of journalism, the increasing involvement of citizens in content generation, the interaction between news providers and news consumers and the diverse interpretations of news and news audiences.

New technologies generating new business models of journalism

Based on a political economy analysis of the new media environment, Freedman (2010, p. 35) argues that what we used to know as the established business model for news dissemination is in serious danger. Traditional media such as newspapers, news magazines, network television and other news providers are seen to be losing their audiences essentially because the key characteristics of the Internet – immediacy and interactivity – are attracting younger news consumers to the new media and driving them away from the traditional media. The ability of the Internet to target key audiences at minimum cost has helped to whittle down newspapers' advertising revenue. In essence, the features of the Internet allow online advertisers to aim their products more precisely at a specific online audience (Freedman, 2010, pp. 35, 38). The loss of consumers of traditional media comes at a cost for traditional media: the drop in huge advertising revenue. Advertisers usually place their products in a medium that can deliver the right kind of audience. The younger audiences attracted to the Internet underline the shifting attention of advertisers to online media audiences.

Freedman (2010, p. 39) acknowledges the disturbing influence of the Internet on the prevailing business models on which traditional media operated and survived for decades.

> The internet's ability to connect advertisers directly to consumers without the mediation of a newspaper (or, to a lesser extent, a television channel) raises the possibility that the historic link between advertising and editorial will be broken and, with it, the model that underpinned the delivery of news for many years.

The evolving relationship between media organizations and advertisers has been the subject of commentary and critical analysis by scholars and researchers (see Chapter 8 for in-depth analysis of the market-driven relationship between media organizations and advertisers). The relationship is boosted when media sell audiences to advertisers who then pay a price for marketing their products to the audiences. For example, journalists are part of business enterprises whose primary objective is to make money. As Gasher and Gabriele (2004, p. 314) argued: 'If the editorial side of newspaper publishing is governed by a bond between the newspaper and its community, so is the business side'. Drawing on Dallas Smythe, the authors elaborate further: 'Newspapers, specifically, assemble each day an audience of predictable size and known demographic characteristics, by providing a comprehensive package of news, information and opinion, and sell access to that audience to advertisers' (Smythe, 1994, cited in Gasher & Gabriele, 2004, p. 314).

It is not only declining advertising revenue that is threatening traditional media in the electronic age. There are other factors. 'The rapid increase in free papers, the emergence of 24-hour television news and the popularization of online and mobile platforms have all contributed to a far more volatile and unstable environment for news organizations' (Freedman, 2010, p. 36). It has also been argued that the business-oriented nature of the Internet, and the competition for younger and technologically skilled audiences, may be drawing traditional print media to adopt more business-focused approaches to news. The danger of newspapers moving in this direction lies in the fear that journalists are likely to lose their independence and the ability to make ethical decisions while gathering and reporting news (Phillips et al., 2010, p. 59).

Although the Internet is threatening the financial base of newspapers in particular and traditional media in general, newspapers and other media have responded by developing strategies to help them to overcome the threats posed by the Internet. These include setting up online sites, cutting operating costs and maximizing productivity (one example is multi-skilling which requires journalists to report and produce news across multiple platforms), product expansion such as acquiring new businesses and branching out into territories previously dominated by the Internet, such as setting up 'online classified advertising sites in an attempt to win back some of the revenue they have lost to the Internet' (Freedman, 2010, p. 43), as well as entering into joint venture agreements and collaborations.

> The business model of online journalism appears to be one in which audiences largely refuse to pay for content, advertising revenue is dominated by search engines and pure-play companies, cannibalization remains a concern (just as it does in the recorded music industry) and traffic goes more and more to internet portals and aggregators who invest virtually nothing in original news content and simultaneously fail to expand significantly the range of source material. (Freedman, 2010, p. 47)

Changing demographics of media audiences

Research shows that the Internet is more appealing, as a news source, to the younger generation than the traditional news media (Flanagin & Metzger, 2001; Lauf, 2001; Coleman & McCombs, 2007; Obijiofor & Hanusch, 2010). Flanagin and Metzger (2001, p. 174) reported in their study of American university students' use of different communication media that, 'Of all channels, the Internet was the most highly used for getting information, over other technologies such as newspapers, television, books, and magazines'. What this suggests is a growing shift away from traditional news media as the primary source of news and information to the younger generation. Other research shows that age or generational difference affects media selection and use. A study by Coleman and McCombs (2007, p. 495) found that the younger generation (those aged between 18 and 34) 'used the Internet significantly more often' than they used the traditional news sources such as newspapers and television. Conversely, the older generation used the traditional sources of news more frequently than they used the Internet. This supports evidence that age differences are reflected in media use. Evidence of the impact of age on newspaper reading habits in Europe was also reported by Lauf (2001). In a study of the determinants of newspaper readership for political information in Europe, Lauf (p. 238) found that 'The strongest determinant of daily reading is age: an increasing number of young people do not read newspapers daily any more to inform themselves about current politics'. In all the European countries he studied, Lauf found that 'age has become the strongest predictor for the daily use of newspapers as a source of political information' (p. 238).

In a more recent study of individual and national differences in newspaper readers in Europe, Elvestad and Blekesaune (2008, p. 442) reported that individual characteristics such as 'gender, age, education and household income' accounted for differences in newspaper reading although the effect varied across countries. Their study, based on data taken from the second round of the 2004/2005 European Social Survey (ESS) of 24 countries, also showed that: men devoted more time to newspaper reading than women; people with higher education spent more time on newspaper reading than those with lower level of education; people in households with high income read more than people in households with low income; 'and older people read more than younger people' (Elvestad & Blekesaune, 2008, p. 442). In terms of time devoted to newspaper reading by people in individual countries, Elvestad and Blekesaune found that, on the whole, people in Ireland devoted the largest amount of time to newspaper reading, compared to people in other European nations. This finding challenges other scholars such as Hallin and Mancini (2004) who categorized Ireland as belonging to 'the lower end of the European table of newspaper reading based on circulation per 1000' (Elvestad & Blekesaune, 2008, p. 431). The United Kingdom also emerged as one of the countries where the average time devoted to newspaper reading was among the uppermost. One of the surprising aspects of the findings was that Norwegians devoted 'less time than the Irish in newspaper reading, but almost 96 percent read newspapers on an average day' (Elvestad & Blekesaune, 2008, p. 431). The study showed that Greece had the smallest proportion of newspaper readers and it was also the country where people devoted the least amount of time to newspaper reading.

There are at least three ways in which the Internet is seen to pose a major threat to newspapers. These include the loss of breaking news function, declining newspaper readership owing to technology-based leisure activities and decline in advertising revenue (Thottam, 1999, p. 217). However, Obijiofor and Green (2001, p. 96) argue that while news consumers may rush to the Internet for bits of breaking news, the same appetite for news will drive media audiences to seek newspapers and other reliable traditional media for more detailed background information and analysis. This was evident in the way the media reported the 11 September 2001 terrorist attacks on New York and Washington. 'Many people watched the events on cable and satellite television but many people also read the next day's newspapers for background details and analysis' (Obijiofor & Green, 2001, p. 96).

Ethical challenges and dilemmas

While traditional methods of news reporting and production have given way to new means of journalism practice, clearly there are ethical challenges, such as journalists relying on web-based information without bothering to cross-check and verify facts. Thus, the increasing use of the Internet and e-mail by journalists to access news sources has raised ethical questions and also promoted complacency (Wu & Hamilton, 2004). The difficulty is compounded by the fact that anybody can set up an e-mail address with a pseudonym (Green, 1997). The fact that information is online does not necessarily imply that the information is factual or accurate (Weise, 1997; Sundar, 1998). 'The Net is a place of intrigue, rumor and fabrication. The first time you see one of the elaborate false reports or supposed trial tran-scripts that litter the on-line world, it seems impossible that anyone would spend so much time creating hoaxes' (Weise, 1997, p. 160). Sundar (1998, p. 55) concurs: 'The internet has made it possible for gossip and rumour to not only gain wide circulation but also attain the status of "news".' Specifically, Weise (1997, p. 162) points out one of the dangers of relying on web-based information as fact.

> Becoming enmeshed in the on-line world means stumbling onto lies presented as gospel truth and sprinkled with enough factoids to make them sound plau-sible. Because they come so crisply typed and seemingly authentically worded, the danger is that the unwary will treat them with less caution than they would a missive composed on an old typewriter and delivered in a hand-addressed envelope.

Indeed, Kruckeberg (1995, p. 80) has argued that 'Emerging use of tel-ecomputer technology as a "news" medium will significantly add to the con-fusion, not only about what constitutes news, but about who reasonably may be considered a bona fide and credible journalist'. In the new digital environ-ment, he points out that 'the role of the journalist and that of the press as an institution are destined to be changed in significant ways, with accompanying ethical ramifications' (1995, p. 81).In a study of the Nigerian press coverage of the Niger Delta conflict, Obijiofor (2009) found that new technologies were used by journalists in ways that breached ethical and professional codes of practice. The study found that while government sources were contacted directly, the journalists relied on e-mail and web-based information to report the conflict, especially the activities of the Niger Delta militants. Although, the style of reporting adopted by Nigerian journalists who covered the Niger Delta conflict may have been influenced by the difficulties the journalists experienced in contacting the Niger Delta activists directly, owing to fears the activists might have for their safety, Obijiofor (2009) identified a redeeming feature of this form of reporting:

> One notable aspect of this style of reporting is that new technologies such as e-mail and the Internet now serve as a forum through which marginalised groups and minorities such as the Niger Delta activists tell their stories and communicate their problems to the rest of the world... e-mail and Internet technologies are highly valuable means of communication adopted by the Niger Delta activists. The Niger Delta activists use these technologies as tools for their economic, social and political emancipation in their struggle for self-determination. (2009, p. 197)

Nevertheless, ethical codes were violated when Nigerian newspaper journalists received web-based messages from anonymous sources and published the information without verifying the sources, as well as the authenticity of the information. In journalism practice, source attribution is an important and credible element of news reporting. As Sundar (1998, p. 56) points out: 'Getting quotes and attributing them to credible sources are essential aspects of journalistic practice, regardless of the medium of news delivery'. A study of the effect of source attribution on perception of online news stories found that online stories that contained source attributions were rated highly by readers in terms of credibility and quality in comparison to stories without quotes (Sundar, 1998). Based on his research results, Sundar concluded that, 'poorly sourced stories on the Internet will be evaluated negatively by readers. Given the ease of digital publishing, online news sites often carry developing stories without complete and thorough source attribution' (Sundar, 1998, pp. 63–4). Surely, technologies cannot be held responsible for dishonourable practices by journalists. Unscrupulous journalistic practices have arisen essentially because of the way journalists use the technologies. Aronson (1971) alluded to similar abuses to which the telephone was subjected soon after its invention. 'The telephone as an instrument of communication is morally neutral, though the uses to which it is put are surely not' (Aronson, 1971, p. 158). Some of the common ethical infractions such as plagiarism of material posted online and digital manipulation of photographs are already having negative impacts on the integrity and credibility of journalists and their news organizations.

Garrison (2000) has also underscored serious ethical problems engendered by technological changes in journalism: 'Sources on the telephone or two-way radio, for instance, may not be who they say they are supposed to be. Human sources have been known to be unreliable, to lie, and even to engage in elaborate hoaxes' (Garrison, 2000, p. 501). Other problems such as anonymity and accountability on the web, as well as 'verification, reliability, sourcing, and credibility' (Garrison, 2000, p. 510) pose critical problems for journalists who gather news online. For example, in a survey of US newspaper journalists' use of online resources between 1994 and 1998, Garrison (2000, p. 506) reported that, 'When asked what they believed were the most common problems of Web sites for journalists, the respondents listed lack of verification most often (54.1%). Similarly, data show unreliable information (44.9%), badly sourced information (44.3%), and lack of site credibility (43.8%) were also important concerns of the respondents'. In terms of credibility of online news sites, Yau and Al-Hawamdeh (2001) argue that credible and well-established media organizations such as CNN, the British Broadcasting Corporation (BBC) and the *New York Times* – all of which have online sites – enjoy higher credibility than websites established by lesser known organizations and individuals. For these established media organizations and online news providers, credibility matters. Credibility is the unique selling point that distinguishes well-known media organizations from their lesser known online counterparts. In this context, Yau and Al-Hawamdeh (2001) contend that, 'If the news industry hopes to prosper online, it will be because recognized branded news sites are accessed for their credibility as sources of information'. The way in which the use of new technologies in journalism can be problematic was evident in the aftermath of the death of Iranian protester Neda Agha-Soltan in June of 2009 (Schraven, 2010, in Hanusch, 2010c, p. 156). Agha-Soltan had died on camera in front of *YouTube* audiences around the world, and soon journalists were scrambling for more information about the life of a woman who had suddenly become synonymous with the struggle for political reforms in Iran. Photos of Agha-Soltan circulated on the Internet and at some point someone found a publicly available photo of a Neda Soltani on the social networking site Facebook. The image was quickly circulated on the Internet and published by the mainstream media. Soltani was a different person to Agha-Soltan, however, and she was very much alive. Soltani tried to correct the error but to no avail. She contacted the Voice of America with a current photo of herself to prove she was not Agha-Soltan, but instead the new photo was circulated widely as a new photo of the dead Agha-Soltan. Soltani eventually fled her home country because of Iranian government pressure on her to expose what it saw as Western lies and propaganda. Nevertheless, her image and even name are still regularly used, wrongly, in connection with the death of Agha-Soltan. As Hanusch (2010c, p. 156) has pointed out, the case 'demonstrates how difficult it is to stop a story once it reaches the Internet, where it is duplicated with amazing speed across countless websites'.

There are arguments about whether technological transformations that spawned 24-hour news coverage, as well as real-time reporting, have increased or diminished public knowledge of current affairs. Bucy et al. (2007, p. 155) contend that despite the emergence of mobile technologies, satellite systems and the Internet, 'the American public remains markedly uninformed about current events'. This is partly attributable to the phenomenon known as information overload. This suggests that despite the deluge of information generated through multiple sources, there remains 'a widening *knowledge gap* that reflects a digital news divide between well-informed and poorly informed information-age news consumers' (Bucy et al., 2007, p. 156). Beyond increasing and decreasing public knowledge of current affairs, in different societies, new technologies are also believed to facilitate greater democratization of information, on one hand and, at the same time, serve as tools for the suppression of public opinion in non-democratic countries. An analysis of how new technologies serve to promote democracy and at the same time dictatorship identifies, for example, the merits and drawbacks of mobile telephony.

> Mobile phones are everywhere and relatively cheap and can serve as a grassroots communication device in regions with otherwise weak infrastructure; on the other hand they can also quite easily be censored, switched off by the authorities, be used to spread the wrong values, or incite violence. (Karstens, 2009)

African journalists adapting to technological changes

Some of the issues examined in relation to technological changes in journalism practice include whether new technologies have increased wider access to news from developing countries (see also Chapter 6). Nigerian and Singaporean journalists believe the Internet has allowed them to diversify their sources of news and to rely less on Western news sources, such as international news agencies (Obijiofor, 2001). Thus, the Internet has opened up a variety of news sources for journalists, including the official websites of established newspapers in developing and developed countries, as well as radio and television news on the web (Obijiofor & Green, 2001). These points raise questions about access to new technologies, in particular limited training opportunities in various newsrooms, especially in

West African newsrooms where technological diffusions are slow. Based on evidence from his study, Obijiofor (2003) distilled two critical arguments about new technologies and journalism practice in Ghana and Nigeria. First, ability to use new technologies requires constant training and re-training to enable journalists to keep up with the pace of technological changes. Second, lack of access to computers and other communication technologies affects journalists' knowledge and understanding of how to use technology in their job. Obijiofor (2003) argued that lack of access to new technologies and lack of training and re-training opportunities are likely to have a negative impact on the ability of African journalists to function effectively.

Questions have been raised about whether the introduction of new technologies in journalism has positively or adversely affected the image of Africa in the Western media. Nearly 30 years after the end of the debate over a New World Information and Communication Order (NWICO) which dominated intellectual discussion at UNESCO in the 1970s and the early 1980s, it is appropriate to examine whether Africa's image in Western media has improved or deteriorated owing to the advent of new technologies. Harding (2003, p. 69) believes there is a link between new technologies and media images of Africa. 'The various images of Africa have of course been dependent on two main factors: firstly, the development of technology and subsequent access to it; and secondly, the ideology and ethos informing the use of the technology.' More significantly, Harding (2003) argues that in the twenty-first century, the projection of Africa to local, national and Western media audiences through the combined use of visual media platforms such as national television, African films and video-movie have helped Africans to achieve complete control over representations of themselves, as well as what they choose to release into the public domain. Additionally, new media technologies have helped to challenge and transform Africa's images that are portrayed in Western media, such as images of war, violence and poverty.

Similarly, new technologies are being harnessed by people in different countries in positive ways. For example, the Internet has helped to diffuse knowledge of Japanese society to youths in the United States, thus serving as an ambassador for Japanese people and culture. Through the Internet, American youngsters are able to 'discover...alluring pictures of Japanese landscape, festivals, fashions, and sports. They download Japanese pop music from their computers, and zoom in on images of Japanese youngsters participating in a globalizing youth culture, enjoying themselves at rock concerts and discos' (Gerbert, 2001, p. 111). For Indigenous people across the world, the

Internet has enabled them to tell their stories to the world, to represent themselves and their culture in a more appropriate and accurate way. Iseke-Barnes (2002, p. 194) argues that Aboriginal and Indigenous people in Canada are using the World Wide Web to resist dominant stories and misrepresentations of themselves. 'Indigenous cyberspace participants can use this medium to challenge dominant stereotypes and discourses, engaging in dialogue which enables resistance activities to be articulated, shared, and acknowledged' (2002, p. 194). Delgado-P (2002) takes up this theme in his discussion of new technologies and the South American native people. He states that the web has enabled the global community to be more informed about the issues that confront Indigenous people. 'The web has made the world more aware of the various problems faced by indigenous peoples...The voices of more indigenous peoples are being heard; indigenous organizations are able to mobilize global support for local causes' (Delgado-P, 2002).

Convergence: For good or bad?

Technological convergence (the integration of print, broadcast and online media practices and routines) is a major feature of technological changes in journalism practice. While Bromley (1997) sees technological convergence (e.g. reporting and producing across multiple platforms) as having a disruptive influence over journalists' ability to uphold their professional skills, Deuze (2008, p. 9) states that convergence is often perceived as an additional burden imposed on journalists 'and the technology-driven enterprise frustrates and confuses many of the newsworkers involved'. Bromley (1997, p. 346) had argued that 'Multi-skilling contains the potential for the final fragmentation of journalism'. This view is not shared by some scholars who have cited intense competition and media mergers as posing more serious threats to journalism practice in the twenty-first century (see Hallin, 1996; Franklin, 1997; Bourdieu, 1998). Deuze (2008, p. 9) notes that, although convergence comes in various forms, it is influenced by both internal ('practices, rituals, routines, cultures') and external factors such as 'regulation, competition, stakeholders, publics'.

Feist (2001, p. 709) predicted at the turn of the century that, 'As the Internet, print and television converge, the traditional methods by which people learn about the world they live in will change forever'. This is already happening. Not only has digitalization resulted in a reduction in broadcasting tools (especially television broadcasting equipment), it has also reduced the cost of transmitting and broadcasting images and photos.

Feist illustrates how technological changes have transformed the broadcast industry:

> Just a few years ago, up-linking broadcast-quality television pictures to a satel-lite required a truckload of equipment. At the end of the Persian Gulf War, ABC and CBS showed live pictures of U.S. troops entering Kuwait. To get those pictures on the air, the networks used four trucks, a ton of equipment, and a portable satellite dish. Today, such a transmission requires only a few suitcases of gear. (Feist, 2001, p. 710)

In fact, digitalization has significantly alleviated the burden imposed by the equipment that broadcast news reporters carry with them in the process of reporting and producing news. See Chapter 6 for a detailed discussion of this phenomenon as it affects foreign correspondents. The change from analogue to digital transmission of broadcast signals has also facilitated the transmis-sion of more images with smaller equipment at a reduced cost (Feist, 2001, p. 710). These technological transformations account largely for the ability of the broadcast industry to engage in real-time ('live') coverage of news events. 'Around the world, the shrinking costs of small satellite receiving dishes and the rapid expansion of cable television have allowed hundreds of millions of people to see the broadcasts of CNN, the British Broadcasting Company (BBC) (sic), and other Western television news organizations' (Feist, 2001, p. 710). Indeed, new technologies have facilitated wider access to global television menu. Above all, the emergence of 24-hour news programs, the desire to 'break the news' (i.e. to be 'first with the news'), and the growth of Internet news sites have spawned intense competition among media organizations and other non-traditional news providers (Feist, 2001, p. 712). 'Each of the new services competes for market share among attentive viewers who in the past had only the networks to watch if they wanted to feel informed' (Utley, 1997, p. 7).

Technological changes have affected the broadcast media in much the same way as they have influenced the online news industry. O'Sullivan (2005, p. 65) makes the point that issues such as 'Objectivity, reader power, accountability and transparency, the right to reply, access to audience, new ways of telling stories – questions concerning all of these and more are thrown up when we consider the new forms of news'. His study of Irish online news which was based on personal observations and discussions with online content providers (i.e. journalists) showed that:

> although superficial consideration of online news has promised many enhance-ments, few were seriously implemented in online media. The opportunity to

provide context-rich content, by means of hyperlinking, was spurned; bulletin boards were sparsely implemented, multimediality was almost non-existent, and production standards were a mixed bag. (O'Sullivan, 2005, p. 65)

In a study of the differential effects of exposure of news consumers to print and online versions of the *New York Times*, Tewksbury and Althaus (2000, p. 457) found that 'Internet-based papers provide fewer cues about news story importance and give readers more control over story selection'. Based on this finding, they argue that 'readers of an online paper may acquire less information about national, international, and political events than would print paper readers' (Tewksbury & Althaus, 2000, p. 457). However, a study of the print and online versions of two newspapers in the Netherlands – *de Telegraaf* and *de Gelderlander* – found, surprisingly, that the print versions of the two newspapers carried more stories than the online versions (d'Haenens et al., 2004, p. 368). This seems to run against the results of previous research by Tewksbury and Althaus (2000) which found a greater number of news articles in online newspapers than the print version because the online newspapers had unlimited space to accommodate more stories. In the print industry, technological changes have allowed reporters and photographers to cover news events from any location and to send their reports to the newsroom from that location (Feist, 2001, p. 710). Physical presence in the newsroom is no longer a precondition for submission of news copy (Henningham, 1995). As Feist (2001, p. 710) points out, '... a digital photograph can be transmitted by wireless telephone or satellite phone from any point on the globe. That image can be published in a newspaper or magazine, or it can be published immediately on a Web site'.

Just as the Internet has helped journalists to improve the speed and efficiency of news reporting and fact gathering, the Internet has also led to what has been described as 'cannibalization of copy' (Phillips, 2010, p. 95). This is the practice whereby reporters rewrite news stories that had been reported in other news media often without further verification or cross-checking. This practice has serious implications for the integrity of journalists and the credibility of their organizations. One obvious consequence of cannibalization of copy is homogenization of news reports across media (see also Redden & Witschge, 2010, pp. 173–9). Homogenization of news ensures there is no diversity of views and news. It undermines the quality of media content. Poor quality of news and similarity of news content can lead to consumers' loss of news appetite. An examination of traditional and alternative online news outlets (Redden & Witschge, 2010) revealed that a large amount of the news content was homogeneous. Homogeneity in news content is driven by intense competition among media, a culture of immediacy and real-time news reporting, as well as constant updating of news material leading to journalists re-using the same or similar news material (Redden & Witschge, 2010, p. 174). Media organizations that engage in homogenization of copy do so at their own peril. New technologies such as the Internet enable news consumers to cross-check facts and details and to make decisions regarding what they want to read on the web, when to read that information and which particular medium to patronize. Consequently, news consumers who are dissatisfied with the quality of service provided by a particular traditional news medium can readily look for alternative news sources elsewhere. In the new electronic environment, the notion of loyalty to a particular news medium has become untenable. This is already happening.

Conclusion

New technologies have transformed journalistic practices in many ways. However, the new technologies do not have homogeneous impact on newsrooms across cultures. This is because in different cultures, ordinary citizens and professional journalists use new technologies to produce media contents in different ways.

Another impact of new technologies is the interlocking relationship that exists between professional journalists (the news providers) and news consumers. For example, the increasing avenues provided to news consumers to comment on or rate contents of online newspapers underlines the growing consciousness on the part of media organizations to improve their relationship with their audiences. It also reflects greater appreciation of the phenomenon known as citizen journalists. In different parts of the world, ordinary citizens have contributed to media coverage of major events such as the Asian tsunami of 26 December 2004 and the terrorist bombings in London in July 2005.

There are also other ways through which technological changes pose serious challenges to journalists and their news organizations. For example, multiple news sources imply that journalists no longer enjoy the monopoly and control over news and information as they did prior to the emergence of the Internet. Online journalism is open to all players, who constantly contest, challenge or modify professional journalism conventions of 'objectivity', accuracy and fairness. This has also raised questions about the role of journalists as gatekeepers. Do journalists and editors still serve as gatekeepers of news and entertainment in light of multiple platforms of news dissemination and the fact that ordinary citizens also serve as content producers?

One of the principles of journalism practice enjoins journalists to be truthful, fair, accurate and balanced in their reporting. However, debate persists on the ability of journalists to uphold these professional values in the new media environment in which emphasis is placed on real-time reporting. Real-time news reporting undermines fair and accurate reporting. To be first with the news does not necessarily mean that the news is complete and accurate. Additionally, the increasing use of the Internet and e-mail by journalists to access news sources has raised ethical questions and also promoted complacency among journalists. Ethical codes are breached when journalists rely on unverified e-mail and web-based information.

While the world may be celebrating the introduction of new technologies in journalism practice, we must keep in mind that journalists in less-developed societies are still grappling with problems of access to technologies. Without access to new technologies, and without a basic knowledge of how to use the technologies, these journalists stand the risk of lagging behind their colleagues in other cultures and indeed are likely to lag behind new developments in technology. These issues must be addressed at the management level of each media organization. News organizations have the moral obligation to equip their editorial staff with the new technological tools that are essential for survival in the twenty-first century and beyond.

DISCUSSION QUESTIONS

1. To what extent has the phenomenon of 'citizen journalism' diminished or enhanced the role of editors and journalists as gatekeepers?
2. Identify and analyse the three main features of the Internet that distinguish online journalism from traditional forms of journalism.
3. Discuss the various ways through which journalists are interacting with news consumers in the digital era. What are the implications of this development for civic deliberation?
4. Explain how the Internet and newer forms of media are threatening the financial bases of traditional mainstream media. Discuss this with specific focus on the situation in your own country.
5. What are the major ethical challenges and dilemmas that have emerged as a result of technological transformations in journalistic practices?

Bibliography

Adam, Gordon and Lina Holguin (2003) 'The media's role in peace-building: Asset or liability?', Paper presented at the Our Media 3 Conference, Barranquilla, Colombia, 19–21 May.

Adam, G. Stuart (2001) 'The education of journalists', *Journalism*, 2(3), pp. 315–39.

Adoni, Hanna and Sherrill Mane (1984) 'Media and the social construction of reality: Toward an integration of theory and research', *Communication Research*, 11(3), pp. 323–40.

Aggarwala, Narinder K. (1979) 'What is development news?' *Journal of Communication*, 29(2), pp. 180–1.

Agostini, Angelo (2009) 'The Italian journalism education landscape', in Georgios Terzis (ed.) *European Journalism Education*, pp. 277–88. Bristol, Intellect.

Ahlers, Douglas (2006) 'News consumption and the new electronic media', *The Harvard International Journal of Press/Politics*, 11(1), pp. 29–52.

al-Kasim, Faisal (1999) 'Crossfire: The Arab version', *International Journal of Press/Politics*, 4(3), pp. 93–7.

Allan, Stuart (1999) *News Culture*, Buckingham, Open University Press.

Allan, Stuart (2006) *Online News: Journalism and the Internet*, Maidenhead, Open University Press.

Allan, Stuart and Barbie Zelizer (eds) (2004) *Reporting War: Journalism in Wartime*, London, Routledge.

Allen, Tim and Jean Seaton (eds) (1999) *The Media of Conflict: War Reporting and Representations of Ethnic Violence*, London and New York, Zed Books.

Altmeppen, Klaus-Dieter (2010) 'The gradual disappearance of foreign news on German television: Is there a future for global, international, world or foreign news?', *Journalism Studies*, 11(4), pp. 567–76.

Altschull, J. Herbert (1995) *Agents of Power: The Media and Public Policy*, White Plains, NY, Longman.

Amanpour, Christiane (1996) 'Television's role in foreign policy', *The Quill*, 84(3), pp. 16–17.

Amin, Hussein (2002) 'Freedom as a value in Arab media: Perceptions and attitudes among journalists', *Political Communication*, 19(2), pp. 125–35.

Anyanwu, Christine (2001) 'In Nigerian newspapers, women are seen, not heard', *Nieman Reports*, 55(4), pp. 68–71.

Aronson, Sidney H. (1971) 'The sociology of the telephone', *International Journal of Comparative Sociology*, 12(3), pp. 153–67.

Atton, Chris (2002) *Alternative Media*, London, Sage.

Atton, Chris and James F. Hamilton, (2008) *Alternative Journalism*, London, Sage.

Ayish, Muhammad I. (2002) 'Political communication on Arab world television: Evolving patterns', *Political Communication*, 19(2), pp. 137–54.

Ball, Amanda, Mark Hanna and Karen Sanders (2006) 'What British journalism students think about ethics and journalism', *Journalism & Mass Communication Educator*, 61(1), pp. 20–32.

Banda, Fackson, Catherine M. Beukes-Amiss, Tanja Bosch, Winston Mano, Polly McLean and Lynette Steenveld (2007) 'Contextualising journalism education and training in Southern Africa', *Ecquid Novi: African Journalism Studies*, 28(1&2), pp. 156–75.

Barnett, Steven (2008) 'On the road to self-destruction', *British Journalism Review*, 19(2), pp. 5–13.

Beaudoin, Christopher E. and Esther Thorson (2001) 'LA Times offered as model for foreign news coverage', *Newspaper Research Journal*, 22(1), pp. 80–93.

Becker, Jonathan (2004) 'Lessons from Russia: A neo-authoritarian media system', *European Journal of Communication*, 19(2), pp. 139–63.

Benesch, Susan (2004) 'Inciting genocide, pleading free speech', *World Policy Journal*, 21(2), pp. 62–9.

Bennett, W. Lance (2001) *News: The Politics of Illusion*, 4th edn, New York, Addison, Wesley, Longman.

Berger, Guy (2007) 'In search of journalism education excellence in Africa: Summary of the 2006 Unesco project', *Ecquid Novi: African Journalism Studies*, 28(1&2), pp. 149–55.

Berger, Guy (2009) 'How the Internet impacts on international news: Exploring paradoxes of the most global medium in a time of "hyperlocalism"', *International Communication Gazette*, 71(5), pp. 355–71.

Berger, Guy and Corinne Matras (2007) *Criteria and Indicators for Quality Journalism Training Institutions & Identifiying Potential Centres of Excellence in Journalism Training in Africa*, Paris, UNESCO.

Berger, Peter L. and Thomas Luckmann (1966) *The Social Construction of Reality: A Treatise in the Sociology of Knowledge*, London, Allen Lane.

Best, Samuel J., Brian Chmielewski and Brian S. Krueger (2005) 'Selective exposure to online foreign news during the conflict with Iraq', *The Harvard International Journal of Press/Politics*, 10(4), pp. 52–70.

Bjørnsen, Gunn, Jan Fredrik Hovden and Rune Ottosen (2007) 'Journalists in the making: Findings from a longitudinal study of Norwegian journalism students', *Journalism Practice*, 1(3), pp. 383–403.

Blankenberg, Ngaire (1999) 'In search of real freedom: Ubuntu and the media', *Critical Arts*, 13(2), pp. 42–65.

Bläsi, Burkhard (2004) 'Peace journalism and the news production process', *Conflict & Communication Online*, 3(1/2).

Bleske, Glen L. (1991) 'Ms. Gates takes over: An updated version of a 1949 case study', *Newspaper Research Journal*, 12(4), pp. 88–97.

Blumler, Jay G., Jack M. McLeod and Karl Erik Rosengren (1992) 'An introduction to comparative communication research', in Jay G. Blumler, Jack M. McLeod and Karl Erik Rosengren (eds) *Comparatively Speaking: Communication and Culture Across Space and Time*, pp. 3–18. Newbury Park, CA, Sage.

Bogart, Leo (1995) *Commercial Culture: The Media System and the Public Interest*, New York, Oxford University Press.

Bogart, Leo (2000) *Commercial Culture: The Media System and the Public Interest*, New Brunswick, NJ, Transaction Publishers.

Bogart, Leo (2004) 'Reflections on content quality in newspapers', *Newspaper Research Journal*, 25(1), pp. 40–53.

Bonney, Bill and Helen Wilson (1983) *Australia's Commercial Media*, Melbourne, Macmillan.

Botha, Nicolene and Arnold S. de Beer (2007) 'South African journalism education: Working towards the future by looking back', *Ecquid Novi: African Journalism Studies*, 28(1&2), pp. 198–205.

Bourdieu, Pierre (1998) *On Television and Journalism*, London, Pluto Press.

Bourgault, Louise Manon (1995) *Mass Media in Sub-Saharan Africa*, Indiana, Indiana University Press.

Boyd-Bell, Susan (2007) *Experiential Learning in Journalism Education – A New Zealand Case Study*, Auckland, AUT University.

Bratic, Vladimir (2006) 'Media effects during violent conflict: Evaluating media contributions to peace building', *Conflict & Communication Online*, 5(1).

Bratic, Vladimir (2008) 'Examining Peace-Oriented Media in Areas of Violent Conflict', *The International Communication Gazette*, 70(6), pp. 487–503.

Breed, Warren (1955) 'Social control in the newsroom: A functional analysis', *Social Forces*, 33, pp. 326–35.

Bromley, Michael (1997) 'The end of journalism? Changes in workplace practices in the press and broadcasting in the 1990s', in Michael Bromley and Tom O'Malley (eds) *A Journalism Reader*, pp. 330–50. London, Routledge.

Bromley, Michael (2009) 'The United Kingdom journalism education landscape', in Terzis, George (ed.) *European Journalism Education*, pp. 47–66. Bristol, Intellect.

Bruns, Axel (2005) *Gatewatching: Collaborative Online News Production*, New York, Peter Lang.

Bucy, Erik P., Walter Gantz and Zheng Wang (2007) 'Media technology and the 24-hour news cycle', in Carolyn A. Lin and David J. Atkin (eds) *Communication Technology and Social Change: Theory and Implications*, pp. 143–63. Mahwah, NJ, Lawrence Erlbaum.

Caballero, María Cristina (2000) 'The Colombian press under siege', *The Harvard International Journal of Press/Politics*, 5(3), pp. 90–5.

Calabrese, Andrew and Barbara Ruth-Burke (1992) 'American identities: Nationalism, the media, and the public sphere', *Journal of Communication Inquiry*, 16(2), pp. 52–73.

Calhoun, Craig (1992) 'Introduction: Habermas and the public sphere', in Craig Calhoun (ed.) *Habermas and the Public Sphere*, pp. 1–48. Cambridge, MA, MIT Press.

Campbell, W. Joseph (2000) 'Not likely sent: The Remington-Hearst "Telegrams"', *Journalism & Mass Communication Quarterly*, 77(2), pp. 405–22.

Campbell, W. Joseph (2003) 'African cultures and newspapers', in Shannon E. Martin and David A. Copeland (eds) *The Function of Newspapers in Society: A Global Perspective*, pp. 31–46. Westport, CT, Praeger.

Cann, David J. and Philip B. Mohr (2001) 'Journalist and source gender in Australian Television news', *Journal of Broadcasting & Electronic Media*, 45(1), pp. 162–74.

Carey, James W. (2000) 'Some personal notes on US journalism education', *Journalism*, 1(1), pp. 12–23.

Carter, Cynthia, Gill Branston and Stuart Allan (eds) (1998a) *News, Gender and Power*, London, Routledge.

Carter, Cynthia, Gill Branston and Stuart Allan (1998b) 'Setting new(s) agendas: An introduction', in Cynthia Carter, Gill Branston and Stuart Allan (eds) *News, Gender and Power*, pp. 1–9. London, Routledge.

Chalaby, Jean K. (1996) 'Journalism as an Anglo-American invention: A comparison of the development of French and Anglo-American journalism, 1830s–1920s', *European Journal of Communication*, 11(3), pp. 303–26.

Chambers, Deborah, Linda Steiner and Carole Fleming (2004) *Women and Journalism*, London, Routledge.

Chambers, Simone and Anne Costain (2000) 'Introduction', in Simone Chambers and Anne Costain (eds) *Deliberation, Democracy, and the Media*, pp. xi–xiv. Lanham, MD, Rowman & Littlefield.

Chan, Joseph Man (1996) 'Whither mass communication education in Asia?', *Asia Pacific Media Educator*, 1, pp. 16–27.

Chang, Li-jing Arthur and Brian L. Massey (2010) 'Work motivation and journalists in Taiwan and the US: An integration of theory and culture', *Asian Journal of Communication*, 20(1), pp. 51–68.

Chang, Tsan-Kuo, Pat Pat Berg, Anthony Ying-Him Fung, Kent D. Kedl, Catherine A. Luther and Janet Szuba (2001) 'Comparing nations in mass communication research, 1970–97: A critical assessment of how we know what we know', *International Communication Gazette*, 63(5), pp. 415–34.

Charon, Jean-Marie (2003) 'Journalist training in France', in Romy Fröhlich and Christina Holtz-Bacha (eds) *Journalism Education in Europe and North America*, Cresskill, Hampton Press.

Chengju, Huang (2001) 'The development of a semi-independent press in post-Mao China: An overview and a case study of Chengdu Business News', *Journalism Studies*, 1(4), pp. 649–64.

Chia, Lynette Clarice (2007) *Foreign News Coverage in Four Online Newspapers*, Unpublished Bachelor of Arts (Honours) thesis. Brisbane, The University of Queensland.

Christensen, Christian (2004) 'Political victims and media focus: The killings of Laurent Kabila, Zoran Djindjic, Anna Lindh and Pim Fortuyn', *Journal for Crime, Conflict and the Media*, 1(2), pp. 23–40.

Christians, Clifford G. (2004) 'Ubuntu and communitarianism in media ethics', *Ecquid Novi: African Journalism Studies*, 25(2), pp. 235–56.

Cohen, Bernard (1963) *The Press and Foreign Policy*, Princeton, NJ, Princeton University Press.

Coleman, Renita and Maxwell McCombs (2007) 'The young and the agenda-less? Exploring age-related differences in agenda setting on the youngest generation, baby boomers, and the civic generation', *Journalism & Mass Communication Quarterly*, 84(3), pp. 495–508.

Conboy, Martin (2009) 'A parachute of popularity for a commodity in freefall?', *Journalism*, 10(3), pp. 306–8.

Cook, Bernie (2001) 'Over my dead body: The ideological use of dead bodies in network news coverage of Vietnam', *Quarterly Review of Film and Video*, 18(2), pp. 203–16.

Cottle, Simon (2006) *Mediatized Conflict: Developments in Media and Conflict Studies*, Maidenhead, Open University Press.

Cottle, Simon (2009) 'Journalism studies: Coming of (global) age?', *Journalism*, 10(3), pp. 309–11.

Craft, Stephanie and Wayne Wanta (2004) 'Women in the newsroom: Influences of female editors and reporters on the news agenda', *Journalism & Mass Communication Quarterly*, 81(1), pp. 124–38.

Croteau, David and William Hoynes (2006) *The Business of Media: Corporate Media and the Public Interest*, Thousand Oaks, CA, Pine Forge Press.

Dahlberg, Lincoln (2004) 'The Habermasian public sphere: A specification of the idealized conditions of democratic communication', *Studies in Social and Political Thought*, 10, pp. 2–18.

Dahlgren, Peter and Colin Sparks (eds) (1991) *Communication and Citizenship: Journalism and the Public Sphere*, London, Routledge.

de Beer, Arnold S. and John C. Merrill (eds) (2004) *Global Journalism: Topical Issues and Media Systems*, Boston, Pearson.

de Bruin, Marjan (2000) 'Gender, organizational and professional identities in journalism', *Journalism*, 1(2), pp. 217–38.

de Bruin, Marjan and Karen Ross (eds) (2004) *Gender and Newsroom Cultures: Identities at Work*, Cresskill, Hampton Press.

de Burgh, Hugo (2000) 'Chinese journalism and the Academy: The politics and pedagogy of the media', *Journalism Studies*, 1(4), pp. 549–58.

de Burgh, Hugo (2003) 'Skills are not enough: The case for journalism as an academic discipline', *Journalism*, 4(1), pp. 95–112.

de Burgh, Hugo (ed.) (2005) *Making Journalists: Diverse Models, Global Issues*, London and New York, Routledge.

Delano, Anthony (2000) 'No sign of a better job: 100 years of British journalism', *Journalism Studies*, 1(2), pp. 261–72.

Delano, Anthony (2003) 'Women journalists: What's the difference?', *Journalism Studies*, 4(2), pp. 273–86.

Delgado-P., Guillermo (2002) 'Solidarity in cyberspace: Indigenous peoples online; have new electronic technologies fulfilled the promise they once seemed to hold for indigenous peoples? The answers are yes, and no', *NACLA Report on the Americas*, 35(5), pp. 49–52.

de M. Higgins, Vanessa, Teresa Correa, Maria Flores and Sharon Meraz (2008) 'Women and the news: Latin America and the Caribbean', in Paula Poindexter, Sharon Meraz and Amy Schmitz Weiss (eds) *Women, Men, and News*, pp. 239–66. New York and London, Routledge.

Dennis, Everett (1988) 'Whatever happened to Marse Robert's dream? The dilemma of American journalism education', *Gannett Center Journal*, 2(2), pp. 1–22.

De Swert, Knut and Marc Hooghe (2010) 'When do women get a voice? Explaining the presence of female news sources in Belgian news broadcasts (2003–5)', *European Journal of Communication*, 25(1), pp. 69–84.

Deuze, Mark (2002) 'National news cultures: A comparison of Dutch, German, British, Australian, and U.S. journalists', *Journalism & Mass Communication Quarterly*, 79(1), pp. 134–49.

Deuze, Mark (2003) 'The web and its journalisms: Considering the consequences of different types of news media online', *New Media & Society*, 5, pp. 203–30.

Deuze, Mark (2004) 'Global journalism education', in Arnold S.de Beer and John C. Merrill (eds) *Global Journalism: Topical Issues and Media Systems*, 4th edn, pp. 128–41. Boston, Pearson.

Deuze, Mark (2005) 'What is journalism?: Professional identity and ideology of journalists reconsidered', *Journalism*, 6(4), pp. 442–64.

Deuze, Mark (2006) 'Global journalism education: A conceptual approach', *Journalism Studies*, 7(1), pp. 19–34.

Deuze, Mark (2007) *Media Work*, Cambridge, Polity.

Deuze, Mark (2008) 'Understanding journalism as newswork: How it changes, and how it remains the same', *Westminster Papers in Communication and Culture*, 5(2), pp. 4–23.

Deuze, Mark (2009) 'The people formerly known as the employers', *Journalism*, 10(3), pp. 315–18.

Deuze, Mark, Christoph Neuberger and Steve Paulussen (2004) 'Journalism education and online journalists in Belgium, Germany, and The Netherlands', *Journalism Studies*, 5(1), pp. 19–29.

d'Haenens, Leen (2003) 'Editorial: Determinants of international news production', *Gazette*, 65(1), pp. 5–7.

d'Haenens, Leen, Nicholas Jankowski and Ard Heuvelman (2004) 'News in online and print newspapers: Differences in reader consumption and recall', *New Media & Society*, 6(3), pp. 363–82.

Dinh, Hang (2004) 'Vietnam's journalism training and education challenge of a free market economy', *Asia Pacific Media Educator*, 15, pp. 181–91.

Djerf-Pierre, Monika (2007) 'The gender of journalism: The structure and logic of the field in the twentieth century', *Nordicom Review*, 28 (Jubilee Issue), pp. 81–104.

Donsbach, Wolfgang and Thomas E. Patterson (2004) 'Political news journalists: Partisanship, professionalism, and political roles in five countries', in Frank Esser and Barbara Pfetsch (eds) *Comparing Political Communication: Theories, Cases, and Challenges*, pp. 251–70. New York, Cambridge University Press.

Dorroh, Jennifer (2007/2008) 'Armies of one: Are ABC's new one-person foreign bureaus a model for covering the world in the digital age?', *American Journalism Review*, 29(6), pp. 12–13.

el-Nawawy, Mohammed (2007) 'Between the newsroom and the classroom: Education standards and practices for print journalism in Egypt and Jordan', *International Communication Gazette*, 69(1), pp. 69–90.

Elvestad, Eiri and Arild Blekesaune (2008) 'Newspaper readers in Europe: A multilevel study of individual and national differences', *European Journal of Communication*, 23(4), pp. 425–47.

Entman, Robert (1991) 'Framing US coverage of international news: Contrasts in narratives of the KAL and Iran Air incidents', *Journal of Communication*, 41(4), pp. 6–27.

Entman, Robert (1993) 'Framing: Toward clarification of a fractured paradigm', *Journal of Communication*, 43(4), pp. 51–8.

Erickson, Emily and John Maxwell Hamilton (2007) 'Happy landings: A defense of parachute journalism', in David D. Perlmutter and John Maxwell Hamilton(eds) *From Pigeons to News Portals: Foreign Reporting and the Challenge of New Technology*, pp. 130–49. Baton Rouge, LA, Louisiana State University Press.

Esser, Frank (1998) 'Editorial structures and work principles in British and German newsrooms', *European Journal of Communication*, 13(3), pp. 375–405.

Esser, Frank (2003) 'Journalism training in Great Britain: A system rich in tradition but currently in transition', in Romy Fröhlich and Christina Holtz-Bacha (eds) *Journalism Education in Europe and North America*, Cresskill, Hampton Press.

Ettema, James E., D. Charles Whitney and Daniel B. Wackman (1987) 'Professional mass communicators', in Charley R. Berger and Steven H. Chaffee (eds) *Handbook of Communication Science*, pp. 747–80. Beverly Hills, CA, Sage.

Fawcett, Liz (2002) 'Why peace journalism isn't news', *Journalism Studies*, 3(2), pp. 213–23.

Feist, Samuel (2001) 'Facing down the global village: The media impact', in Richard L. Kugler and Ellen L. Frost (eds) *The Global Century: Globalization and National Security*, pp. 709–25. Washington, DC, National Defense University Press.

Fenton, Natalie (ed.) (2010a) *New Media, Old News: Journalism and Democracy in the Digital Age*, London, Sage.

Fenton, Natalie (2010b) 'Drowning or waving? New media, journalism and democracy', in Natalie Fenton (ed.) *New Media, Old News: Journalism and Democracy in the Digital Age*, pp. 3–16. London, Sage.

Fenton, Tom (2005) *Bad News: The Decline of Reporting, the Business of News, and the Danger to Us All*, New York, Reagan Books.

Ferreira, Leonardo and Donn J. Tillson (2000) 'Sixty-five years of journalism education in Latin America', *The Florida Communication Journal*, 27(1&2), pp. 61–79.

Flanagin, Andrew J. and Miriam J. Metzger (2001) 'Internet use in the contemporary media environment', *Human Communication Research*, 27(1), pp. 153–81.

Fourie, Pieter J. (2008) 'Ubuntuism as a framework for South African media practice and performance: Can it work?', *Communicatio: South African Journal for Communication Theory and Research*, 34(1), pp. 53–79.

Franklin, Bob (1997) *Newszak and News Media*, London, Arnold.

Franklin, Bob (2008) 'The future of newspapers', *Journalism Studies*, 9(5), pp. 630–41.

Franks, Suzanne (2005) 'Lacking a clear narrative: Foreign reporting after the Cold War', *The Political Quarterly*, 76(1), pp. 91–101.

Freedman, Des (2010) 'The political economy of the 'new' news environment', in Natalie Fenton (ed.) *New Media, Old News: Journalism and Democracy in the Digital Age*, pp. 35–50. London, Sage.

Freedman, Eric (2007) 'After the Tulip Revolution: Journalism education in Kyrgyzstan', *Asia Pacific Media Educator*, 18, pp. 171–84.

Frère, Marie-Soleil (2007) *The Media and Conflicts in Central Africa*, Boulder, CO, Lynne Rienner.

Friedlander, Peter G. (2009) 'The Hindi newspaper revolution: Teaching reading of print and online news media', *Electronic Journal of Foreign Language Teaching*, 6(1), pp. 254–67.

Frith, Simon and Peter Meech (2007) 'Becoming a journalist: Journalism education and journalism culture', *Journalism*, 8(2), pp. 137–64.

Fröhlich, Romy (2007) 'Three steps forward and two back?: Women journalists in the Western world between progress, standstill, and retreat', in Pamela J. Creedon and Judith Cramer (eds) *Women in Mass Communication*, 3rd edn, pp. 161–76. Thousand Oaks, Sage.

Fröhlich, Romy and Christina Holtz-Bacha (eds) (2003a) *Journalism Education in Europe and North America: An International Comparison*, Cresskill, Hampton Press.

Fröhlich, Romy and Christina Holtz-Bacha (2003b) 'Summary: Challenges for today's journalism education', in Romy Fröhlich and Christina Holtz-Bacha (eds) *Journalism Education in Europe and North America: An International Comparison*, pp. 307–23. Cresskill, Hampton Press.

Fröhlich, Romy and Christina Holtz-Bacha (2003c) 'Journalism education in Germany: A wide range of different ways', in Romy Fröhlich and Christina Holtz-Bacha (eds) *Journalism Education in Europe and North America*, pp. 187–205. Cresskill, Hampton Press.

Fröhlich, Romy and Christina Holtz-Bacha (2009) 'The German journalism education landscape', in Georgios Terzis (ed.) *European Journalism Education*, Bristol, Intellect, pp. 131–48.

Fröhlich, Romy and Sue A. Lafky (2008) 'Introduction', in Romy Fröhlich and Sue A. Lafky (eds) *Women Journalists in the Western World: What Surveys Tell Us*, pp. 1–9. Cresskill, Hampton Press.

Gallagher, Margaret (1981) *Unequal Opportunities - The Case of Women and the Media*, Paris, UNESCO.

Gallagher, Margaret (1995) *An Unfinished Story: Gender Patterns in Media Employment*, Paris, UNESCO.

Gallagher, Margaret (2001) *Gender Setting: New Agendas for Media Monitoring and Advocacy*, London and New York, Zed Books.

Gallagher, Margaret (2005) *Global Media Monitoring Project 2005*, London, World Association for Christian Communication.

Gallagher, Margaret (2008) 'At the millennium: Shifting patterns in gender, culture and journalism', in Romy Fröhlich and Sue A. Lafky (eds) *Women Journalists in the Western World: What Surveys Tell Us*, pp. 201–16. Cresskill, Hampton Press.

Gallagher, Margaret (2010) *Global Media Monitoring Project 2010*, London, World Association for Christian Communication.

Galtung, Johan (1969) 'Violence, peace, and peace research', *Journal of Peace Research*, (6), pp. 167–91.

Galtung, Johan (1998) 'Peace journalism: What, why, who, how, when, where', Paper presented in the workshop, "What are journalists for?" TRANSCEND, Taplow Court, UK, 3–6 September.

Galtung, Johan (2002) 'Peace journalism: A challenge', in Wilhelm Kempf and Heikki Luostarinen (eds) *Journalism and the New World Order, Vol. 2: Studying War and the Media*, pp. 259–72. Göteborg, Nordicom.

Galtung, Johan and Tord Höivik (1971) 'Structural and direct violence: A note on operationalization', *Journal of Peace Research*, (8), pp. 73–6.

Galtung, Johan and Mari Holmboe Ruge (1965) 'The structure of foreign news', *Journal of Peace Research*, 2(1), pp. 64–91.

Galtung, Johan and Mari Holmboe Ruge (1970) 'The structure of foreign news: The presentation of the Congo, Cuba and Cyprus crises in four foreign newspapers', in

Jeremy Tunstall (ed.) *Media Sociology: A Reader*, pp. 259–98. London: Constable & Co. Ltd.

Garnham, Nicholas (1990) *Capitalism and Communication: Global Culture and the Economics of Information*, London, Sage.

Garrison, Bruce (2000) 'Journalists' perceptions of online information-gathering problems', *Journalism & Mass Communication Quarterly*, 77(3), pp. 500–14.

Gasher, Mike and Sandra Gabriele (2004) 'Increasing circulation? A comparative news-flow study of the Montreal *Gazette's* hard-copy and on-line editions', *Journalism Studies*, 5(3), pp. 311–23.

Gaunt, Philip (1992) *Making the Newsmakers: International Handbook on Journalism Training*, Westport, CT, Greenwood Press.

Gerbert, Elaine (2001) 'Images of Japan in the digital age', *East Asia: An International Quarterly*, 19(1), pp. 95–122.

Getlin, Josh (1999) 'The republic of entertainment', *Nieman Reports*, Summer, pp. 68–9.

Gieber, Walter (1956) 'Across the desk: A study of 16 telegraph editors', *Journalism Quarterly*, 33(3), pp. 423–32.

Giffard, C. Anthony (1975) 'Ancient Rome's Daily Gazette', *Journalism History*, 2(4), pp. 106–09, 32.

Gilboa, Eytan (2005) 'The CNN effect: The search for a communication theory of international relations', *Political Communication*, 22(1), pp. 27–44.

Green, Kerry (1997) 'Online and undercover: Discovering the boundaries', *Australian Journalism Review*, 19(2), pp. 24–30.

Green, Kerry (2005) 'Journalism education: Towards a better understanding', *Australian Journalism Review*, 27(1), pp. 185–94.

Griffin, Michael (1999) 'The great war photographs: Constructing myths of history and photojournalism', in Bonnie Brennen and Hanno Hardt (eds) *Picturing the Past: Media, History, and Photography*, pp. 122–57. Urbana, University of Illinois.

Gross, Peter and Timothy Kenny (2008) 'The long journey ahead: Journalism education in Central Asia', *Problems of Post-Communism*, 55(6), pp. 54–60.

Grove, Steve (2008) 'YouTube: The flattening of politics', *Nieman Reports*, 62(2), pp. 28–30.

Gunter, Barrie (2003) *News and the Net*, Mahwah, New Jersey, Lawrence Erlbaum Associates.

Gunther, Marc (1999) 'The transformation of network news', *Nieman Reports*, Summer, pp. 20–32.

Gutiérrez Villalobos, Sonia (2005) 'Pro-conflict and pro-cooperation coverage: The San Juan River conflict', *Conflict & Communication Online*, 4(1).

Habermas, Jürgen (1989) *The Structural Transformation of the Public Sphere: An Enquiry into a Category of Bourgeois Society*, Cambridge, MA, MIT Press.

Hachten, William A. (1981) *The World News Prism: Changing Media, Clashing Ideologies*, Ames, Iowa State University Press.

Hachten, William A. (1996) *The World News Prism: Changing Media of International Communication*, 4th edn, Ames, Iowa State University Press.

Hackett, Robert A. (2006) 'Is Peace Journalism possible? Three frameworks for assessing structure and agency in news media', *Conflict & Communication Online*, 5(2).

Hafez, Kai (2009) 'Let's improve 'global journalism'!', *Journalism*, 10(3), pp. 329–31.

Hallin, Daniel C. (1986) *The Uncensored War: The Media and Vietnam*, New York, Oxford University Press.

Hallin, Daniel C. (1996) 'Commercialism and professionalism in the American news media', in James Curran and Michael Gurevitch (eds) *Mass Media and Society*, 2nd edn, pp. 218–37. London, Arnold.

Hallin, Daniel C. (2000) 'Commercialism and professionalism in the American news media', in James Curran and Michael Gurevitch, (eds) *Mass Media and Society*, 3rd edn, pp. 218–37. London, Arnold.

Hallin, Daniel C. and Paolo Mancini (2004) *Comparing Media Systems: Three Models of Media and Politics*, Cambridge, Cambridge University Press.

Hallin, Daniel C. and Stylianos Papathanassopoulos (2002) 'Political clientelism and the media: Southern Europe and Latin America in comparative perspective', *Media, Culture & Society*, 24(2), pp. 175–95.

Halloran, James D. (1998) 'Social science, communication research and the Third World', *Media Development*, 45(2), pp. 43–6.

Hamelink, Cees J. (2008) 'Media between warmongers and peacemakers', *Media, War & Conflict*, 1(1), pp. 77–83.

Hamilton, John Maxwell and Eric Jenner (2003) 'The new foreign correspondence', *Foreign Affairs*, 82(5), pp. 131–8.

Hamilton, James T. (2004) *All the News that's Fit to Sell: How the Market Transforms Information into News*, Princeton, NJ, Princeton University Press.

Hammond, William M. (1989) 'The press in Vietnam as agent of defeat: A critical examination', *Reviews in American History*, 17(2), pp. 312–23.

Hanitzsch, Thomas (2004) 'Journalists as peacekeeping force? Peace journalism and mass communication theory', *Journalism Studies*, 5(4), pp. 483–95.

Hanitzsch, Thomas (2005) 'Journalists in Indonesia: Educated but timid watchdogs', *Journalism Studies*, 6(4), pp. 493–508.

Hanitzsch, Thomas (2007a) 'Deconstructing journalism culture: Towards a universal theory', *Communication Theory*, 17(4), pp. 367–85.

Hanitzsch, Thomas (2007b) 'Situating peace journalism in journalism studies: A critical appraisal', *Conflict & Communication Online*, 6(2).

Hanitzsch, Thomas (2008) 'Comparing media systems: Recent development and directions for future research', *Journal of Global Mass Communication*, 1(3/4), pp. 111–17.

Hanitzsch, Thomas (2009) 'Comparative journalism studies', in Karin Wahl-Jorgensen and Thomas Hanitzsch (eds) *The Handbook of Journalism Studies*, pp. 413–27. New York, Routledge.

Hanitzsch, Thomas (2011) 'Populist disseminators, detached watchdogs, critical change agents and opportunist facilitators: Professional milieus, the journalistic field and autonomy in 18 countries', *International Communication Gazette*, accepted for publication.

Hanitzsch, T., Maria Anikina, Rosa Berganza, Incilay Cangoz, Mihai Coman, Basyouni Hamada, Folker Hanusch, Christopher D. Karadjov, Claudia Mellado, Sonia Virginia Moreira, Peter G. Mwesige, Patrick Lee Plaisance, Zvi Reich, Josef Seethaler, Elizabeth A. Skewes, Dani Vardiansyah Noor, and Kee Wang Yuen (2010) 'Modeling perceived influences on journalism: Evidence from a cross-national survey of journalists', *Journalism & Mass Communication Quarterly*, 87(1), pp. 5–22.

Hanitzsch, Thomas, Folker Hanusch, Claudia Mellado Ruiz, Maria Anikina, Rosa Berganza, Incilay Cangoz, Mihai Coman, Basyouni Hamada, Maria Elena Hernandez, Christopher D. Karadjov, Sonia Virginia Moreira, Peter G. Mwesige, Patrick Lee Plaisance, Zvi Reich, Josef Seethaler, Elizabeth A. Skewes, Dani Vardiansyah Noor and Edgar Kee Wang Yuen (2011) 'Mapping journalism cultures across nations: A comparative study of 18 countries', *Journalism Studies*, 12(3), pp. 273–93.

Hanitzsch, Thomas, Josef Seethaler, Elizabeth A. Skewes, Maria Anikina, Rosa Berganza, Incilay Cangoz, Mihai Coman, Basyouni Hamada, Folker Hanusch, Maria Elena Hernandez Ramirez, Christopher D. Karadjov, Claudia Mellado, Sonia Virginia Moreira, Peter G. Mwesige, Patrick Lee Plaisance, Zvi Reich, Dani Vardiansyah Noor and Kee Wang Yuen (2011) 'Worlds of journalism: Journalistic cultures, professional autonomy and perceived influences across 18 nations', in David H. Weaver and Lars Willnat (eds) *The Global Journalist*.

Hanusch, Folker (2008a) 'Valuing those close to us: A study of German and Australian quality newspapers' reporting of death in foreign news', *Journalism Studies*, 9(3), pp. 341–56.

Hanusch, Folker (2008b) 'Mapping Australian journalism culture: Results from a survey of journalists' role perceptions', *Australian Journalism Review*, 30(2), pp. 97–109.

Hanusch, Folker (2009) 'A product of their culture: Using a value systems approach to understand the work practices of journalists', *International Communication Gazette*, 71(7), pp. 613–26.

Hanusch, Folker (2010a) 'Cultural influences on journalism practice: On the importance of cultural values for comparative journalism research', Paper presented at the International Conference Comparing Journalism: Theory, Methodology, Findings, Eichstätt, Germany, 9–11 July.

Hanusch, Folker (2010b) 'The dimensions of travel journalism: Exploring new fields for journalism research beyond the news', *Journalism Studies*, 11(1), pp. 68–82.

Hanusch, Folker (2010c) *Representing Death in the News: Journalism, Media and Mortality*, Basingstoke, Palgrave Macmillan.

Harcup, Tony and Deirdre O'Neill (2001) 'What is news? Galtung and Ruge revisited', *Journalism Studies*, 2(2), pp. 261–80.

Harding, Frances (2003) 'Africa and the moving image: Television, film and video', *Journal of African Cultural Studies*, 16(1), pp. 69–84.

Hargreaves, Ian (2000) 'Is there a future for foreign news?', *Historical Journal of Film, Radio and Television*, 20(1), pp. 55–61.

Harrison, Jackie and Lorna M. Woods (2001) 'Defining European public service broadcasting', *European Journal of Communication*, 16(4), pp. 477–504.

Harrison, Jackie, Karen Sanders, Christina Holtz-Bacha, Raquel Rodriguez Diaz, Serra Görpe, Salma Ghanem and Chioma Ugochukwu (2008) 'Women and the news: Europe, Egypt and the Middle East, and Africa', in Paula Poindexter, Sharon Meraz and Amy Schmitz Weiss (eds) *Women, Men, and News*, pp. 175–211. New York and London, Routledge.

Hartley, John (2000) 'Communicative democracy in a redactional society: The future of journalism studies', *Journalism Studies*, 1(1), pp. 39–48.

Hau'ofa, Epeli (1993) 'Our sea of islands', in Epeli Hau'ofa, Eric Waddell and Vijay Naidu (eds) *A New Oceania: Rediscovering Our Sea of Islands*, Suva, University of the South Pacific.

Bibliography

Hawkins, Virgil (2002) 'The other side of the CNN factor: The media and conflict', *Journalism Studies*, 3(2), pp. 225–40.

Hendrickson, Richard D. (2006) 'Publishing e-mail addresses ties readers to writers', *Newspaper Research Journal*, 27(2), pp. 52–68.

Henningham, John (1993) 'Characteristics and attitudes of Australian journalists', *Electronic Journal of Communication*, 4.

Henningham, John (1995) 'Australian journalists' reactions to new technology', *Prometheus*, 13(2), pp. 225–38.

Herscovitz, Heloiza G. (2004) 'Brazilian journalists' perceptions of media roles, ethics and foreign influences on Brazilian journalism', *Journalism Studies*, 5(1), pp. 71–86.

Hess, Stephen (1996) 'Media mavens', *Society*, 33(3), pp. 70–8.

Hickey, Neil (1998) 'Money lust: How pressure for profit is perverting journalism', *Columbia Journalism Review*, 37(2), pp. 28–36.

Hiebert, Ray and Peter Gross (2003) 'Remedial education: The remaking of Eastern European journalists', in Romy Fröhlich and Christina Holtz-Bacha (eds) *Journalism Education in Europe and North America*, pp. 257–82. Cresskill, Hampton Press.

Hirst, Martin (2010) 'Journalism education "down under": A tale of two paradigms', *Journalism Studies*, 11(1), pp. 83–98.

Hjarvard, Stig (2002) 'The study of international news', in Klaus Bruhn Jensen (ed.) *A Handbook of Media and Communication Research*, pp. 91–7. London, Routledge.

Hochheimer, John L. (2001) 'Journalism education in Africa', *Critical Arts*, 15(1), pp. 97–116.

Hofstede, Geert (1980) *Culture's Consequences: International Differences in Work-Related Values*, Beverly Hills, Sage.

Hofstede, Geert (2001) *Culture's Consequences: Comparing Values, Behaviors, Institutions, and Organizations Across Nations*, 2nd edn, London, Sage.

Hofstede, Geert and Gert Jan Hofstede (2005) *Cultures and Organizations: Software of the Mind*, 2nd edn, New York, McGraw-Hill.

Hoge, James F. (1997) 'Foreign news: Who gives a damn?', *Columbia Journalism Review*, 36(4), pp. 48–52.

Holman, Kate (1992) *Women in the News: International Survey of Women's Rights in Journalism*, Brussels, International Federation of Journalists.

Howard, Ross (2003) *Conflict Sensitive Journalism: A Handbook*, Vancouver, IMPACS.

Huang, Chengju (2002) *From Communism to Commercialism: Media and Social Transformation in China*, Unpublished PhD thesis. St. Lucia, The University of Queensland.

Hume, Ellen (2007) *University Journalism Education: A Global Challenge*, Washington, DC, Center for International Media Assistance.

Hurwitz, Roger (1999) 'Who needs politics? Who needs people? The ironies of democracy in cyberspace', *Contemporary Sociology*, 28(6), pp. 655–61.

Inglehart, Ronald (1997) *Modernization and Postmodernization: Cultural, Economic and Political Change in 43 Societies*, Princeton, NJ, Princeton University Press.

International Federation of Journalists (2009) *Getting the Balance Right: Gender Equality in Journalism*, Brussels, International Federation of Journalists.

Iriekpen, Davidson (2009) 'Concern, anger over new anti-media Bill', *This Day*, 16 November, viewed 23 October 2010, http://allafrica.com/stories/200911160001.html.

Iseke-Barnes, Judy M. (2002) 'Aboriginal and indigenous people's resistance, the Internet, and education', *Race, Ethnicity and Education*, 5(2), pp. 171–98.

Jakubowicz, Karol (2009) 'The Eastern European/Post-Communist media model countries: Introduction', in George Terzis (ed.) *European Journalism Education*, pp. 349–56. Bristol, Intellect.

Jankowski, Nicholas W. and Martine van Selm (2000) 'Traditional news media online: An examination of added values', *Communications*, 25(1), pp. 85–101.

Janowitz, Morris (1975) 'Professional models in journalism: The gatekeeper and the advocate', *Journalism Quarterly*, 52(4), pp. 618–26.

Johansen, Peter, David H. Weaver and Christopher Dornan (2001) 'Journalism education in the United States and Canada: Not merely clones', *Journalism Studies*, 2(4), pp. 469–83.

Joseph, Ammu (2007) 'The gender factor' in Nalini Rajan (ed.) *21st Century Journalism in India*, pp. 29–44. New Delhi, Sage.

Josephi, Beate (2007) 'Internationalizing the journalistic professional model: Imperatives and impediments', *Global Media and Communication*, 3(3), pp. 300–6.

Josephi, Beate (2009) 'Journalism education', in Karin Wahl-Jorgensen and Thomas Hanitzsch (eds) *The Handbook of Journalism Studies*, pp. 42–56. New York and London, Routledge.

Joye, Stijn (2010) 'Around the world in 8 pages? A longitudinal analysis of international news coverage in Flemish newspapers (1986–2006)', viewed 3 October 2010, http://biblio.ugent.be/input/download?func=downloadFile&fileOId=940470.

Karan, Kavita (2001) 'Journalism education in India', *Journalism Studies*, 2(2), pp. 294–99.

Kariel, Herbert G. and Lynn A. Rosenvall (1995) *Places in the News: A Study of News Flows*, Ottawa, Carleton University Press.

Karstens, Eric (2009) 'The Internet: Tool of tyranny or democracy?', European Journalism Centre, June 10, 2009, viewed 25 October 2010, http://www.ejc.net/magazine/article/the_internet_tool_of_tyranny_or_democracy/.

Kasoma, Francis (1996) 'The foundations of African ethics (Afriethics) and the professional practice of journalism: The case for society-centred media morality', *Africa Media Review*, 10(3), pp. 93–116.

Katovsky, Bill and Timothy Carlson (2003) *Embedded: The Media at War in Iraq*, Guilford, CT, Lyons Press.

Kempf, Wilhelm (2002) 'Conflict coverage and conflict escalation', in Wilhelm Kempf and Heikki Luostarinen (eds) *Journalism and the New World Order. Volume II: Studying War and the Media*, pp. 59–72. Göteborg, Nordicom.

Kempf, Wilhelm (2003) 'Konstruktive Berichterstattung - ein sozialpsychologisches Forschungs- und Entwicklungsprogramm [Constructive reporting - a social psychological research and development program]', *Conflict & Communication Online*, 2(2).

Kempf, Wilhelm (2006) 'Acceptance and impact of de-escalation-oriented conflict coverage', *Diskussionsbeiträge der Projektgruppe Friedensforschung Konstanz*, 60.

Kempf, Wilhelm (2007) 'Peace journalism: A tightrope walk between advocacy journalism and constructive conflict coverage', *Conflict & Communication Online*, 6(2).

Khouri, Rami G. (2001) 'Arab satellite TV: Promoting democracy or autocracy?', Media Monitors Network, viewed 12 September 2010, www.mediamonitors.net/Khouri13.html.

Kim, Eun-Gyoo and James W. Hamilton (2006) 'Capitulation to capital? OhmyNews as alternative media', *Media, Culture & Society*, 28(4), pp. 541–60.

Kim, Hun Shik, Seow Ting Lee and Crispin C. Maslog (2008) 'Peacemakers or warmongers? Asian news media coverage of conflicts', *Journal of Global Mass Communication*, 1(3/4), pp. 251–70.

Kim, Kyung-Mo and Youn-Jung Kim (2005) 'Coverage difference of female newsmakers among national newspapers: Influences of journalist gender and gender ratio in the newsroom', *Korean Journalism and Information Studies*, 29, pp. 7–41, 273.

Kim, Kyung-Hee and Youngmin Yoon (2009) 'The influence of journalists' gender on newspaper stories about women Cabinet members in South Korea', *Asian Journal of Communication*, 19(3), pp. 289–301.

Kim, Yung Soo and James D. Kelly (2008) 'A matter of culture: A comparative study of photojournalism in American and Korean newspapers', *International Communication Gazette*, 70(2), pp. 155–73.

Kirkpatrick, Rod (1996) '75 years of tertiary journalism studies', *Australian Studies in Journalism*, 5, pp. 256–64.

Kitch, Carolyn (2002) 'Women in journalism', in W. David Sloan and Lisa Mullikin Parcell (eds) *American Journalism: History, Principles, Practices*, pp. 87–96. Jefferson, NC, McFarland & Company.

Knickmeyer, Ellen (2005) 'Darfur fits into a pattern of reporting neglect', *Nieman Reports*, 59(2), pp. 113–14.

Knudson, Jerry W. (1987) 'Journalism education's roots in Latin America are traced', *Journalism Educator*, 41(4), pp. 22–4, 33.

Knudson, Jerry W. (1996) 'Licensing journalists in Latin America: An appraisal', *Journalism & Mass Communication Quarterly*, 73(4), pp. 878–89.

Köcher, Renate (1986) 'Bloodhounds or missionaries: Role definitions of German and British journalists', *European Journal of Communication*, 1, pp. 43–64.

Kohut, Andrew (2002) 'The press shines at a dark moment', *Columbia Journalism Review*, 40(5), pp. 54–5.

Koponen, Juhani (2003) 'The structure of foreign news revisited', in Nando Malmelin (ed.) *Välittämisen tiede. Viestinnän näkökulmia yhteiskuntaan, kulttuuriin jakansalaisuuteen. [The science of mediation and caring. Communicational viewpoints of society, culture and citizenship].* pp. 144–66. Helsinki, Helsingin yliopisto.

Kovach, Bill (1999) 'Looking inside the business of journalism', *Nieman Reports*, Summer (2).

Kruckeberg, Dean (1995) 'International journalism ethics', in John C. Merrill (ed.) *Global Journalism: Survey of International Communication*, 3rd edn, pp. 77–87. White Plains, NY, Longman.

Lambeth, Edmund B. (1995) 'Global media philosophies', in John C. Merrill (ed.) *Global Journalism: Survey of International Communication*, 3rd edn, pp. 3–18. White Plains, NY, Longman.

Lauf, Edmund (2001) 'The vanishing young reader: Sociodemographic determinants of newspaper use as a source of political information in Europe, 1980–98', *European Journal of Communication*, 16(2), pp. 233–43.

Lavie, Aliza (1997) *The Agenda as Shaped by Female and Male Editors in Israel's Print Press*, MA Thesis. Ramat Gan, Israel, Bar-Ilan University.

Lavie, Aliza and Sam Lehman-Wilzig (2003) 'Whose news?: Does gender determine the editorial product?', *European Journal of Communication*, 18(1), pp. 5–29.

Lavie, Aliza and Sam Lehman-Wilzig (2005) 'The method is the message: Explaining inconsistent findings in gender and news production research', *Journalism*, 6(1), pp. 66–89.

Lee, Seow Ting (2009) 'Peace journalism', in Lee Wilkins and Clifford G. Christians (eds) *The Handbook of Mass Media Ethics*, pp. 258–75. New York, Routledge.

Lee, Seow Ting and Crispin C. Maslog (2005) 'War or peace journalism? Asian newspaper coverage of conflicts', *Journal of Communication*, 55(2), pp. 311–29.

Lee, Seow Ting, Crispin C. Maslog and Hun Shik Kim (2006) 'Asia's local conflicts and the war in Iraq: A comparative framing analysis', *The International Communication Gazette*, 68(5–6), pp. 499–518.

Lehrer, Jim (1999) 'Blurring the lines hurts journalism', *Nieman Reports*, Summer, pp. 65–6.

Lerner, Daniel (1958) *The Passing of Traditional Society: Modernizing the Middle East*, Glencoe, IL, The Free Press.

Leung, Kwok and Michael H. Bond (2004) 'Social axioms: A model for social beliefs in multi-cultural perspective', *Advances in Experimental Social Psychology*, 36, pp. 119–97.

Lewin, Kurt (1947) 'Frontiers in group dynamics: II. Channels of group life; social planning and action research', *Human Relations*, 1(2), pp. 143–53.

Lewin, Kurt (1951) *Field Theory in Social Science: Selected Theoretical Papers*, New York, Harper.

Liebler, Carol M. and Susan J. Smith (1997) 'Tracking gender differences: A comparative analysis of network correspondents and their sources', *Journal of Broadcasting & Electronic Media*, 41(1), pp. 58–68.

Lim, Y. S. and J. Y. Uhm (2005) 'Examining gender equity consciousness and attitude of female journalists in managerial positions', *Media, Gender, Culture*, 3, pp. 144–81.

Livingston, Steven (2007) 'The Nokia effect: The reemergence of amateur journalism and what it means for international affairs', in David D. Perlmutter and John Maxwell Hamilton (eds) *From Pigeons to News Portals: Foreign Reporting and the Challenge of New Technology*, pp. 47–69. Baton Rouge, LA, Louisiana State University Press.

Livingstone, Sonia (2003) 'On the challenges of cross-national comparative media research', *European Journal of Communication*, 18(4), pp. 477–500.

Löffelholz, Martin (ed.) (2004) *Krieg als Medienereignis II: Krisenkommunikation im 21. Jahrhundert (War as a Media Event II: Crisis Communication in the 21st Century)*, Wiesbaden, VS Verlag für Sozialwissenschaften.

Lont, Cynthia (1995) *Women and Media: Content, Careers, and Criticism*, Belmont, CA, Wadsworth Publishing.

Loyn, David (2007) 'Good journalism or peace journalism', *Conflict & Communication Online*, 6(2).

Lugo-Ocando, Jairo (ed.) (2008) *The Media in Latin America*, Maidenhead, Open University Press.

Lumby, Catharine (1994) 'Feminism and the media: The biggest fantasy of all', *Media Information Australia*, 72, pp. 49–54.

Lünenborg, Margret (1993) '"Wendezeiten': Women's journalism in East and West Germany', Paper presented at the IAMCR conference 'Europe in Turmoil: Global Perspectives', Dublin, 25–26 June.

Lutes, Jean Marie (2002) 'Into the madhouse with Nellie Bly: Girl stunt reporting in late nineteenth-century America', *American Quarterly*, 54(2), pp. 217–53.

Lynch, Jake (2007) 'Peace journalism and its discontents', *Conflict & Communication Online*, 6(2).

Lynch, Jake and Annabel McGoldrick (2005) *Peace Journalism*, Stroud, Hawthorn Press.

Macdonald, Isabel (2006) 'Teaching journalists to save the profession', *Journalism Studies*, 7(5), pp. 745–64.

Mancini, Paolo (2005) 'Is there a European model of journalism?', in Hugo de Burgh (ed.) *Making Journalists: Diverse Models, Global Issues*, pp. 77–93. London, Routledge.

Martin, L. John and Anju Grover Chaudhary (1983) *Comparative Mass Media Systems*, New York, Longman.

Maslog, Crispin C. (2000) *A Manual on Peace Reporting in Mindanao*, Manila, Philippine Press Institute.

Maslog, Crispin C., Seow Ting Lee and Hun Shik Kim (2006) 'Framing analysis of a conflict: How five Asian countries covered the war in Iraq', *Asian Journal of Communication*, 16(1), pp. 19–39.

Massey, Brian L. and Li-jing Arthur Chang (2002) 'Locating Asian values in Asian journalism: A content analysis of Web newspapers', *Journal of Communication*, 52(4), pp. 987–1003.

Massey, Doreen (1998) *Space, Place and Gender*, London, Polity Press.

May, Albert L. (2008) 'Campaign 2008: It's on YouTube', *Nieman Reports*, 62(2), pp. 24–8.

McCurdy, Patrick M. and Gerry Power (2007) 'Journalism education as a vehicle for media development in Africa: The AMDI project', *Ecquid Novi: African Journalism Studies*, 28(1&2), pp. 127–47.

McGoldrick, Annabel (2006) 'War journalism and 'objectivity'', *Conflict & Communication Online*, 5(2).

McManus, John (1995) 'A market-based model of news production', *Communication Theory*, 5(4), pp. 301–38.

McManus, John H. (1992) 'What kind of commodity is news?', *Communication Research*, 19(6), pp. 787–805.

McManus, John H. (2009) 'The commercialization of news', in Karin Wahl-Jorgensen and Thomas Hanitzsch (eds) *The Handbook of Journalism Studies*, pp. 218–233. New York, Routledge.

McQuail, Denis (1994) *Mass Communication Theory: An Introduction*, 3rd edn, London, Sage.

McQuail, Denis (2005) *McQuail's Mass Communication Theory*, 5th edn, London, Sage.

McRobbie, Angela (1996) 'More! New sexualities in girls' and women's magazines', in James Curran, David Morley and Valerie Walkerdine (eds) *Cultural Studies and Communications*, pp. 172–95. London, New York, Arnold.

McSweeney, Brendan (2002) 'Hofstede's model of national cultural differences and their consequences: A triumph of faith - A failure of analysis', *Human Relations*, 55(1), pp. 89–118.

Meadows, Michael, Susan Forde, Jacqui Ewart and Kerrie Foxwell (2007) *Community Media Matters: An Audience Study of the Australian Community Broadcasting Sector.*

Brisbane, Griffith University. Accessed on Sunday, 16 January 2011 at: www.griffith. edu.au/__.../Susan-Ford-Community-Media-matters-Exec-Sum- and-Chapt-1.pdf

Media Studies Journal (1999) 'Preface', *Media Studies Journal*, 13(1), pp. xiii–xiv.

Medsger, Betty (2005) 'The evolution of journalism education in the United States', in Hugo de Burgh (ed.) *Making Journalists: Diverse Models, Global Issues*, pp. 205–26. London and New York, Routledge.

Melki, Jad (2009) 'Journalism and media studies in Lebanon', *Journalism Studies*, 10(5), pp. 672–90.

Mellor, Noha (2005) *The Making of Arab News*, Lanham, MD, Rowman and Littlefield.

Mellor, Noha (2008) 'Arab journalists as cultural intermediaries', *The International Journal of Press/Politics*, 13(4), pp. 365–483.

Melone, Sandra, Georgios Terzis and Ozsel Beleli (2002) 'Using the media for conflict transformation: The common ground experience', in Martina Fischer and Norbert Ropers (eds) *Berghof Handbook for Conflict Transformation*, Berlin, Berghof Research Center for Constructive Conflict Management, viewed 19 May 2011, http://www. berghof-handbook.net/uploads/download/melone_hb.pdf.

Merrill, John C. (ed.) (1983) *Global Journalism: A Survey of the World's Mass Media*, New York, Longman.

Merrill, John C. (ed.) (1995) *Global Journalism: Survey of International Communication*, White Plains, NY, Longman.

Meyer, Philip (1987) *Ethical Journalism*, New York, Longman.

Miralles, Ana Maria (2010) 'Citizen voices: Public journalism made in Colombia', in Angela Romano (ed.) *International Journalism and Democracy: Civic Engagement Models From Around the World*, pp. 136–50. New York, Routledge.

Mishra, Smeeta, Xin Chen, Yi-Ning Katherine Chen and Kyung-Hee Kim (2008) 'Women and the news: India and Asia', in Paula Poindexter, Sharon Meraz and Amy Schmitz Weiss (eds) *Women, Men, and News*, pp. 212–38. New York and London, Routledge.

Moreira, Sonia Virginia and Carla Leal Rodrigues Helal (2009) 'Notes on media, journalism education and news organizations in Brazil', *Journalism*, 10(1), pp. 91–107.

Mosco, Vincent (2000) 'Webs of myth and power: Connectivity and the new computer technopolis', in Andrew Herman and Thomas Swiss (eds) *The World Wide Web and Contemporary Cultural Theory*, pp. 37–60. New York, Routledge.

Mowlana, Hamid (1997) *Global Information and World Communication: New Frontiers in International Relations*, 2nd edn, London, Sage.

Mowlana, Hamid, George Gerbner and Herbert I. Schiller (eds) (1992) *Triumph of the Image: The Media's War in the Persian Gulf – A Global Perspective*, Boulder, Westview Press.

Murphy, Sharon M. and James F. Scotton (1987) 'Dependency and journalism education in Africa: Are there alternative models', *Africa Media Review*, 1(3), pp. 11–35.

Mwangi, Susan W. (2007) *The Impact of Commercialisation of the Media on the Content of the Conglomerate-Owned Community Newspapers in South Africa: A Study of Four Community Newspapers from the Caxton CTP Publishers Stable*, Unpublished Master of Journalism and Media Studies Thesis. Johannesburg, University of the Witwatersrand.

Mwesige, Peter G. (2004) 'Disseminators, advocates and watchdogs: A profile of Ugandan journalists in the new millennium', *Journalism*, 5(1), pp. 69–96.

Naím, Moisés (2007) 'The YouTube effect', *Foreign Policy*, 158, pp. 103–4.

Nerone, John C. (ed.) (1995) *Last Rights: Revisiting Four Theories of the Press*, Urbana, University of Illinois Press.

Nguyen, An (2006) 'The status and relevance of Vietnamese journalism education: An empirical analysis', *Asia Pacific Media Educator*, 17, pp. 41–55.

Nohrstedt, Stig A. and Rune Ottosen (eds) (2005) *Global War – Local Views*, Goteborg, Nordicom.

Nordenstreng, Kaarle (2006) 'Four Theories of the Press reconsidered', in Nico Carpentier, Pille Pruulmann-Vengerfeldt, Kaarle Nordenstreng, Maren Hartmann, Peeter Vihalemm and Bart Cammaerts (eds) *Researching Media, Democracy and Participation: The Intellectual Work of the 2006 European Media and Communication Doctoral Summer School*, pp. 35–45. Tartu, Estonia, Tartu University Press.

Nordenstreng, Kaarle (2009) 'Soul-searching at the crossroads of European journalism education', in Georgios Terzis (ed.) *European Journalism Education*, pp. 511–17. Bristol, Intellect.

Nordenstreng, Kaarle and S. T. Kwame Boafo (1988) *Promotion of Textbooks for the Training of Journalists in Anglophone Africa: Final Report of an IDPC Project*, Budapest, Mass Communication Research Centre.

Nordenstreng, Kaarle, Aggrey Brown and Michael Traber (1998) 'Overview', in Kaarle Nordenstreng (ed.) *Inventory of Textbooks in Communication Studies Around the World: Final Report of the Project*, Tampere, University of Tampere.

North, Louise (2009a) *The Gendered Newsroom: How Journalists Experience the Changing World of Media*, Cresskill, Hampton Press.

North, Louise (2009b) 'Rejecting the 'F-word': How 'feminism' and 'feminists' are understood in the newsroom', *Journalism*, 10(6), pp. 739–57.

Nyamnjoh, Francis B. (2005) 'African journalism: Modernity, Africanity', *Rhodes Journalism Review*, 25, pp. 3–6.

Obijiofor, Levi (2001) 'Singaporean and Nigerian journalists' perceptions of new technologies', *Australian Journalism Review*, 23(1), pp. 131–51.

Obijiofor, Levi (2003) 'New technologies and journalism practice in Nigeria and Ghana', *AsiaPacific MediaEducator*, 14, pp. 36–56.

Obijiofor, Levi (2009) 'Journalism in the digital age: The Nigerian press framing of the Niger Delta conflict', *Ecquid Novi: African Journalism Studies*, 30(2), pp. 175–203.

Obijiofor, Levi and Kerry Green (2001) 'New technologies and future of newspapers', *AsiaPacific MediaEducator*, 11, pp. 88–99.

Obijiofor, Levi and Folker Hanusch (2003) 'Foreign news coverage in five African newspapers', *Australian Journalism Review*, 25(1), pp. 145–64.

Obijiofor, Levi and Folker Hanusch (2010) 'Students' perceptions and use of the Internet as a news channel', Paper presented at the Second World Journalism Education Congress, Grahamstown, South Africa, 5–7 July.

Ogundimu, Folu F., Olusola Yinka Oyewo and Lawrence Adegoke (2007) 'West African journalism education and the quest for professional standards', *Ecquid Novi: African Journalism Studies*, 28(1&2), pp. 191–6.

Okoko Tom, Tervil (2008) *Enhancing Gender Equality in the Media in Eastern Africa*, Djibouti, Eastern Africa Journalists Association.

Olorunyomi, Dapo (1998) 'Defiant publishing in Nigeria', in Nancy J. Woodhull and Robert W. Snyder (eds) *Journalists in Peril*, pp. 57–63. New Brunswick, USA, Transaction Publishers.

Orgeret, Kristin Skare and Helge Rønning (eds) (2009) *The Power of Communication: Changes and Challenges in African Media*, Oslo, Oslo Academic Press.

Oso, Lai (1991) 'The commercialization of the Nigerian press: Development and implications', *Africa Media Review*, 5(3), pp. 41–51.

O'Sullivan, John (2005) 'Delivering Ireland: Journalism's search for a role online', *Gazette*, 67(1), pp. 45–68.

Overholser, Geneva (1998) 'Editor Inc.', *American Journalism Review*, 20(10), pp. 48–65.

Ozgunes, Neslihan and George Terzis (2000) 'Constraints and remedies for journalists reporting national conflict: The case of Greece and Turkey', *Journalism Studies*, 1(3), pp. 405–26.

Palacios, Margarita and Javier Martinez (2006) 'Liberalism and conservatism in Chile: Attitudes and opinions of Chilean women at the start of the twenty-first century', *Journal of Latin American Studies*, 38(1), pp. 1–34.

Papathanassopoulos, Stylianos (2009) 'The Mediterranean/Polarized pluralist media model countries: Introduction', in Georgios Terzis (ed.) *European Journalism Education*, pp. 219–28. Bristol, Intellect.

Papoutsaki, Evangelia and Steve Sharp (2006) 'A journalism-education perspective on communication needs in the South Pacific', *Australian Studies in Journalism*, (16), pp. 101–28.

Parks, Michael (2002) 'Foreign news: What's next? Past failures, future promises', *Columbia Journalism Review*, 40(5), pp. 52–7.

Paschalidis, Gregory (1999) 'Images of war and the war of images', *Gramma: Journal of Theory and Criticism*, 7, pp. 121–52.

Patterson, Thomas E. and Wolfgang Donsbach (1996) 'News decisions: Journalists as partisan actors', *Political Communication*, 13, pp. 455–68.

Pauli, Carol (1999) 'Professionalism and African values at *The Daily Nation* in Kenya', Paper presented at the Association for Education in Journalism and Mass Communication National Convention, New Orleans, August 4–7.

Paulussen, Steve and Pieter Ugille (2008) 'User generated content in the newsroom: Professional and organisational constraints on participatory journalism', *Westminster Papers in Communication & Culture*, 5(2), pp. 24–41.

Pavlik, John V. (1997) 'The future of online journalism: Bonanza or blackhole?', *Columbia Journalism Review*, 36(2), pp. 30–1.

Pavlik, John V. (1999) 'New media and news: Implications for the future of journalism', *New Media & Society*, 1(1), pp. 54–9.

Peleg, Samuel (2006) 'Peace journalism through the lense of conflict theory: Analysis and practice', *Conflict & Communication Online*, 5(2).

Peleg, Samuel (2007) 'In defense of peace journalism – a rejoinder', *Conflict & Communication Online*, 6(2).

Perlmutter, David D. and John Maxwell Hamilton (eds) (2007) *From Pigeons to News Portals: Foreign Reporting and the Challenge of New Technology*, Baton Rouge, LA, Louisiana State University Press.

Peters, Bettina (2001) *Equality and Quality: Setting Standards for Women*, Brussels, International Federation of Journalists.

Peterson, Theodore (1956) 'The Social Responsibility Theory', in Fred S. Siebert, Theodore Peterson and Wilbur Schramm *Four Theories of the Press: The Authoritarian,*

Libertarian, Social Responsibility and Soviet Communist Concepts of What the Press Should Be and Do, pp. 73–103. Illinois, The University of Illinois.

Phillips, Angela (2005) 'Who's to make journalists?', in Hugo de Burgh (ed.) *Making Journalists: Diverse Models, Global Issues*, pp. 227–44. London and New York, Routledge.

Phillips, Angela (2010) 'Old sources: New bottles', in Natalie Fenton (ed.) *New Media, Old News: Journalism and Democracy in the Digital Age*, pp. 87–101. London, Sage.

Phillips, Angela, Nick Couldry and Des Freedman (2010) 'An ethical deficit? Accountability, norms, and the material conditions of contemporary journalism', in Natalie Fenton (ed.) *New Media, Old News: Journalism and Democracy in the Digital Age*, pp. 51–67. London, Sage.

Picard, Robert G. (1982/1983) 'Revisions of the 'Four Theories of the Press' model', *Mass Communication Review*, 10(1/2), pp. 25–8.

Picard, Robert G. (2004) 'Commercialism and newspaper quality', *Newspaper Research Journal*, 25(1), pp. 54–65.

Pintak, Lawrence and Jeremy Ginges (2008) 'The mission of Arab journalism: Creating change in a time of turmoil', *The International Journal of Press/Politics*, 13(3), pp. 193–227.

Pintak, Lawrence and Jeremy Ginges (2009) 'Inside the Arab newsroom: Arab journalists evaluate themselves and the competition', *Journalism Studies*, 10(2), pp. 157–77.

Porto, Mauro P. and Daniel C. Hallin (2009) 'Media and democratization in Latin America', *International Journal of Press/Politics*, 14(3), pp. 291–5.

Prado, Paola and Sallie Hughes (2009) 'Media diversity and gender (in)equality in Latin American broadcast news', Paper presented at the Congress of the Latin American Studies Association, Rio de Janeiro, June 11–14.

Preston, Paschal (2009) *Making the News: Journalism and News Cultures in Europe*, London, Routledge.

Rainey, James (2005) 'Portraits of war: When words weren't enough', *Los Angeles Times*, 21 May, http://articles.latimes.com/2005/may/21/nation/na-warphotos21, viewed 10 January 2011.

Rajan, Nalini (ed.) (2005) *Practising Journalism: Values, Constraints, Implications*, New Delhi, Sage.

Rajan, Nalini (ed.) (2007) *21st Century Journalism in India*, New Delhi, Sage.

Ramaprasad, Jyotika (2001) 'A profile of journalists in post-independence Tanzania', *Gazette*, 63(6), pp. 539–56.

Ramaprasad, Jyotika and Naila Nabil Hamdy (2006) 'Functions of Egyptian journalists: Perceived importance and actual performance', *International Communication Gazette*, 68(2), pp. 167–85.

Ramaprasad, Jyotika and James D. Kelly (2003) 'Reporting the news from the world's rooftop: A survey of Nepalese journalists', *International Communication Gazette*, 65(3), pp. 291–315.

Ramaprasad, Jyotika and Shafiqur Rahman (2006) 'Tradition with a twist: A survey of Bangladeshi journalists', *International Communication Gazette*, 68(2), pp. 148–65.

Rao, Shakuntala (2009) 'Glocalization of Indian journalism', *Journalism Studies*, 10(4), pp. 474–88.

Redden, Joanna and Tamara Witschge (2010) 'A new news order? Online news content examined', in Natalie Fenton (ed.) *New Media, Old News: Journalism and Democracy in the Digital Age*, pp. 171–86. London, Sage.

Reese, Stephen D. (2009) 'The future of journalism in emerging deliberative space', *Journalism*, 10(3), pp. 362–64.

Reese, Stephen D. and Jane Ballinger (2001) 'The roots of a sociology of news: Remembering Mr. Gates and social control in the newsroom', *Journalism & Mass Communication Quarterly*, 78(4), pp. 641–58.

Reese, Stephen D. and Jeremy Cohen (2000) 'Educating for journalism: The professionalism of scholarship', *Journalism Studies*, 1(2), pp. 213–27.

Richter, Simone (1999) Journalisten zwischen den Fronten. Kriegsberichterstattung am Beispiel Jugoslawien [Journalists between the fronts. War reporting in the example of Yugoslavia]. Opladen/Wiesbaden, Westdeutscher Verlag.

Riffe, Daniel, Charles F. Aust, Ted C. Jones, Barbara Shoemake and Shyam Sundar (1994) 'The shrinking foreign newshole of the New York "Times"', *Newspaper Research Journal*, 15(3), pp. 74–89.

Robie, David (2001) 'Newsrooms and organisations', in David Robie (ed.) *The Pacific Journalist: A Practical Guide*, pp. 147–75. Suva, University of the South Pacific.

Robie, David (2004) *Mekim Nius: South Pacific Media, Politics and Education*, Suva, USP Book Centre.

Robinson, Gertrude J. (2005) *Gender, Journalism, and Equity. Canadian, U.S., and European Perspectives*, Cresskill, Hampton Press.

Robinson, Gertrude J. (2008) 'Journalism as a symbolic practice: The gender approach in journalism research', in Martin Löffelholz and David Weaver (eds) *Global Journalism Research: Theories, Methods, Findings, Future*, pp. 79–89. Malden, MA, Blackwell.

Robinson, Gertrude J. and Armande Saint-Jean (1998) 'Canadian women journalists: The "other half" of the equation', in David H. Weaver (ed.) *The Global Journalist: News People Around the World*, pp. 351–72. Cresskill, NJ, Hampton Press.

Robinson, Piers (2002) *The CNN Effect: The Myth of News, Foreign Policy and Intervention*, London, Routledge.

Rokeach, Milton (1973) *The Nature of Human Values*, New York, Free Press.

Romano, Angela (1998) 'Normative theories of development in journalism: State versus practitioner theories in Indonesia', *Australian Journalism Review*, 20(2), pp. 60–87.

Rønning, Helge (2005) 'African journalism and the struggle for democratic media', in Hugo de Burgh (ed.) *Making Journalists: Diverse Models, Global Issues*, pp. 157–79. London, Routledge.

Rooney, Dick (2003) 'Rethinking the journalism curriculum in PNG', *Asia Pacific Media Educator*, 14, pp. 76–91.

Rooney, Richard (2007) 'Revisiting the journalism and mass communication curriculum: Some experiences from Swaziland', *Ecquid Novi: African Journalism Studies*, 28(1&2), pp. 207–21.

Rooney, Richard, Evangelia Papoutsaki and K. Pamba (2004) 'A country failed by its media: A case study from Papua New Guinea', Paper presented at the 13th AMIC Annual Conference, Impact of New and Old Media on Development in Asia, Bangkok, 1–3 July.

Ross, Karen (2001) 'Women at work: Journalism as en-gendered practice', *Journalism Studies*, 2(4), pp. 531–44.

Ross, Karen and Carolyn M. Byerly (eds) (2004) *Women and Media: International Perspectives*, Malden, MA, Blackwell.

Ross, Susan Dente (2006) '(De)Constructing conflict: A focused review of war and peace journalism', *Conflict & Communication Online*, 5(2).

Rugh, William A. (2004) *Arab Mass Media: Newspapers, Radio, and Television in Arab Politics*, Westport, CT, Praeger.

Rush, Ramona R. (1989) 'Communications at the crossroads: The gender gap connection', in Ramona R. Rush and Donna Allen (eds) *Communications at the Crossroads: The Gender Gap Connection*, pp. 3–19. Norwood, NJ, Ablex.

Rush, Ramona R. (2004) 'Three decades of women and mass communications research: The ratio of recurrent and reinforced residuum hypothesis revisited', in Ramona R. Rush, Carol E. Oukrop and Pamela J. Creedon (eds) *Seeking Equity for Women in Journalism and Mass Communication: A 30-year Update*, pp. 263–73. Mahwah, NJ, Lawrence Erlbaum.

Rush, Ramona R., Elizabeth Buck and Christine Ogan (1982) 'Women and the communications revolution: Can we get there from here?', *Chasqui*, 4(July–September), pp. 88–97.

Rush, Ramona R., Carol E. Oukrop and Katharine Sarikakis (2005) 'A global hypothesis for women in journalism and mass communications: The ratio of recurrent and reinforced residuum', *International Communication Gazette*, 67(3), pp. 239–53.

Ryszka, Franciszek (2002) 'The extermination of the Jews and the leading newspapers of the Third Reich: *Völkischer Beobachter* and *Das Reich*', in Robert Moses Shapiro (ed.) *Why Didn't the Press Shout? American and International Journalism During the Holocaust*, pp. 297–314. Jersey City, KTAV.

Sakr, Naomi (ed.) (2004) *Women and Media in the Middle East: Power through Self-Expression*, London, I.B. Tauris.

Sakr, Naomi (2005) 'The changing dynamics of Arab journalism', in Hugo de Burgh (ed.) *Making Journalists: Diverse Models, Global Issues*, pp. 142–56. London, Routledge.

Sakr, Naomi (2008) 'Women and media in Saudi Arabia: Rhetoric, reductionism and realities', *British Journal of Middle Eastern Studies*, 35(3), pp. 385–404.

Sanders, Karen, Mark Hanna, Maria Rosa Berganza and Jose Javier Sanchez Aranda (2008) 'Becoming journalists: A comparison of the professional attitudes and values of British and Spanish journalism students', *European Journal of Communication*, 23(2), pp. 133–52.

Schorr, Daniel (1998) 'CNN effect: Edge-of-seat diplomacy', *The Christian Science Monitor*, November 27, p. 11.

Schramm, Wilbur (1956) 'The Soviet Communist Theory', in Fred S. Siebert, Theodore Peterson and Wilbur Schramm *Four Theories of the Press: The Authoritarian, Libertarian, Social Responsibility and Soviet Communist Concepts of What the Press Should Be and Do*, pp. 105–46. Urbana, University of Illinois Press.

Schraven, David (2010) *'Das zweite Leben der Neda Soltani'*, 6 February, viewed 10 February 2010, http://sz-magazin.sueddeutsche.de/texte/anzeigen/32571/das-zweite-leben-der-neda-soltani.

Schultz, Julianne (1994a) 'Media convergence and the Fourth Estate', in Julianne Schultz (ed.) *Not Just Another Business: Journalists, Citizens and the Media*, pp. 15–33. Leichhardt, NSW, Pluto Press Australia.

Schultz, Julianne (1994b) 'The paradox of professionalism', in Julianne Schultz (ed.) *Not Just Another Business: Journalists, Citizens and the Media*, pp. 35–51. Leichhardt, NSW, Pluto Press Australia.

Schwartz, Shalom H. (2004) 'Mapping and interpreting cultural differences around the world', in H. Vinken, J. Soeters and P. Ester (eds) *Comparing Cultures: Dimensions of Culture in a Comparative Perspective*, pp. 43–73. Leiden, Brill.

Schwartz, Shalom H. (2007) 'Value orientations: Measurement, antecedents and consequences across nations', in Roger Jowell (ed.) *Measuring Attitudes Cross-nationally: Lessons from the European Social Survey*, pp. 169–203. Los Angeles, Sage; Centre for Comparative Social Surveys.

Search for Common Ground (2010a) 'Radio for Peacebuilding Africa: The project', Search for Common Ground, viewed 6 June 2010, http://www.radiopeaceafrica.org/index. cfm?lang=en&context_id=1&context=about&cont_menu_id=3&page=theproject.

Search for Common Ground (2010b) 'Studio Ijambo', Search for Common Ground, viewed 6 June 2010, http://www.sfcg.org/programmes/burundi/burundi_studio.html.

Seib, Philip (2007) 'The real-time challenge: Speed and the integrity of international news coverage', in David D. Perlmutter and John Maxwell Hamilton (eds) *From Pigeons to News Portals: Foreign Reporting and the Challenge of New Technology*, pp. 150–66. Baton Rouge, LA, Louisiana State University Press.

Servaes, Jan (2002) 'Intercultural communications and cultural diversity', Paper presented at the International Relations and Cross-cultural Communication Conference, Beijing, 12–14 April.

Shafer, Richard and Eric Freedman (2003) 'Obstacles to the professionalization of mass media in post-Soviet Central Asia: A case study of Uzbekistan', *Journalism Studies*, 4(1), pp. 91–103.

Shaw, Ibrahim Seaga (2009) 'Towards an African journalism model: A critical historical perspective', *International Communication Gazette*, 71(6), pp. 491–510.

Sheridan Burns, Lynette (2001) 'Reflections: Development of Australian journalism education', *Asia Pacific Media Educator*, 14, pp. 57–75.

Shinar, Dov (2003) 'The peace process in cultural conflict: The role of the media', *Conflict & Communication Online*, 2(1).

Shoemaker, Pamela J. (1991) *Communications Concepts 3: Gatekeeping*, Newbury Park, Sage.

Shoemaker, Pamela J. and Stephen D. Reese (1996) *Mediating the Message: Theories of Influences on Mass Media Content*, 2nd edn, White Plains, Longman.

Shoemaker, Pamela and Tim P. Vos (2009a) *Gatekeeping Theory*, New York, Routledge.

Shoemaker, Pamela J. and Tim P. Vos (2009b) 'Media Gatekeeping', in Don W. Stacks and Michael B. Salwen (eds) *An Integrated Approach to Communication Theory and Research*, 2nd edn, pp. 75–89. New York, Routledge.

Siebert, Fred S. (1956a) 'The Authoritarian Theory', in Fred S. Siebert, Theodore Peterson and Wilbur Schramm *Four Theories of the Press: The Authoritarian, Libertarian, Social Responsibility and Soviet Communist Concepts of What the Press Should Be and Do*, pp. 9–37. Urbana, University of Illinois Press.

Siebert, Fred S. (1956b) 'The Libertarian Theory', in Fred S. Siebert, Theodore Peterson and Wilbur Schramm *Four Theories of the Press: The Authoritarian, Libertarian, Social Responsibility and Soviet Communist Concepts of What the Press Should Be and Do*, pp. 39–71. Urbana, University of Illinois Press.

Siebert, Fred S., Theodore Peterson and Wilbur Schramm (1956) *Four Theories of the Press: The Authoritarian, Libertarian, Social Responsibility and Soviet Communist Concepts of What the Press Should Be and Do*, Urbana, University of Illinois Press.

Silverstone, Roger (1999) *Why Study the Media?* London, Sage.

Singer, Jane B. (1997) 'Still guarding the gate? The newspaper journalist's role in an on-line world', *Convergence: The Journal of Research into New Media Technologies*, 3(1), pp. 72–89.

Singer, Jane B. (2005) 'The socially responsible existentialist: A normative emphasis for journalists in a new media environment', *Journalism Studies*, 7(1), pp. 2–18.

Singer, Jane B. (2006) 'Stepping back from the gate: Online newspaper editors and the co-production of content in Campaign 2004', *Journalism & Mass Communication Quarterly*, 83(2), pp. 265–80.

Skinner, David, Mike J. Gasher and James Compton (2001) 'Putting theory to practice: A critical approach to journalism studies', *Journalism*, 2(3), pp. 341–60.

Skjerdal, Terje S. and Charles Muriru Ngugi (2007) 'Institutional and governmental challenges for journalism education in East Africa', *Ecquid Novi: African Journalism Studies*, 28(1&2), pp. 176–89.

Soderlund, Walter C., Stuart H. Surlin and Walter I. Romanow (1989) 'Gender in Canadian local television news: Anchors and reporters', *Journal of Broadcasting & Electronic Media*, 33(2), pp. 187–96.

Sparks, Colin (2000) 'Media theory after the fall of European communism: Why the old models from East and West won't do any more', in James Curran and Myung-Jin Park (eds) *De-Westernizing Media Studies*, pp. 35–49. London, Routledge.

Spencer, Graham (2005) *The Media and Peace: From Vietnam to the 'War on Terror'*, Basingstoke, Palgrave Macmillan.

Splichal, Slavko (1995) *Media Beyond Socialism*, Boulder, CO, Westview Press.

Spohrs, Monika (2006) 'Über den Nachrichtenwert von Friedensjournalismus - Ergebnisse einer experimentellen Studie', *Conflict & Communication Online*, 5(1).

Spyridou, Paschalia-Lia and Andreas Veglis (2008) 'The contribution of online news consumption to critical-reflective journalism professionals: Likelihood patterns among Greek journalism students', *Journalism*, 9(1), pp. 52–75.

Sreberny-Mohammadi, Annabelle (1982) 'More bad news than good: International news reporting', *Media Information Australia*, 23, pp. 87–90.

Sreberny-Mohammadi, Annabelle, Kaarle Nordenstreng and Robert L. Stevenson (1984) 'The world of the news study', *Journal of Communication*, 34(1), pp. 134–8.

Steiner, Linda (1998) 'Newsroom accounts of power at work', in Cynthia Carter, Gill Branston and Stuart Allan (eds) *News, Gender and Power*, pp. 145–59. London, Routledge.

Steiner, Linda (2009) 'Gender in the newsroom', in Karin Wahl-Jorgensen and Thomas Hanitzsch (eds) *The Handbook of Journalism Studies*, pp. 116–29. New York, Routledge.

Stephenson, Hugh (1997) 'Journalism education and the groves of academe', in Jan Bierhoff and Mogens Schmidt (eds) *European Journalism Training in Transition: The Inside View*, pp. 23–25. Maastricht, European Journalism Centre.

Stephenson, Hugh and Pierre Mory (1990) *Journalism Training in Europe*, Brussels, European Commission.

Stevenson, Robert L. (1997) 'Remapping the world', viewed 5 October 2010, http://www.ibiblio.org/newsflow/results/Newsmap.htm.

Sundar, S. Shyam (1998) 'Effect of source attribution on perception of online news stories', *Journalism & Mass Communication Quarterly*, 75(1), pp. 55–68.

Sun, Wanning (1996) 'In Search of new frameworks: Issues in the study of Chinese media in the era of reform', *Media International Australia*, 79, pp. 40–8.

Sutcliffe, John B., Walter C. Soderlund, Kai Hildebrandt and Martha F. Lee (2009) 'The reporting of international news in Canada: Continuity and change, 1988–2006', *American Review of Canadian Studies*, 39(2), pp. 131–46.

Tait, Richard (2000) 'The future of international news on television', *Historical Journal of Film, Radio and Television*, 20(1), pp. 51–3.

Taylor, Philip M. (1992) *War and the Media: Propaganda and Persuasion in the Gulf War*, Manchester, Manchester University Press.

Taylor, Philip M. (2000) 'News and the grand narrative: Some further reflections', *Historical Journal of Film, Radio and Television*, 20(1), pp. 33–6.

Terzis, George (2008) 'Journalism education crossing national boundaries: De-mainstreaming binary oppositions in reporting the 'other'', *Journalism*, 9(2), pp. 141–62.

Terzis, Georgios (ed.) (2009) *European Journalism Education*, Bristol, Intellect.

Tewksbury, David and Scott L. Althaus (2000) 'Differences in knowledge acquisition among readers of the paper and online versions of a national newspaper', *Journalism & Mass Communication Quarterly*, 77(3), pp. 457–79.

The Economist (1999) 'Caught in the web: Internet may mean end of newspaper industry', July 17, p. 17.

Thompson, Allan (ed.) (2007) *The Media and the Rwanda Genocide*, London, Pluto Press.

Thottam, George (1999) 'The future of newspapers: Survival or extinction', *Media Asia*, 26(4), pp. 216–21.

Tomaselli, Keyan G. (2003) ' "Our Culture" vs "Foreign Culture": An essay on ontological and professional issues in African Journalism', *Gazette*, 65(6), pp. 427–41.

Tomaselli, Keyan G. and Marc Caldwell (2002) 'Journalism education: Bridging media and cultural studies', *Communicatio*, 28(1), pp. 22–8.

Trammell, Kaye Sweetser and David D. Perlmutter (2007) 'Bloggers as the new 'foreign' correspondents: Personal publishing as public affairs', in David D. Perlmutter and John Maxwell Hamilton (eds) *From Pigeons to News Portals: Foreign Reporting and the Challenge of New Technology*, pp. 70–88. Baton Rouge, LA, Louisiana State University Press.

Tuinstra, Fons (2004) 'Caught between the Cold War and the Internet', *Nieman Reports*, 58(3), pp. 100–3.

Tully, James (2005) 'The media effect', in John Henderson and Greg Watson (eds) *Securing a Peaceful Pacific*, pp. 294–97. Christchurch, Canterbury University Press.

Tumber, Howard (2009) 'Covering war and peace', in Karin Wahl-Jorgensen and Thomas Hanitzsch (eds) *The Handbook of Journalism Studies*, pp. 386–97. New York, London, Routledge.

Tumber, Howard and Jerry Palmer (2004) *Media at War: The Iraq Crisis*, London, Sage.

Turner, Graeme (2000) ''Media wars': Journalism, cultural and media studies in Australia', *Journalism*, 1(3), pp. 353–65.

UNESCO (2007) *Model Curricula for Journalism Education*, Paris, UNESCO.

UNESCO (2008) *Consultation Meeting: Capacity Building for Potential Centres of Excellence in Journalism Training in Africa*, Paris, UNESCO.

Ureneck, Lou (1999) 'Newspapers arrive at economic crossroads', *Nieman Reports*, Summer, pp. 3–19.

Ursell, Gillian D.M. (2001) 'Dumbing down or shaping up?: New technologies, new media, new journalism', *Journalism*, 2(2), pp. 175–96.

Utley, Garrick (1997) 'The shrinking of foreign news: From broadcast to narrowcast', *Foreign Affairs*, 76(2), pp. 2–10.

van Zoonen, Liesbet (1991) 'A tryanny of intimacy? Women, femininity and television news', in C. Sparks and P. Dahlgren (eds) *Communication and Citizenship: Journalism and the Public Sphere in the New Media Age*, pp. 217–35. London, Routledge.

van Zoonen, Liesbet (1994) *Feminist Media Studies*, London, Sage.

van Zoonen, Liesbet (1998) 'One of the girls?: The changing gender of journalism', in Cynthia Carter, Gill Branston and Stuart Allan (eds) *News, Gender and Power*, pp. 33–46. London, Routledge.

Vilanilam, John V. (2005) *Mass Communication in India: A Sociological Perspective*, New Delhi, Sage.

Volz, Yong Z. and Chin-Chuan Lee (2009) 'American pragmatism and Chinese modernization: Importing the Missouri model of journalism education to modern China', *Media, Culture & Society*, 31(5), pp. 711–30.

Waisbord, Silvio (2000) 'Media in South America: Between the rock of the state and the hard place of the market', in James Curran and Myung-Jin Park (eds) *De-Westernizing Media Studies*, pp. 50–62. London, Routledge.

Wall, Melissa (2009) 'Africa on YouTube: Musicians, tourists, missionaries and aid workers', *International Communication Gazette*, 71(5), pp. 393–407.

Wasserman, Herman and Arnold S. de Beer (2004) 'Covering HIV/AIDS. Towards a heuristic comparison between communitarian and utilitarian ethics', *Communicatio: South African Journal for Communication Theory and Research*, 30(2), pp. 84–98.

Wasserman, Herman and Arnold S. de Beer (2009) 'Towards de-Westernizing journalism studies', in Karin Wahl-Jorgensen and Thomas Hanitzsch (eds) *The Handbook of Journalism Studies*, pp. 428–38. New York, Routledge.

Weaver, David H. (ed.) (1998a) *The Global Journalist: News People Around the World*, Cresskill, NJ, Hampton Press.

Weaver, David H. (1998b) 'Journalists around the world: Commonalities and differences', in David H. Weaver (ed.) *The Global Journalist: News People Around the World*, pp. 455–80. Cresskill, NJ, Hampton Press.

Weaver, David H. (2003) 'Journalism education in the United States', in Romy Fröhlich and Christina Holtz-Bacha (eds) *Journalism Education in Europe and North America: An International Comparison*, pp. 49–64. Cresskill, Hampton Press.

Weaver, David H. and G. Cleveland Wilhoit (1986) *The American Journalist*, Bloomington, University of Indiana Press.

Weaver, David H. and G. Cleveland Wilhoit (1996) *The American Journalist in the 1990s: US News People at the End of an Era*, Mahwah, NJ, Erlbaum.

Weaver, David H., Randal A. Beam, Bonnie J. Brownlee, Paul S. Voakes and G. Cleveland Wilhoit (2007) *The American Journalist in the 21st century: U.S. News People at the Dawn of a New Millennium*, Mahwah, Lawrence Erlbaum.

Weibull, Lennart (2009) 'The Northern European/Democratic Corporatist media model countries: Introduction', in George Terzis (ed.) *European Journalism Education*, pp. 69–77. Bristol, Intellect.

Weischenberg, Siegfried, Malik, Maja and Scholl, Armin (2006) Die Souffleure der Mediengesellschaft: Report über die Journalisten in Deutschland [Prompters of the media society: Report about journalists in Germany]. Konstanz, UVK.

Weise, Elizabeth (1997) 'Does the Internet change news reporting? Not quite', *Media Studies Journal*, 11(2), pp. 159–63.

West, Darrell M. (2001) *The Rise and Fall of the Media Establishment*, Boston, Bedford/ St. Martin's.

White, David Manning (1950) 'The 'Gate Keeper': A case study in the selection of news', *Journalism Quarterly*, 27, pp. 383–96.

Whitney, Charles D., Randall S. Sumpter and Denis McQuail (2004) 'News media production: Individuals, organizations, and institutions', in John D. H. Downing, Denis McQuail, Philip Schlesinger and Ellen A. Wartella (eds) *The Sage Handbook of Media Studies*, pp. 393–409. Thousand Oaks, CA, Sage.

Whitt, Jan (2008) *Women in American Journalism: A New History*, Champaign, IL, University of Illinois Press.

Williams, Bruce A. and Michael X. Delli Carpini (2004) 'Monica and Bill all the time and everywhere: The collapse of gatekeeping and agenda setting in the new media environment', *The American Behavioral Scientist*, 47(9), pp. 1208–30.

Williams, Francis (1969) *The Right to Know: The Rise of the World Press*, London, Longmans.

Winfield, Betty H., Takeya Mizuno and Christopher E. Beaudoin (2000) 'Confucianism, collectivism and constitutions: Press systems in China and Japan', *Communication Law and Policy*, 5(3), pp. 323–47.

Witt-Barthel, Annegret (2006) 'EFJ survey: Women journalists in the European integration process', viewed 9 August 2010, http://www.ifj.org/assets/docs/118/144/bad0a76-d2b7b90.pdf.

Wolfsfeld, Gadi (1997) 'Promoting peace through the news media: Some initial lessons from the Oslo peace process', *Harvard International Journal of Press/Politics*, 2(4), pp. 52–70.

Wolfsfeld, Gadi (2004) *Media and the Path to Peace*, Cambridge, Cambridge University Press.

Wolter, Ines (2006) 'Determinants on international news coverage', in Nico Carpentier, Pille Pruulmann-Vengerfeldt, Kaarle Nordenstreng, Maren Hartmann, Peeter Vihalemm and Bart Cammaerts (eds) *Researching Media, Democracy and Participation: The Intellectual Work of the 2006 European Media and Communication Doctoral Summer School*, pp. 59–71. Tartu, Estonia, Tartu University Press.

World Association of Newspapers (2006) 'New editorial concepts. Shaping the future of the newspaper project', 1 August 2006, viewed 4 February 2010, http://www.wan-press.org/article11575.html.

World Association of Newspapers (2009) 'Newspaper circulation grows despite economic downturn: WAN', viewed 24 September 2010, http://www.wan-press.org/article18148.html.

World Journalism Education Council (2007) 'Declaration of principles', viewed 11 July 2010, http://wjec.ou.edu/principles.html.

World Journalism Education Council (2010) 'About the World Journalism Education Council', viewed 11 July 2010, http://wjec.ou.edu/aboutwjec.html.

Wu, H. Denis (2007) 'A brave new world for international news? Exploring the determinants of the coverage of foreign nations on US websites', *The International Communication Gazette*, 69(6), pp. 539–51.

Wu, H. Denis and John Maxwell Hamilton (2004) 'US foreign correspondents: Changes and continuity at the turn of the century', *International Communication Gazette*, 66(6), pp. 517–32.

Xu, Xiaoge (2005) *Demystifying Asian Values in Journalism*, Singapore, Marshall Cavendish.

Xu, Yu, Leonard L. Chu and Guo Zhongshi (2002) 'Reform and challenge: An analysis of China's journalism education under social transition', *International Communication Gazette*, 64(1), pp. 63–77.

Yau, Joanne Teoh Kheng and Suliman Al-Hawamdeh (2001) 'The impact of the Internet on teaching and practicing journalism', *The Journal of Electronic Publishing*, 7(1).

Yemma, John (2007) 'Instant connection: Foreign news comes in from the cold', in David D. Perlmutter and John Maxwell Hamilton (eds) *From Pigeons to News Portals: Foreign Reporting and the Challenge of New Technology*, pp. 110–29. Baton Rouge, Louisiana, Louisiana State University Press.

Yong, Zhang (2000) 'From masses to audience: Changing media ideologies and practices in reform China', *Journalism Studies*, 1(4), pp. 617–35.

Zelizer, Barbie and Stuart Allan (eds) (2002) *Journalism After September 11*, London and New York, Routledge.

Zhou, Xiang (2008) 'Cultural dimensions and framing the internet in China: A cross-cultural study of newspapers' coverage in Hong Kong, Singapore, the US and UK', *International Communication Gazette*, 70(2), pp. 117–36.

Zhu, Jian-Hua, David H. Weaver, Ven-hwei Lo, Chongshan Chen and Wei Wu (1997) 'Individual, organizational, and societal influences on media role perceptions: A comparative study of journalists in China, Taiwan, and the United States', *Journalism & Mass Communication Quarterly*, 74(1), pp. 84–96.

Zurawik, David and Christina Stoehr (1993) 'Money changes everything', *American Journalism Review*, 15(3), pp. 26–30.

Name Index

Subject Index

Aboriginal, *see* Indigenous
accreditation of journalists, 68–9, 73, 82
accuracy, 170, 180–1, 184
Acta Diurna Populi Romani, 131
adversarial role of journalism, 44, 47–8, 58
advertising, 33, 42, 157–67, 172, 175–6, 185, 186–7
advocacy journalism, 21, 28, 30, 140, 142
Afghanistan, 113, 124
African
  culture, 53
  media systems, 24–7
  values, 52–3
Agha-Soltan, Neda, 191
Algeria, 31, 45, 66
Al Jazeera, 31, 32
alternative journalism, 182–4
American
  Broadcasting Company (ABC), 113, 195
  Civil War, 131
  model of journalism education, 63–4
  newspapers, 161
    see also individual newspapers
  Revolution, 88
Anglo-American journalism, 4, 26, 37, 67
Angola, 143
apprenticeships in journalism, 78
Arab
  journalism, 30–3
  journalists, 46
  values, 46
Argentina, 29, 66, 78
Asian
  Conflicts, 147–8
  tsunami of 2004, 118, 184
  values, 51–2
Associated Press, 34, 111
audience
  appeal, 163
  attitudes, 136, 140
  research, 42, 179

Australia, 7, 41, 44, 45, 57–8, 65, 70–1, 73, 78, 101, 165, 170, 177, 183
Austria, 41, 78, 93, 150
authoritarian
  countries, 28–30, 32, 53, 67, 76, 85
  press system, 15
autonomy, 81, 118–19, 171

bad news, 34, 40
Bahrain, 31
Balkans, 11, 132
Baltic, 93–4
Bangladesh, 46, 48
Belgium, 3, 23, 69, 111
blog, 117–18, 156, 178, 182, 184
Bosnia, 126–7, 134, 144
Botswana, 94
Brazil, 2, 8, 28, 29, 41, 46, 47, 66, 78, 95, 102, 106
Britain, 3, 7, 19, 21–3, 26, 44–6, 58, 64, 68–9, 78–9, 85, 88, 93, 95–6, 100, 113–14, 135, 164, 173, 188
British Broadcasting Corporation (BBC), 124, 191, 195
Broadcast media, 20–2, 28, 105, 112–13, 122–4, 126–8, 143, 156, 164, 183, 194–5
Brunei, 52
Bulgaria, 41, 97
Burundi, 143–4
business
  elites, 42, 50
  models of journalism, 157–61, 166–9

Cable News Network (CNN), 124
CNN Effect, 126–8
cable television, 124, 128, 162, 195
cadetships, *see* apprenticeships
Cameroon, 66, 75
Canada, 22, 45, 45–6, 78, 92–3, 101, 111, 122, 194